adapted from a drawing by Maresco Pearce

CUESTA DEL ALCÁZAR

ZOCODOVER

Arch of La Sangre

SANTA CRUZ

North Terrace

ZIG ZAG

ZIG ZAG

Footbridge

GOBIERNO

Stable Approach

End of Stable Approach

STABLE Nº 4

LA CONCEPCIÓN

CALLE DEL CARMEN

Wheat Store

J.P.

THE SIEGE OF THE ALCÁZAR

THE
SIEGE
OF THE
ALCÁZAR

Cecil D. Eby

Random House · New York

TO

Tom and Theodosia

Only he who attempts the absurd is capable of achieving the impossible.

—MIGUEL DE UNAMUNO

Spaniards are accustomed to living for great and spectacular ends.

—GERALD BRENAN

CONTENTS

THE SIEGE OF THE ALCÁZAR

TOLEDO—JULY, 1936

TOLEDO, THE ADMINISTRATIVE CENTER of a poor province and rich diocese of Spain, lies forty miles south of Madrid. The highway, asphalt over cobblestone, is a good one by Spanish standards, but the landscape through which it passes is undulating and monotonous. The violent sun has drained color as well as water from the parched soil and has left only exaggerated contrasts like those seen in overexposed photographs. Sunglasses are required equipment for the traveler crossing this glaring plain of New Castile.

Few villages intrude upon this naked landscape shimmering in the midsummer heat, and beyond the outskirts of Madrid there are no factories. Perhaps the last reminder of the twentieth century is the pueblo of Getafe, which in 1936 boasts the busiest airport in Spain, but there are only a few silent trimotors on the airstrips off to the left. Beyond Getafe, time seems measured in the past tense only, if measured at all. No matter what the map says, the region looks African. Beside the road are irrigation wells—rattling affairs worked by burro or man—which date from the Moslem occupation a thousand years ago and are still in use. But the most numerous inhabitants of the region are magpies, which feast upon dung dropped by the burros at the wells or upon the carcasses of animals killed on the highway. The brilliant black-and-white plumage of this nervous bird seems an indelible emblem of the sharp contrasts of Spain itself—certainly more so than the customary *sol y sombra* dichotomy. For where, in the pitiless sunlight of New Castile, is there shade?

Halfway to Toledo a low ridge of cubes appears to float on the horizon like distant islands. This turns out to be the little town of Illescas, magical at a distance and miserable within. The Madrid road dodges through grubby, narrow streets past flaked white-washed houses. Guidebooks allude to five of El Greco's paintings in a chapel, but the door is bolted and the priest nowhere to be found. No matter. In this poor village it is difficult—even a little irreverent—to keep one's mind on art. The newest, most artistic object in town is an enameled tin sign nailed to a wall in the town plaza, advertising a Spanish cognac called Veterano. Underneath it, leaning on their bolt-action Mausers, stand two men of the Civil Guard in green linen summer uniforms with black patent-leather belts. Neither the fancy liquor nor these particular guards are native products, and the villagers cannot afford the one or trust the other.

As it nears Toledo the road passes through geometrical groves of pine and olive before descending gradually to the Tagus River valley through a wide ravine. Two miles out, the first landmark of the city is, appropriately, the walled cemetery which, sur-rounded by dark green cypress, stands on the slope where El Greco painted his somber landscapes of the Imperial City. After a curve in the road the city pops into view, still capped by the two buildings which dominate El Greco's paintings—the cathedral and the castle, the latter better known by its Moorish name, El Alcázar. Toledo is, wrote the Spanish novelist Pérez Galdós, "a city speared upon a peak—the Alcázar the point." Beyond the city, in the distance, are the blue ridges of the Montes de Toledo, a wild and rarely visited region plagued by wolves and malaria.

What remains is anticlimatic. Clustered around the bull ring are the one-story brick shanties of Las Covachuelas, the northern-most *barrio* of Toledo. Farther along is the Hospital of Cardinal Tavera, a vast, cold edifice built of immense granite blocks. A broad park of eucalyptus trees separates the hospital from the walls of the city, which formerly guarded Toledo from northern attack. The Madrid road enters the city proper by passing under the escutcheon of a Habsburg spread eagle carved above the Bisagra Gate. Stenciled on the wall are the words "Blasphemy and Begging Are Forbidden in This City." The road winds up a steep incline, passes remains of an Arabic wall, and abruptly terminates among the café tables, *mazapán* stands, and souvenir shops (steel letter openers and damascene ashtrays) of the Plaza Zocodover, hub of the city. The steep slope continues beyond the Zocodover, and on either side branches a cartographer's nightmare—a network of narrow lanes twisting in strange arabesques, where sense of distance as well as direction is hopelessly lost except to the denizens of these streets who seem to know the way by a kind of extra sense.

Directly above the arcades of the Zocodover looms the Alcázar on top of the hill—once a Moorish fort, later the palace of Charles V, and now the most prestigious military academy in Iberia. In the Middle Ages the Alcázar was a primitive fortress, more walls than a castle, where the early mayors—like El Cid—dispensed the king's justice. But a succession of rulers, beginning with Charles V, embarrassed by its clumsy heaviness, unleashed their favorite architects upon the drab exterior. Covarrubias imposed a thin Renaissance veneer upon the elephantine bulk of the north front, which has since been considered the main façade. Then Herrera, creator of the Escorial, plastered the south face with brick and mortar, but in the end provided little more than an orderly ensemble of neatly spaced windows. The west and east sides have wisely been left alone, and the latter still shows a machicolated wall and three small round turrets of indeterminate age.

Efforts to destroy the Alcázar availed as little as those to beautify it. Burned by the English during the War of the Spanish Succession and by the French in the Napoleonic Wars, it was abandoned for half a century. Between 1867 and 1882 it was rebuilt for use as a military school, only to burn again five years later. Reconstruction followed as if by habit. This time the interior was buttressed with steel girders so that it became, as one Academy superintendent said, "absolutely indestructible." A monument to both the sentimentality and the stubbornness of the Spanish temperament, the Alcázar is also a symbol of the temporal power which Spain, in the epoch of Charles V, held over an empire vast enough to have aroused the envy of a Roman. This empire has vanished, but the symbol remains.

Standing upon the highest of Toledo's seven hills, the Alcázar's rectangular granite bulk dwarfs the rest of the town. Tiny windows penetrate the gray walls, which in some places are twelve feet thick. At each of the four corners is a square tower, crowned by a pyramidical steeple pierced by a tall, lance-sharp spire. The four walls form a large courtyard bordered by two levels of arcades. On a marble pedestal in the center stands a bronze statue of Charles V, a squat, powerful figure with the bulldog jaw of the Habsburgs, trampling a squirming Moor. Below is an inscription (which has become the unofficial motto for three generations of cadets): "If you should see my horse and my standard fall in battle, raise up my standard first." On the south side of the courtyard a regal stairway—with steps fifty feet wide and each monolithic—leads up to the second story.

Although the Army holds that the Alcázar is an edifice of unusual architectural significance (a view not shared by many art critics), the local military authorities do not welcome visitors, except those dignitaries important enough to carry persuasive letters of introduction with them to Toledo. These would begin their tour of inspection at the Gobierno Militar, a plain office building housing the military governor of the province, as well as an overflow of riding horses from the Academy in the basement stables. The Gobierno stands at the foot of the Alcázar hill, below the north terrace, and it is connected by a footbridge with the east esplanade. From the Gobierno, starting at the iron gate, a serpentine road called the Zig Zag winds up a steep escarpment to the north terrace. The view here is fine, though conducive to arrogance. Everything, except the cathedral across town and a few church towers closer in, lies below: the Zocodover, the Gobierno, and the Santa Cruz, the last an abandoned hospital converted into a museum, facing the Gobierno across the narrow Calle del Carmen. Intervening buildings conceal the Bisagra Gate from sight, but Tavera Hospital can be clearly seen. Beyond the squalid hovels of the Covachuelas district, which from this perspective resembles a heap of unglazed and broken crockery, lies a wind-swept and water-cut wasteland relieved here and there by occasional olive groves along the Madrid road.

On the east side of the Alcázar is the infantry parade ground, a flat and dusty expanse of packed earth officially known as the east esplanade. Beneath the southeast tower and connected with it by a covered stone passageway is the Capuchinos, a nondescript old monastery converted into cadets' quarters, and the terrace between the Capuchinos and the south wall is called the Plaza de Capuchinos. Beside it is the Comedor, the dining hall, a modern building of steel and glass. Farther east, at a lower level, is an immense field house called the Picadero, which is used as the riding academy. There is a wide terrace here as well, with a ramp leading up gradually to the east esplanade above. A few improvised stables clutter the terrace. Just to the south of the Picadero lies the last dependency of the Alcázar, a pseudo-Gothic barracks for the permanent troop section assigned to the Academy. The Santiago, as this building is called, perches on the edge of the steep ravine above the Tagus, which roars through a deep, narrow gorge a hundred feet below. The city of Toledo is almost girdled by this noisy, swirling river, which functions as a moat and seals the city from infantry attack on all sides except the northern. And the northern, unmoated approaches to Toledo are walled.

To the south and west the Alcázar is shouldered by the plebeian bulk of the city. Ancient brick shanties push up to the walls of the Capuchinos, and an open common called the Corralillo runs up to the back windows of the Comedor. Peasants from outlying districts tether their animals, prohibited in the Zocodover, among the weeds and rubbish of the Corralillo. In the houses near by live some of the poorest citizens of Toledo, many of them within spitting distance of the Alcázar. In their minds the hated Army and the proud cadets have perpetuated their misery.

Descending to the Zocodover is a wide street, the Cuesta del Alcázar, which runs along the canyonlike west face of the Academy. On this side is the carriage gate, a service entrance now in disuse, which connects with a large catacomb running completely around the Alcázar at cellar level. On this level, too, are classrooms lit by clerestory windows, and various service rooms. There is yet another cellar below this one but only on the east and south sides, since the site is uneven. Because the original builders of the Alcázar were constructing a broad edifice on the tipped peak of a hill, much of the foundation consists of rubble and fill. Nowhere is this more noticeable than along the west side of the north terrace, which drops fifty feet to the Cuesta del Alcázar.

Though the Alcázar is a formidable symbol of military power, as a fortress it is nearly valueless. If the city came under attack, an enemy could enter either of the principal gates (Bisagra below or Cambrón farther west), and under cover of sinuous streets, reach positions only yards away from the Alcázar, without being detected by anyone inside the building. Once besieged, its inhabitants would have no way out. Early Spanish writers proudly compared the Alcázar to an impregnable eagle's nest, but modern artillerymen would not be awed by ancient metaphor. Deathtrap might be a more fitting word. For a visitor in 1936, the Alcázar is like a cardboard castle, and the ubiquitous sentries with shining bayonets and the booted officers with long red sashes are merely military hocus-pocus. He suspects that this martial pomp is an attempt to prevent the outsider from discovering what the insider already knows—that the once mighty Alcázar has become a showpiece.

There is no question that the golden age of the Academy has passed. Earlier in the century a thousand cadets were in residence at a time. Many of its graduates are listed as dedicated enemies of the five-year-old Republic. One is the deposed king, Alfonso XIII, forced to flee the country in 1931 and now eagerly waiting to be recalled. Another is General Francisco Franco, the former Army chief, hated by many Spaniards for his rough efficiency in squashing the revolt of the Asturian miners two years ago. Because of his alleged role in the plot against the Republic—rumored to be the major objective of the Unión Militar Española, a secret organization of military officers—General Franco is now languishing at an obscure post in the Canary Islands, far from the Spanish mainland.

The Republic, apprehensive about the Army's support of Rightist factions, has cut down the number of cadets to a hundred or so. In July of 1936 all of them are on leave. On hand are a few dozen officer-instructors, who live in the city, and two companies of conscripts—for the most part orderlies, sweeps, or paper-shufflers lacking even rudimentary military instruction. The fact is that the Army is not eager to instruct such men in handling weapons, since eventually they will return to their villages where they might put their knowledge to use, should an insurrection occur. With the cadets away and the staff billeted with their families in the city, the Alcázar is little more than a deserted museum, its empty rooms haunted by ghosts of the past. The walls of the Hall of Honor are covered with the names, carved in marble, of those who have died in battle; most of them tell the same story: "Killed in Morocco." The latter chapters of Spanish military annals record nothing more impressive than this obscure little war which the average foreigner has never heard of.

More important, from a military standpoint, is the Fábrica Nacional, although this is less an arms factory than an assemblage of workshops in the valley northwest of town. The fact that an armory exists here at all proves the tenacity of tradition in Spain. At one time Toledo steel blades were famous throughout the world, but while their reputation lingers on, the quality has fallen off. In any case, the use of cold steel, whether in affairs of love or war, has become infrequent even in Spain. Heavy armament is largely produced in Seville or elsewhere. The workshops scattered among the silver-poplar groves by the Tagus specialize in less destructive weaponry such as cartridges, sabers, grenades, and dress swords.

The grenades fare badly. A new and cheaper model is being developed here, but red tape has tangled production. While thousands of necessary screws are being stock-piled and miles of steel wire turned into springs, the Ministry of War has not yet sent instructions to manufacture the remaining parts—or if the order was sent, it has been lost en route. The director, Colonel Soto, is a trusted Republican (he is said to be a personal friend of President Manuel Azaña's himself), but he is powerless against the bureaucratic apathy of the Ministry.

Between the arms factory and the Madrid road lies another military establishment, though of far less consequence. This is the Central School of Physical Education. Its director is sixty-year-old Colonel José Moscardó, a Blimpish career officer who, by his own admission, has long been more interested in his soccer teams than in military training. With the possible exception of the Archbishop, Moscardó loathes the Republic—to him a synonym for Marxism—more ardently and more outspokenly than anyone else in the province. His views are well known in Republican circles, but the aging colonel is allowed to keep his post. The directorship of the Central School is not thought of as an important position, and even fanatical colonels with forty years of service to Spain have a right to enjoy their sinecure. A soccer coach posing a threat to the Republic? Such an idea is preposterous.

Aside from the churches and their art, Toledo has little else to offer. The hotels are rumored to be bad, so that few tourists fail to return to Madrid after nightfall. Guidebooks praise the open-air restaurants near the Central School, singling out, in particular, Venta de Aires, a favorite of minor Bourbons when in town. Now Toledo is a stagnant provincial town with its face turned away from the future—which offers it nothing—and toward the past. There is a saying here that when God created the sun He first placed it above Toledo, and many Toledanos deplore His wisdom in later moving it. For centuries the city was the nominal capital of Spain, and Philip II has never been entirely forgiven for carrying away the court to an upstart village called Madrid, a step which hastened the decay of the old Visigothic capital. Tradition is here an obsession. Even now the city casts the majority of its votes for the Conservative candidates, who believe in Life Everlasting, rather than for those of the Popular Front, or "Reds," who promise merely an earthly paradise.

The principal products and exports of the city are soldiers and priests, the quality of whom is widely celebrated; it imports nearly everything else, particularly tourists, who come from every portion of the globe to genuflect before the art objects and religious relics of the cathedral and other churches. In Toledo there are more canvases of El Greco per square foot than anywhere else in the world—perhaps the same can be said of priests, for the city is a major center of seminaries. For the Spanish Liberals, Toledo has become a special target of attack: this city has only slightly more than thirty thousand people, yet it supports ninety churches and eighteen convents. The Archbishop of Toledo, who also bears the title Primate of Spain, is not only the most important ecclesiastic in the country but also an outspoken opponent of the Second Republic, which to him is synonymous with lawlessness, godlessness, and Communism. In 1931 the Conservatives were shocked when the Republican government banished Archbishop Pedro Segura from the country for pronouncements clearly opposed to democratic ideals; and a few months later the Liberals were, in turn, outraged when the Archbishop sneaked back into the country without permission. His successor, Cardinal Isidoro Goma, is a more circumspect man.

If by day Toledo belongs to the priests, by night it is given over to the soldiers. Cadets from the Alcázar inherit the arcades and cafés of the Zocodover, where they stroll or sit in small groups, their white-gloved hands resting lightly upon the hilts of dress swords. In fine weather the Academy band plays light opera and noisy marches from the concrete bandstand in the middle of the square. Although the government has remedied the scandalous overemphasis of the military arm (which in the years of the Monarchy consumed 51 percent of the national budget), there are nevertheless many who voice the widely held opinion that the Army is not really an army but a police force—and an inefficient one at that. The officers, they say, are remarkable only for their magnificent uniforms; few of them have battlefield experience, for Spain has not participated in a war within living memory, except, of course, the colonial affair with the United States and the prolonged conflict with the Riffian tribes of Spanish Morocco (who almost always thrashed the Spaniards in the field).

Throughout Spain a furious and open hostility is growing toward both the priests and the soldiers. "In Spain there are two Spains," says a proverb, "one that works and does not eat, and the other that eats but does not work." So far as the laborer is concerned, the clergy and the Army are clearly in the second category. With its Alcázar and its cathedral, Toledo is a symbol of that Spain.

From the low, thyme-scented mountains south of town, the view of Toledo beyond the horseshoe curve of the Tagus gorge is a magnificent, even classical, Spanish scene. The aspect is more African than European, particularly the low, ocher-colored houses which seem to sprout like warts on the hillsides. In texture the landscape resembles wrinkled human skin; in color it recalls faded blood. Such a country is tragic—youthfulness and joy seem to have disappeared from it altogether. Even its folklore is grim:

there is, for example, in Spanish the phrase *"noche toledana,"* a night when one is unable to sleep because of some terrible event that has happened or is expected to happen.

Balanced on the steep slopes of the south bank of the river are the *cigarrales*, groomed patrician estates among terraced olive groves. From any of these the blunt towers of the Alcázar can be seen looming above the other buildings of the city. But the city is as silent and as motionless as a city of the dead—not even barking dogs can be heard above the roar of the river in its gorge. Toledo once made history, and its memories are enough to keep a historian busy for his lifetime. But what could possibly happen again in this weary little town?

1

THE RISING

AT A LITTLE before ten o'clock in the morning of July 18, 1936, Colonel José Moscardó left his home in the patrician Santa Clara quarter of Toledo and drove rapidly north along the Madrid road. As director of the Army's Central School of Physical Education, a sprawling collection of brick buildings on the edge of the city, Moscardó was ex-officio Spanish commissioner for the Olympic Games scheduled to begin in Berlin in a few days. His son Pepe, a lieutenant, was in Barcelona at the time, making last-minute preparations for the journey that both of them would take together, the son as his father's aide-de-camp. For more than a year the colonel had eagerly been waiting for the trip to Germany. It came after seven uneventful years in Toledo, where he had been farmed out to two comfortable but dreary assignments, first as head of the Infantry Orphans' School and then as director of the Central School. The sixty-year-old officer was fond of adventure and new places, but except for his service in Morocco, where he had been garrisoned for twenty years, he, like most career officers in peacetime Spain, had reached his declining years without having tasted much of either.

Despite his pleasant anticipations of the trip, Moscardó was deeply troubled. Throughout the morning the radio broadcasts had been hinting that African garrisons of the Army, which consisted largely of the crack Tercios of the Foreign Legion and the Regulares of the Moors, had revolted the previous night against the Republican government. Further, it seemed that General Francisco Franco had secretly deserted his post in the Canary Islands and had flown to Morocco, where he would doubtless call for a general revolt of the Army on the Spanish mainland. It was still too early for the newspapers, but Moscardó had little use for newspapers, in any case. Those published by parties supporting the Popular Front coalition were filled with glaring lies, while those representing the Monarchist or ecclesiastical factions were emasculated by the Republican censors—or so their editors claimed.

The government-controlled Unión Radio in Madrid was of little help. Although it had alluded vaguely to "disturbances" in Morocco, it had nevertheless concluded each broadcast with the monotonous chant: ". . . but the government has the situation well in hand." To Moscardó, this meant nothing either—unless perhaps the opposite. What was he, a senior officer of the Army, supposed to do? It was urgent that he confer with colleagues in Madrid, men who could be depended on to tell him what was truly afoot in Africa, but he dared not talk over the telephone, which might be tapped at the Toledo exchange. Thus it was that Moscardó left his wife, María Guzmán, in the care of his youngest sons, Luis and Carmelo, and raced toward Madrid in his small black Ford.

It was not that he or any officer doubted that a rising of the military arm against the Republic would come eventually— Spanish political events have nearly always been controlled by the Army. The First Republic, a tepid experiment in the 1870's, was inaugurated the way it was abolished—by a military coup. Thus it seemed that history was repeating itself in 1932 when General José Sanjurjo, hero of the Moroccan wars a decade before, attempted to overthrow the Second Republic, but this time the result was disastrous. Because the military rising lacked sufficient support of civilian Rightist elements, it was suppressed within hours. Though sentenced to death, Sanjurjo ("The Lion of the Riff") was eventually allowed to go into exile in Portugal, where he fomented a more carefully planned revolution aimed at the overthrow of the Republic. Through an organization known as the Unión Militar Española, an elaborate plan for seizing power had been worked out, and the Army would be supported by most of the classes which traditionally were opposed to liberal movements. It had become clear to the military caste that if it were ever to figure in internal affairs again, it would have to be supported by elements outside its numbers.

Meanwhile the Republic tried to emasculate the Army, which had too long held the balance of power, and the ranks had been thinned by compulsory "retirements" and humiliating demotions. Though he himself had had no part in and bare forewarning of the plot, Moscardó had been demoted temporarily to lieutenant colonel. He took this so hard that his wife feared for his sanity. Although his rank was shortly restored to him, Moscardó had thereafter become almost fanatical in his abhorrence of representative government which respected neither Church, nor Army, nor King.

However, Moscardó would have been an inept plotter—he was too flamboyant, too obvious. The times required men of Machiavellian stamp, and for this reason he was overlooked, or ignored, by the key officers of the Unión Militar Española, the junta plotting the destruction of the Second Spanish Republic. Moscardó was far too inclined to bellow with indignation to any-one who would listen, even to important Republican sympathizers like the American ambassador, Claude Bowers, who had come down to Toledo early in July for a short visit and left with memories of both moon-drenched streets and Moscardó's bile. The colonel's assignment to the Central School showed clearly that the Army honored his long service considerably more than his military abilities. "Teaching," he told his aides, "is not my dominant passion." It was not clear what specific passion he was hinting at, unless it was football.

Compared to his colleagues, Moscardó was a mountain of a man. He was nearly six feet tall, but he carried himself awkwardly and ran to such flesh that he was nicknamed "the Flabby Giant." Since he had difficulty in controlling his nervous hands, he usually kept them tightly locked in his lap; he was painfully conscious of his tendency to make wild gesticulations. Whenever possible he wore a hat in order to conceal his almost totally bald head. His fondness for impeccable full-dress uniforms betrayed vanity and an excess of self-esteem. Except for a wide, sensual mouth and a slightly drooping jaw, his face was bland and easily forgettable. Like many other volatile men, he was none too bright and certainly not stable—bombast was often followed by hesitancy, obstinacy by vacillation. His mother is said to have died insane.

Moscardó was haunted by the specter of failure. Sooner or later all his junior officers would hear him tell of his first military assignment after graduating from the Alcázar in 1896. He had commanded the sentries at the funeral of an indigent white-haired lieutenant who had died without home or family in a shabby Madrid boarding house. There were no other attendants. Moscardó had been profoundly shocked, and he tortured himself by repeating this doleful tale, which seemed to mirror his own insignificance among the military elite. Although he had achieved more prominence than the superannuated lieutenant, he was a failure, too—a fact that no gaudy uniform could conceal. Junior officers at the Central School sensed this, and they genuinely liked the old man who so readily overlooked their wining and wenching. They believed, however, that their future, and the future of Spain, lay in the hands of sleek, forward-looking officers; Moscardó was a myopic anachronism.

As Moscardó's Ford dashed wildly down the Madrid highway, perhaps he recalled a similar frantic errand a few years before. At that time he had been cast in the role of a revolutionary, and he suspected that he had played the fool. It began when a local leader of the Falange called at his office in the Central School. Like many other Conservatives, Moscardó had an ambivalent attitude toward the Falangists. They were mortal enemies of the Popular Front parties—this was good; but they spoke out against both the Church and the Army—this was very bad. The Falangist leader had opened the conference with a request delivered in such a matter-of-fact manner that Moscardó was stunned. "Colonel, I wish to enlist your aid in a march of the Falange, first on Toledo, then on Madrid."

Was this the voice of destiny, of a madman, or of a spy? Fearing a trick or a trap, Moscardó told the Falangist to come back after lunch for an answer. Then he jumped into his car and drove madly to Madrid to report this proposal. Refusing to divulge his mission to the underlings at the Ministry of War, he pounded furiously on desk tops and eventually succeeded in obtaining an interview with General Franco. Although the general had to be torn from a military conference, he was touched by the zeal of the provincial colonel, and perhaps a little amused. Franco instructed Moscardó to remain quietly at his post "until the proper time," although he did not specify when this would be. Meanwhile the Falangist must be discouraged from premature maneuvers. It was late in the afternoon when Moscardó returned to his office, where he dismissed the young visionary of the Falange. Afterward Moscardó felt a little foolish about his precipitate behavior in uncovering the "plot." And to his growing list of public nuisances he added the name of the Falange.

Ever since the Second Republic was proclaimed in 1931, Colonel Moscardó had prayed that the Army would revolt to save Spain from drifting toward Communism, Freemasonry, and atheism. The constitutional government, run by moderates, had attempted to pursue a middle course between two extremes: on the one hand, Monarchists, landowners, industrialists, the clergy, and the military, and on the other, Socialists, Communists, and Anarchists. But the middle way has always been the doomed way in Spain, and the Republic was not able to reconcile such opposites. The power struggle experienced elsewhere in Europe between the Left and the Right began to be felt in Spain. Since each faction was convinced that the other was developing sinister plots to seize the government—and often with good reason—the breach between them opened wider and wider, until Spain consisted of two hopelessly antithetical camps. The various disparate parties of both the Left and the Right began to form coalitions which, a little later, became known as the Popular Front and the National Front.

On this crystalline July morning of 1936 Moscardó must have felt a keen pang of disappointment that the revolt had occurred—if it truly had occurred—just at the time when the Berlin Games were due to begin, for with the shadow of war hanging over Europe it seemed unlikely that he would ever attend another Olympics. Moscardó had few illusions about Spanish athletes, and he particularly regretted that his favorite soccer team would make no showing. But in riding and shooting, Spain could hope to gain medals. Horses and rifles—how important these would become to him, in quite another way, in a matter of days!

He had with him in the Ford a small battered Spanish-German dictionary which he had bought thirty years before to teach himself German between campaigns in Morocco. Like most Spaniards of his caste, Moscardó admired the Germans enormously, even though he found them obnoxious as individuals. Also with him—in fact, inseparable from him—was a small volume of religious poetry, *The Perfect Marriage* by Fray Luis de León.

Along his route the Castilian villages lay quiet in the blinding sunlight. It was not until the Ford had crossed the long bridge over the Manzanares River and had climbed the bluff on the north side that Moscardó realized that Madrid was a bedlam of apprehension and belligerence. Swarms of Madrileños of the lower classes were arguing along the curbs and shouting in the streets. Many of them wore their regular overalls—loose-fitting blue boiler-suits called *monos*—some of which were bedecked with the five-point Communist star. Others had red-and-black scarves, the colors of the Anarchist trade union, tied around their necks. At the Puerta de Toledo a crowd on the sidewalk cheered with clenched fists as an open truck daubed with the letters *UGT* careened around the triumphal arch in the plaza.* None of these crowds appeared to be armed. Moscardó wondered why the military forces had not already seized the city.

Since the Ministry of War was staffed by officers with strong Republican sympathies, Moscardó dared not show himself there for fear of being placed under arrest. Instead, he made some discreet telephone calls and got confirmation that the revolt was

---

* Although the Republican militia were to adopt many devices of the Communists—the red star, the Marxian hagiography, the clenched-fist salute —the Communist party was extremely small at the outbreak of the war. The propaganda of the Rightists, however, eagerly seized upon these manifestations in order to support their claim that they were engaged in a war against Communism. Of outstanding strength in the opening months were the UGT (Unión General de Trabajadores)—the Socialist Trade Union; the CNT (Confederación Nacional del Trabajo)—the Anarcho-Syndicalist Trade Union; and the feared FAI (Federación Anarquista Ibérica)—an Anarchist secret organization and shock force.

under way.* General Franco had joined the African garrisons, who were momentarily expected to cross the Strait of Gibraltar and to commence their march upon Madrid, consolidating other units in southern Spain as they advanced. In the foothills of the Pyrenees, at Pamplona, the revolt led by General Emilio Mola (known as the "brains" of the Army) had been successful, and he was expected to lead a column toward Madrid from the north. Already a motorized column from Valladolid, the stronghold of the Falange, a hundred miles northwest of the capital, was said to be rumbling toward Madrid, and workers there were demanding arms from the government in order to thrust it back before it captured the summits of the Guadarrama Mountains, which lay only twenty miles to the west. Street-fighting was in progress in Barcelona. No one understood why the Army units in Madrid still remained in barracks.

Throughout Spain the philosophy of *mañana* was being supplanted by the exigencies of *hoy*. The proverbial patience of Spaniards had worn down to a fine thread, and this thread had at last snapped. Moscardó realized that if the province of Toledo were to be secured for the insurgents, there was not a minute to lose. The workers at the arms factory, most of them supporters of the Popular Front, might even now be helping themselves to weapons, and packing munition boxes destined for Madrid. Or a telephone call from the Ministry to the Alcázar might irretrievably commit the Academy and its forces to the Republican side. Once this happened, it would be nearly impossible to reverse the decision, particularly if the workmen were armed and the Alcázar occupied. Moscardó knew that the arms factory was the principal military installation in the province, but he was not blind to the symbolic value of the Alcázar. It seemed to him that if this embodiment of Spain's military tradition were taken by armed rabble, then the revolt of the Army would be doomed.

The long-awaited trip to Berlin was canceled. Moscardó did not even take the time to call his son Pepe in Barcelona. But he had little doubt that the mob there had already capitulated to the

* The specific nature of Moscardó's telephone calls has never been disclosed. Perhaps he had been instructed to get in touch with an agent of the Unión Militar Española when the revolt began, or perhaps he was seeking some clue to his correct course of action.

units commanded by General Manuel Goded. The boy would be all right.

Moscardó did, however, telephone Captain Emilio Vela Hidalgo, an instructor of cavalry tactics at the Alcázar. Vela, who was spending his leave in Madrid, was instructed to round up all the cadets he could find and to return with them to Toledo at once. This done, Moscardó hurried back across the plain to the city slumbering beside the Tagus.

Moscardó's call to Captain Vela was unnecessary. All morning Vela had been on the telephone, trying to locate the cadets of the Alcázar, who before going on leave had pledged themselves to keep track of one another in case the revolt came during the summer. But the results were disappointing. If anyone answered the phone, Vela's request to speak with a particular cadet was more often than not answered with ". . . in Santander" or ". . . gone to San Sebastián." These were sea resorts in the north of Spain— they were also conveniently close to the French frontier. In a few cases someone picked up the phone, shouted "*Viva la República!*" and slammed down the receiver. By midafternoon Vela had found only six cadets willing to meet him at a café in the Puerta del Sol and to return to Toledo.

Vela's choice of the point of rendezvous was deliberate. Since the time of Goya, the Puerta del Sol—Madrid's Piccadilly Circus —had been a seismograph of revolution. At the slightest tremor of disturbance in Spain, crowds of Madrileños converged upon the square, collecting in front of the Ministry of the Interior on the south side, headquarters of the hated Civil Guard. At such times Army officers were *personae non grata,* and that is the reason why Vela chose it.

Short, stumpy, and brash, Captain Vela was a whirlwind of energy. The most popular young instructor at the Alcázar, he was respected as one of the most heedless horsemen in Spain. With a massive jaw, always dark with stubble, Vela might have been mistaken for a boxer, although his arms between the elbow and wrist were abnormally short. He walked like a powerful, overgrown dwarf; some of the younger cadets emulated this swagger. He had a violent temper but he held no grudges, since he was inordinately pious. Intoxicated by the mystique of sacri-

fice and violence, he was an ardent Falangist—a rare alignment
for an Army officer in 1936. Just as Moscardó reflected the con-
servatism of Old Spain, so Vela embodied the aspirations of New
Spain. The age of horses was nearing an end; Vela's immediate
ambition was to command a company of tanks. In an army cluttered with ineffectual amateurs, Vela was a professional. Moscardó knew this. His call to Vela was the instinctive clutch of a
tottering man at a strong limb.

Captain Vela had become a minor celebrity two months earlier
when he had nearly fomented his own private revolution in
Toledo. It began in the Zocodover one Saturday night while the
cadets were off duty. A vendor of leftwing newspapers flaunted
his wares in the face of a cadet. Deeply insulted, the cadet slapped
the man sharply with his white cotton gloves, and a crowd of
civilians surrounding him swore they would tear him apart.
Within seconds Captain Vela had cut through the crowd with a
pistol in his hand. The local police quickly restored order, but the
civil governor panicked and, foolishly, telephoned Madrid to report that there had been an uprising among the Academy officers.
Late that same night a commission, headed by a general known to
be loyal to the Republic, came down to Toledo from the Ministry of War and took depositions till dawn. Although the general
reported that the whole affair had been exaggerated, the government, yielding to public demand that the Army be put in its
place, punished the cadet corps by banishing it from the Alcázar
to its camp at Alijares, a bleak upland moor two miles east of
Toledo.

While the cadets were roughing it at Alijares, the Conservatives—especially those in the Army—demanded the re-
moval of the civil governor. Since the punishment of the cadets
was out of all proportion to their offense and the whole incident
was beginning to embarrass the government, a moderate Republican named Manuel González was appointed governor of the
province. His first order allowed the corps of cadets to return,
and he even permitted them to stage a triumphal march through
the Zocodover with Captain Vela at the head. Forbidden
Monarchist banners of red and yellow waved from isolated bal-
conies as the cadets marched up from the Alcántara Bridge. Yet,
antagonism still smoldered underground. Solitary cadets were

beaten up by Leftist gangs if they strayed into the winding streets within the working districts, and Captain Emilio Vela Hidalgo became a target for revenge.

Now, as Vela waited for the cadets, the café across the plaza from the Ministry of the Interior was jammed with blue *monos*, and the square was filled with men and women chanting "Arms! Arms!" A government sound truck blared out reports of the Moroccan rising, interspersed with exhortations to keep calm. A band of Anarchists tried in vain to organize an attack on the Quixote statue in the Plaza de España because the hand of the knight was stretched out flat, as if making the Fascist salute. Elsewhere in Madrid, behind shutters closed to exclude the heat and the clamor, ministers debated which of two terrifying alternatives was the lesser evil: a successful coup by the Army or an uncontrollable rabble in arms. They ignored the dilemma by doing nothing.

The sun was low when Captain Vela and six cadets, all of them in mufti, rolled out of Madrid in a big touring car. At the Manzanares River bridge there was a bad moment when they were stopped by some Socialists who shoved pistols through the windows and demanded to know where they were going.

"To the Alcázar of Toledo," said Vela. Then, to reassure the tightened faces, he added, "To destroy it."

"Pass, brothers," came the reply. Under clenched fists, Vela and the cadets drove off to Toledo.*

Lieutenant Luis Barber did not hear of the rising in Morocco until the early afternoon of July 18, and then quite by chance. His parents' estate lay a few miles west of Toledo, and here he was spending the last days of his emergency leave. An officer of engineers stationed at Morocco, Barber had received permission to attend the funeral of his uncle, José Calvo Sotelo, the most outspoken Rightist in the Spanish parliament, whose assassination on the evening of July 13 had hurled Spain over the brink of bad feelings into the abyss of civil war.

---

* In the weeks ahead, the world would hear much about the defense by the young cadets of the Alcázar. In actual fact there were only eight cadets in the battle, six of whom were brought in by Captain Vela.

This precipitating event, leading to open rebellion, was one in a chain of interconnected political murders in 1936. The Popular Front was victorious in the February elections, but in the four months that followed, Spain seemed to be falling to pieces. In this short period there were 269 political assassinations, 113 general strikes, and 160 churches burned. The government looked on helplessly (or so said the National Front) as carloads of political terrorists—Fascists and Anarchists, for the most part—machine-gunned one another in the streets of Madrid and other cities. In April, on the fifth anniversary of the Republic, a Civil Guard (the police force traditionally allied with the Right) had been killed by an Anarchist. At his funeral there was a riot in which José Castillo, an Assault Guard * (the police force allied with the Left), killed a prominent marquis and Falangist. On July 12, Castillo was murdered near his home by four unidentified gunmen. In retaliation, the next night a band led by an Asalto captain assassinated Calvo Sotelo, and dumped his body beside the cemetery gate. This had an instantaneous effect throughout Spain. Like the assassination of Archduke Ferdinand, it released a force which no one was able to stop and which culminated in war. Three years of incessant street-fighting by *pistoleros* of the Left and the Right (particularly Anarchists and Falangists) had at last felled two victims for whom all Spain would shortly bleed. As a generation of Spanish political theorists had prophesied, Cain must kill Abel once again.

Before leaving Morocco, Lieutenant Barber had been told by a senior officer that in a matter of days General Franco would avenge the murder of his uncle. Being a level-headed young man, Barber did not take this pledge of vengeance very seriously; it sounded too romantic to be true. He reached Madrid too late to attend the funeral in the East Cemetery, where his uncle, draped in monk's hood and gown, was laid to rest under the flat-hand salutes of his weeping followers. He did, however, walk over that

---

* The official name of the Asaltos, or Assault Guards, was the Cuerpo de Seguridad y Asalto. They were organized in 1931 with the specific purpose of defending the interests of the Republic, because the Cuerpo de la Guardia Civil traditionally aligned itself with the Conservative factions. The uniform of the Asaltos consisted of a dark blue tunic, soft peaked cap, and black leather puttees. The force is no longer in existence.

dusty Golgotha several hours later while the grave diggers were finishing their job. In the same place, not far away, was the grave of Lieutenant José Castillo.

From Madrid the lieutenant went to Toledo, where he had lived since boyhood and where he had graduated from the Alcázar. Taking advantage of his short leave, he slept late, dawdled over coffee and newspapers on the terrace of the family estate, and admired the view of the city through the olive trees. The morning of July 18 was no different from any other. At midday Barber strolled over to the city for cigarettes. At the *tabaquería* near the Cambrón Gate, the most sluggish quarter of Toledo, he overheard a broadcast from Unión Radio reporting that the Moroccan garrisons were in revolt. It was clearly impossible for him to make his way through southern Spain and to rejoin his regiment at Melilla, so he decided to wait in Toledo for his regiment to join him. Like most anti-Republican officers, Barber believed that it would be only a matter of a few days before the military coup would restore order throughout the peninsula. After buying a few extra packs of cigarettes, he returned home, rolled up his uniform in a newspaper, and reported to the provincial military headquarters to receive his orders.

Meanwhile not even the imminent fall of the Second Republic interfered with the customary siesta of the city. Toledo, which had seen governments and kings come and go for two thousand years, had grown indifferent to such things. Iberians, Romans, Visigoths, Moors, Jews, Christians—civilizations had passed away, while the Tagus, the sun, and the wrinkled earth remained. Behind a grille at the cathedral there was a revered stone marking the place where the Virgin Mary had touched the earth when she descended from Heaven: for most Toledanos, except perhaps those tainted with the doctrines of Carlos Marx, this stone was more meaningful than indistinct echoes from remote Morocco, Madrid, or Barcelona. Ignore these murmurings and they would go away—like the Iberians, the Romans, the Visigoths, the Moors, and the Jews.

Although the city was siesta-still, Lieutenant Barber found the Gobierno a bedlam, where no one was in charge and no one wanted to be. At the first hints of impending danger, refugees of the Right—professional men, wealthier merchants, minor gentry

—had scurried to safety here, where they flooded the narrow corridors and overflowed into the courtyards. Wives and children of many officers had congregated here as well, though most of the officers had gone above to the Alcázar. The Gobierno resembled the *zoco* of a North African town except that the jewelry boxes, bundles of clothing, chromos of sacred hearts, silverware, bags of food, hunting guns, guitars, accordions, and whimpering children were not for sale. In Stable No. 4, which lay directly beneath the main floor of the Gobierno, horses whinnied and kicked at their concrete stalls, adding to the turmoil above them.

Escaping from this confusion, Barber walked up the Zig Zag to the main entrance on the north terrace, where he was stopped and questioned by the guard before being allowed to join the officers milling about in the courtyard. Up here, nerves seemed steadier. Barber learned that Colonel Abeilhé, superintendent of the Academy, was in Madrid on leave and could not be reached by telephone. In his absence the commanding officers were Lieutenant Colonel Antonio Valencia, an old professor, and Lieutenant Colonel Pedro Romero, chief of the Civil Guard of Toledo Province. It was believed that the Guard would support the military rising, since they had taken part in the quasi-secret mobilization orders a few weeks before. Still, the officers in the courtyard nervously eyed the Tommy-gun guards standing in front of the superintendent's office, where Valencia and Romero were closeted together.

In the meantime Lieutenant Barber could do nothing except change into his uniform and wait for something to happen. In the Spanish Army there were over two hundred generals and countless colonels, and more captains and majors than there were sergeants. History was not made, or even altered, by green lieutenants of the Engineers.

Shortly after three in the afternoon, Colonel Moscardó's dusty black Ford rattled into the Zocodover, where the siesta mood was beginning to wane. From a café radio came a fragmented announcement from Unión Radio, but the marble-top tables at the Café Goya were still deserted. A waiter sloshed an abandoned drink over a potted plant in the plaza—old rituals prevailed over innovations.

After the tumult of Madrid, Moscardó must have found Toledo strangely untouched; here events seemed to be filtered through a thick screen of almost sepulchral indifference.

Turning right into a narrow alleyway opposite the Santa Cruz, Moscardó drove to the Gobierno, where he was stopped briefly by a guard before being allowed to enter the Academy grounds. Then, entering the iron gate, which blocked access to the Zig Zag and the dependencies of the Alcázar, he continued up the long ramp by the Picadero and parked among the school vehicles on the east esplanade. Leaning out of the windows of the Santiago Barracks and watching him listlessly were the soldiers of the troop section. Someone had had the foresight to confine them to quarters so that they could not stir up trouble in the city. Once inside the Alcázar, Moscardó was disturbed by the large numbers of unfamiliar faces in the courtyard. For a moment he feared that a Madrid unit had been sent down to secure Toledo for the Republic, but he was told that these were only stray officers caught in the area while on leave or in transit who had reported to the Academy for assignment during the emergency.

As he moved across the courtyard toward the superintendent's office on the south side, Moscardó accumulated an entourage of officers belonging to the Academy and the Central School. At this time Toledo had no military governor (the Republic had abolished many of the military governorships on the provincial level), but the function was still performed by the ranking officer of the province—until this time the superintendent of the Academy, Colonel Abeilhé. However, since he was in Madrid when the revolt began and had not returned, Moscardó learned that he outranked all officers who had so far reported to the Alcázar. Moscardó and his companions brazenly pushed past the Guards at the office door and found Colonel Valencia sitting in the superintendent's chair next to the telephone and Colonel Romero standing aloof near the window. Despite his advanced age and frail physique, Valencia bounded out of the chair like a man worked by springs; one could only guess at the political sympathies of a fellow officer. Meanwhile Romero, who looked cool and dignified in the braided military cloak he wore even in the heat of July, observed the two men with seeming indifference. While he was experienced in supressing civil disturbances in isolated pueblos, marshaling military insurrections against the government was not in his line.

Moscardó immediately asked whether there had been any telephone calls from the Ministry. Valencia told him that there had been none so far.

In this gloomy office, furnished with cracked leather chairs and fading photographs of previous superintendents in identical wooden frames, Moscardó confirmed the rumors of a military revolt in Africa. He told his colleagues that garrisons throughout Spain were rising against the Republic, and expressed his opinion that General Franco would soon be marching northward from Andalucia with the Army of Africa. At any moment the Madrid garrisons would be in full revolt. Within a few days the Army would have complete control of Spain, at which time it would turn this power over to political elements uncontaminated by anarchy, blasphemy, and Marxism. There was no sound in the room. The spellbound band of officers were standing at the brink—and Moscardó pushed them over.

Throwing both hands high above his head, he shouted, "Gentlemen! The province of Toledo is from this day with the rising! You have the word!" In the crowd someone cheered *"Viva España!"* and the cry was echoed by others. Instantly the news swept out into the patio and erupted into a second volley: "Toledo for General Franco!" Only then were a few dissenting voices heard above the shouting. These men wanted to know how it was possible for them to resist, isolated and unsupported, against the limitless resources of the government. If the Army units in Madrid failed to revolt or were overcome and the Republic sent a column on Toledo, where would they obtain men, arms, munitions, and food for a defense of the city? But Moscardó brightened the darkening mood with his succinct reply: "Don't worry. God will provide." No irony was intended.

In the council of war which followed, in which about a dozen select officers participated, plans for the defense were debated. Moscardó, exhorting the younger men as if they were soccer players, suggested that they announce to the world that Toledo had joined the revolt, for this proclamation from the holy city of the Spanish Army would encourage uncommitted garrisons throughout the country to follow their example. Such a bold act would, in his judgment, contribute psychologically to the rapid success of the rising. Valencia heartily agreed. He liked the prospect of the Alcázar, of which he would officially be the acting superintendent, becoming the symbolic center of the new crusade.*

Romero, a dry Castilian, thought all this foolishness. He was perfectly willing to allow Moscardó and Valencia to have major roles in the Alcázar drama so long as he himself would not have to participate in a farce. Psychology and symbolism meant nothing to Romero. He knew well enough that these officers and professors regarded his Civil Guard as little more than policemen, but he did not care so long as they did not interfere with the century-old responsibility of his corps: the preservation of law and order in the provinces of Spain. After forty years of service in the Civil Guard, Romero's concept of duty amounted almost to passion. In the conference he stood stiffly apart from the others, shaking his head until they noticed him and asked his opinion. His reply was cumbersome, but his blunt logic was irrefutable.

As he saw it, their first duty was to hold Toledo. To accomplish this, they should delay their announcement until the last minute. If the local radio station broadcast the information that the Alcázar had joined the revolt, the government would probably send down a column from Madrid. To resist such an attack, they needed two things: men and ammunition. At present they had neither, but they could get both if they were willing to wait forty-eight hours. Scattered throughout the province were six hundred Civil Guards, and these could be mobilized and concentrated in Toledo by Monday morning. There was plenty of ammunition in the arms factory, but until the Guards arrived they could not get at it. The director, Colonel Soto, was a loyal Republican; the thousand workmen there—all of them members of trade unions—would resist any demand that the ammunition be brought to the Alcázar. The present forces within the Alcázar were too thin to take the factory by direct attack; as a matter of fact, they could not even be expected to hold the city.

There were other matters to be considered. At that moment

* The Nationalists apparently believed that they were engaged in a holy war—to expel the Red infidel from sacred soil. The official name which they gave to the Spanish Civil War was "the War of the Liberation," and the thirty-five-volume official history is titled *Historia de la Cruzada Española.*

the Alcázar forces were estimated at two hundred soldiers and forty officers, but the former were conscripts without much military training, and to make matters worse, were politically unreliable. Most of them came from lower-class backgrounds and might turn their rifles on their officers, if an opportunity arose. Could such boys (their average age was eighteen) be depended on to carry the main burden of the defense? Romero thought not. There were, of course, other smaller groups in Toledo which could be counted on. In the patio at that moment were forty unassigned officers, but half of them were on the retirement list and one of them was, of all things, an Air Force bombardier. There were thirty members of the Academy band, most of them grown fat in long service. Guarding the banks, town hall, radio station, and arms factory were about eighty thinly scattered members of the local Civil Guard contingent. The whole situation was hopeless, at least until the six hundred Guards of the outlying districts arrived in Toledo. Only when this concentration was complete could the Alcázar declare its commitment to the rising. In the meantime they could only pray that the Ministry of War would be so preoccupied with Madrid problems that Toledo would be forgotten.

After listening to Romero's pedantic summation, Moscardó and the other officers abandoned their aspiration to defy the authority of the Republic. There was little they could do except authorize the Civil Guard to fall back to the city. Romero at once picked up the phone and gave the order.

Plans for this movement had been worked out a month before. The password, "Always faithful to his duty," was relayed by telephone, short-wave radio, and motorcyclist to each post in the province. This was the signal for each section head to open a sealed letter already in his possession, which instructed isolated posts to proceed to villages, from villages to towns, and from towns to Toledo. The Guards were ordered to carry or burn all equipment, and to bring their families lest they be taken as hostages.

The order sent, there was nothing any of them could do but wait. Which would appear on the horizon first—the black, patent-leather tricorns of the Civil Guard or the baggy blue *monos* of the Republican militia?

The window of the superintendent's office faced south. In that direction, three hundred miles away, lay Morocco. It had taken seven hundred years to expel the Moors from Spain; now they were returning as the shock force of Franco's Army of Africa. If Moscardó found anything ironic in this situation, he did not take the trouble to articulate it. But when asked to estimate the amount of time they would have to spend in the Alcázar before being relieved, he replied, "Four or five days, unless the rising in Madrid fails. In that event, fifteen days at the outside." Colonel Romero offered no prediction at all.

During the rest of the afternoon the Alcázar command pored over maps of the city, working on a military problem which had never, in fifty years of Academy history, been discussed in the classroom—a plan for the defense of Toledo itself. In the Middle Ages the defensive position of the city had been so advantageous that an Arab saying claimed that Toledo could be taken only by hunger. The Tagus looped around the city like a horseshoe, and since high bluffs rose steeply by the bridges, the only possible direction of attack was from the north, along the Madrid road. At the base of the hill below the Alcázar the city walls ran in an unbroken line across the neck of the Tagus loop like a drawstring on a sack. Moscardó planned to prevent the Republicans from entering the city by placing his men along these walls and by fortifying Tavera Hospital and the Central School buildings, which covered the Madrid road a few hundred meters north of the Bisagra Gate. (Had he commanded a division instead of several companies, or had the enemy been armed only with spears, his plan might have been a valid one, provided that the attackers were not supported by artillery.) If the enemy broke through the walls, the Nationalist forces would then retire into the Alcázar and resist from there. But a siege was not envisioned at this stage, and no one made any effort to bring food and other provisions into the Academy.

Late in the afternoon cheering news came in. Sixty of the Asaltos assigned to the city had suddenly been called to Madrid. They requisitioned ten touring cars and left in a hurry, according to the enraged owners who came up to the Gobierno to report their loss. Since the Asaltos were violently pro-Republican, their departure weakened the ranks of the Popular Front within the city. Further, their sudden recall implied that the government was so distraught by the crisis in Madrid that it had few thoughts to spare for Toledo affairs.

As shadows lengthened in the city, refugees of the Right continued to trickle into the Gobierno. None of them brought evidence that their lives or property had been threatened by workers, but they wished to take no chances. One pious lady was nearly hysterical: she said that a ragged man on the steps of her church had leered at her when she entered, and when she came out, parodied the sign of the cross, making horizontal movement of his hand across his throat as if holding a knife. This lady was in striking contrast to the military wives, who, chatting and knitting, sat under the striped awnings stretched over the inner courtyards. Yet anxious faces revealed that they knew that, this evening, coffee would not be followed by a stroll with their families through the Zocodover to watch the martins darting about in the golden twilight.

In a deserted office of the Gobierno, Moscardó conferred with his wife and his sons Luis and Carmelo. What to do with them was a major problem. He did not like the prospect of keeping them as refugees in the Gobierno, for the place was cramped and inconvenient. If the Republicans attacked the city, they would probably bomb or shell the building, in which case his family would be exposed to grave dangers. Further, he had a lurking fear that a counterrevolutionary faction within the Alcázar—he knew that not everyone was determined to join the rising—might seize them as hostages in order to force him to surrender. It seemed better to let them return home, and if the city were threatened by a besieging force, Luis could find a way of taking them to Madrid, where their identity could not so easily be discovered. As befitted the daughter of a former general of the Civil Guard, Señora Moscardó accepted her husband's decision, but Luis did not wish to leave. Somewhere he had found a rifle and was intoxicated by the prospect of using it. He now had a chance of becoming a real soldier like his two elder brothers Pepe and Miguel, both of them lieutenants. Though twenty-four years old, Luis was more child than man; some said his mind was defective. Moscardó gently took the gun from him and made him promise to look after his mother and the sixteen-year-old Carmelo. Late in the evening they were escorted back to their home on Santa Clara, and the house was provided with an armed guard.

Night had fallen when Captain Vela arrived at the Alcázar with his six cadets. Having expected fifty or sixty, Moscardó was keenly disappointed, but he welcomed each with a handshake and a few words of thanks. Perhaps the others were at that moment pushing through roadblocks throughout Spain in an effort to return to the Alcázar, as promised. Among the cadets was the son of General Cruz Boullosa, Undersecretary of War and a stanch Republican. Vela explained that Cadet Cruz had deliberately disobeyed his father's command not to return to the Academy.

Captain Vela said that they had not seen any troop movements along the highway. The villages en route had seemed normal. He thought that the government would shortly distribute arms to the workers; if this happened before the Madrid garrisons revolted, the doom of the capital would be inevitable. Having reported to Moscardó, Vela slipped out of the fortress on a secret mission of his own. Without Moscardó's knowledge, he intended to make arrangements for the Toledo Falange to join the forces of the Alcázar. These men had been begging for a chance to fight: now they would have it.

At ten in the evening the city was quiet. Some of the Saturday crowd in the Zocodover were walking homeward, while others leaned against open doorways and windows, listening to a broadcast which they had been waiting all day to hear. "La Pasionaria" was speaking to Spain. In a nation where a woman was usually judged by her fancied resemblance to or divergence from the Virgin, Dolores Ibarruri was a rare phenomenon—she was not only a politician but also a Communist. Spain would long remember her speech on that Saturday night. She demanded that the Fascists be destroyed wherever they were found, and appealed to Spanish women to join the struggle with knives and boiling oil, if they had nothing better. Her peroration with the borrowed phrase "It is better to die on your feet than to live on your knees! *No pasarán!*" was the signal for the proletariat to erupt. "*No pasarán!*" ("They shall not pass!") became the rallying cry of the People's Army for the next three years. These words, posted on billboards or scrawled on gutted buildings, became an indelible part of the Spanish landscape. In Madrid the government began to distribute weapons to the workers.

Her speech brought the war to Toledo. In the Zocodover a loose band of workmen fired pistols at the sentinels of the Civil Guard on duty in the square. While screaming bystanders dived beneath café tables, the rifles of the Guards cracked in reply. Hertas, the leader of the workingmen, shouted, "Let's get them!" and charged wildly on the Guards. He was shot dead by two bullets fired almost simultaneously. Within a few minutes, six townspeople, four of whom were not participants in the attack, lay bleeding to death on the cobblestones of the Zocodover, while four Guards were being carried away with minor wounds. Reinforcements from the Alcázar poured into the square, but by this time the rest of the gunmen had dispersed into the city.

At the time of this skirmish, the Falange was holding a meeting at their temporary headquarters in the narrow Calle Nueva, barely a dozen paces from the square. Captain Vela was trying to persuade Pedro Villaescusa, their chief, to ask for asylum in the Alcázar, but without much success. Recruited largely from university cliques, the Falange distrusted the Army, regarding it as reactionary and unenlightened. It believed that the rejuvenation of Spanish society would be effected by spiritual, not muscular means. Most of its doctrines were mere opposition to something else—whether the Church, the Monarchy, or the Popular Front. The nearest they got to an articulate creed was the concept of a "revolutionary elite" which would use the "national essence" to rebuild Spain. Since this was nothing but gibberish to most Spaniards, the Falangist party numbered less than twenty-five thousand members and controlled not a single seat in the Cortes. Yet as a result of hit-and-run tactics in street-fighting during the past three years and its awesome mystique of violence, the Falange had an influence out of all proportion to its size. While Falangists disclaimed cousinship with Italian and German nationalism, they nevertheless shared with them a deep antipathy toward international Communism. However indefinite their convictions, it was clear that their party slogan, "*Arriba, España!*" ("Arise, Spain!"), did not mean acquiescence to the ideals of the Popular Front coalition.

The firing in the Zocodover was more persuasive than was Vela's argument, for a bomb hurled by a Communist, Socialist, or Anarchist—none could say which, since the culprit had not been caught—had destroyed their original headquarters only a few weeks before. Now the sound of gunfire outside seemed to augur another such attack. Some of the Falangists urged an immediate sortie into the square, but Vela remarked that if the Civil Guard were involved in the fighting they would shoot first and look for identity papers later, after the bodies had cooled. The *pistolero* phase of the rebellion had ended. There was a fight to the death brewing in Spain, and if the Falange sought to fight alone, it would bear the brunt of the dying.

The Toledo Falangists knew that they were marked men. They were personally known to the working classes and would be picked off one by one. Vela won his point. With their leaders he worked out a plan of notifying all members of the Falange to assemble that night in the Academy photography laboratory, a small frame building located below the north terrace, near the Zig Zag. Here they would be able to conceal themselves temporarily in a neutral zone between the Alcázar and the city. They could then decide what they preferred to do, without being irretrievably compromised. Captain Vela promised to arrange matters with the sentries posted along the north terrace so that they would not be fired at in the dark. He did not mention Moscardó's ignorance of his plan.

2

THE BLUFF

SUNDAY, July 19, opened with a time-honored custom, early Mass in the chapel of the Alcázar; it was held by a Toledo prelate who left shortly thereafter. At one end of the tiny room the doll-featured madonna, cast from plaster, looked down from the altar. An overflow crowd spilled out on the stairway outside, where Civil Guards stood stiffly at attention with rifles at their sides, ramrod reminders of the solemnity of the service. Most of the crowd were civilians, rumpled and soiled after a fitful sleep in the chairs or on the floors of the Gobierno. They seemed to be grateful for the Mass and doubly grateful for the Guards; in the Alcázar one could attend Mass without having to endure the customary jeers and coarse jokes of the priest-haters who waited at the doors of churches and the cathedral in Toledo. In the front rank of worshipers Moscardó knelt. After Mass he went back to his office on the floor below, where he spent the morning listening to Unión Radio, impatiently waiting for news from Madrid that the Army had seized the city.

At ten o'clock a ringing telephone broke the tension in the office. An aide seized the phone and whispered that General Cruz at the Ministry of War was on the line. Cruz sounded courteous but very formal. He told Moscardó that he was sending two security agents to Toledo at once to bring back his son, and trusted that Moscardó had no objection. It was clear that Cruz was not quite sure whether his son was regarded as a political hostage or not. After Moscardó had replied that this arrangement was entirely suitable, General Cruz added, as if it were a post-script:

"Oh, by the way, I want you to send the munitions in the arms factory to Madrid immediately."

Moscardó realized that he was being given an opportunity to declare his loyalty to the Republic, although Cruz must have known his political beliefs.

"I must have the order in writing."

"Don't you trust me?" snapped General Cruz.

"Of course, General," replied Moscardó, and then played his trump card: "But you know that the order must be given in cipher."

Cruz hung up abruptly, leaving Moscardó with a humming telephone in his hand and a broad smile on his face. His demand for written instructions was legally correct, and by using this technicality he had bought additional time for the Alcázar. A secret weapon had entered the war on the Nationalist side: red tape.

Without intending to do so, General Cruz had raised the confidence of the Alcázar command. If Madrid wanted the munitions, why had they called the Academy, which had no jurisdiction over the arms factory, instead of the factory directly? There was one plausible explanation: the government thought that the forces concentrated in the Alcázar were a great deal stronger than they actually were—strong enough to prevent a shipment of ammunition to Madrid. The factory was a coveted prize but neither side wished to provoke the other to seize it first.

What no one in the Alcázar knew at this time was that other factors were working in their favor. During the first forty-eight hours of the crisis the personnel of the Ministry of War was shaken up three different times because of Cabinet changes and the prevailing suspiciousness within the military hierarchy. In the attendant confusion no particular official was made responsible for obtaining the munitions in Toledo. On the previous day workingmen had organized caravans of automobiles and had started down the Madrid road to seize the arms factory for themselves, but along the way they had run out of gas, got drunk, or turned back to Madrid. The question was asked often enough in the capital, What is going on in Toledo? but no one knew the answer.

Late in the afternoon a Socialist deputy named Prats arrived in Toledo to discover for himself why it had remained so quiet while the rest of Spain was seething. After making contact with some Toledo Socialists, he called on the civil governor of the province, Manuel González. Assisted by his companions, Prats grilled the frightened governor and demanded that he hand over the arms of the Civil Guard and the Academy. The events of the past twenty-four hours had stripped González of what little power he had. With only a few dozen municipal policemen, what could he do? In desperation he fabricated a fantastic story that all the weapons had been melted down into scrap metal. Prats was not amused. He ordered González to explain to the Alcázar that their weapons must be surrendered, adding that unless he returned promptly he would never see his family alive again. González left at once on his absurd mission.

Moscardó received the civil governor with mixed feelings. He had scant use for officials of the Republic, but González had always shown proper respect for the interests of the Army during his administration of the province. It was he who had recalled the cadets to the Alcázar after their temporary exile to Alijares, ordered by his predecessor. And earlier in the year, while civil governor at Albacete, González had ordered the Civil Guard to fire upon peasants who were illegally cutting down trees for firewood in the pueblo of Yeste. The Leftist press had been incensed about the so-called Yeste Massacre, accusing González of having betrayed Republican principles. These principles he retained, but he was not ready to die for them in vain. The national situation was becoming so chaotic that he could not determine whether he was threatened more by the Republicans than by the Nationalists. Sensing his dilemma, Moscardó offered asylum for González and his family in the fortress, but he dared not accept—that would be treason. Then Moscardó outlined a unique plan: at the first opportunity, Alcázar forces would "raid" his home and arrest the González family. In this way they could be brought to safety without compromising his loyalty to the Republic. González returned to Prats and explained that the Alcázar refused to surrender its arms. Immediately Prats hurried back to Madrid with the first direct evidence that the Moscardó clique was hostile to the government.

Except for the call from General Cruz and the visit of Prats, Sunday passed so quietly that Toledo seemed to have regained its mood of slumbering antiquity. Although the troop section remained in quarters, the city was regarded as safe enough for Moscardó to dine at home with his family. Some officers thought that things were preternaturally quiet: they could not recall a Sunday in fair weather when the Zocodover had been so deserted. When the security policemen arrived from Madrid to fetch Cadet Cruz, the young man left the Alcázar without protest or farewell.*

The most explosive event of the day occurred when Moscardó discovered the sixty Falangists hiding in the photography laboratory, below the north terrace. Vela argued that if fighting broke out, the Blue Shirts would be useful to the Alcázar. They could be trained by an officer of the Academy, but would not be given weapons unless conditions became desperate. Although Vela won his point, Colonel Moscardó insisted that they remain where they were for another twenty-four hours. This delay would teach them who was in command of the Alcázar. Without food or water, the Falangists huddled together in the stifling heat throughout that Sunday, patiently learning Moscardó's lesson.

After dark the telephone rang again. This time Colonel Juan Hernández Sarabia,** officer of the day at the Ministry of War, was on the line. He ordered that the munitions at the factory be sent to Madrid in the morning. Again, with serene courtesy, Moscardó expressed his willingness to co-operate, but he regretted a minor technicality: he could do nothing until he received written authorization in code.

"It will be there in the morning, Colonel," said Hernández Sarabia.

The Ministry still seemed unable to decide whether Colonel

---

* Placed in the Montaña Barracks by his father, Cadet Cruz was killed the next day when the barracks was stormed by a Madrid mob.

** Hernández Sarabia later became supreme commander of the Republican armies of the Levant and commanded at the Battle of Teruel.

Moscardó was the most stubborn fool or the smoothest conspirator in Spain. They had to find out quickly. Even if Moscardó were morally committed to the rising, he had not yet made an overt gesture against the Republic; it was not too late for him to realize his folly and to change his mind. The Ministry of War did not regard him as a particularly resolute or dangerous conspirator, just one moderately tainted.

In the bleak light of dawn on Monday a sentry in one of the east towers saw something moving toward Toledo along the Ocaña road, from the east. It looked like a column of men with tanks or armored cars at the front and rear. Instantly the officers, jarred loose from sleep, scrambled up the steel stairways leading to the top of the towers. Observers focused binoculars on the olive groves north of Toledo, prepared to see the slopes near the cemetery blossoming with Republican militia. There was no sign of movement there, but tight files of men were approaching the city from the east. As they came nearer and as the sky lightened, cheers broke out in the towers and spread along the east windows of the Alcázar. The first of the Civil Guards from the province were coming in.

The alleged armored cars turned out to be overloaded wagons and camions bulging with mattresses, furniture, and file cabinets. On top sat women and children wrapped in blankets. By sunrise the roads from Ocaña and Mora were flooded with these gypsy caravans, all of them making for a single point—the Alcázar. The news swept through Toledo and brought townspeople to the Zocodover. Somewhere far off in the city six pistol shots were fired in rapid succession—but whether this was a gesture of rage or joy no one could say.

All day the Guards straggled into Toledo, until there were slightly over six hundred of them. They came on foot, on the backs of horses and mules, in confiscated cars, and in antiquated trucks piled high with possessions. No deserters were reported. Each Guard knew that to be caught in the outlying districts was equivalent to having a death warrant already signed. Founded in the 1830's as a police force to exterminate banditry in the provinces, the Civil Guard had become, because of its brutal efficiency in putting down rural demonstrations, synonymous in the peasant's mind with oppression, tyranny, poverty. In some areas hatred of the men in the patent-leather wing-back hats was so violent that local deputies in the Cortes were forced to ask for the disbandment of the Civil Guard, but no such bill had been passed.

Twenty-three Guards from Tembleque did not make it, through some flaw in the mobilization plan. A railway strike had stopped all trains, and the village was so poor that there were no cars to confiscate. After finally setting out on foot, they were cut off by peasants armed with shotguns and pitchforks, who sprang out of the ground like dragon's teeth in this blighted region of La Mancha. Those taken alive were trussed up and sent to Madrid, where they were imprisoned or executed by a people's tribunal. At another village a squad of Guards were besieged in their *cuartel* by a band of men and women who would not allow them to leave. But when the Guardsmen came out, cheering the Republic and explaining that they had received orders to go to Madrid to fight the Fascists, the villagers believed them and sent them on their way with congratulations and cheers.*

While the Civil Guard were coming into the city, the Alcázar command learned that Colonel Soto had received a direct order to pack the munitions and send them to Madrid. Moscardó phoned Soto at once and urged him to comply with the order to crate them, but to delay shipment. Soto knew that the number of Civil Guards under Moscardó's command was increasing by the hour, and dared not disobey him. Then, too, he was worried about the twenty artillery officers at the factory who were taking a summer training course; while these men had given no firm indication that they supported the rising, they had shown no enthusiasm for the Republic, either. He also suspected that there were spies all around him, and kept a loaded pistol in his desk and

* Revenge followed swiftly. After the Guards had escaped, the peasants turned upon those villagers throughout the province who were—rightly or wrongly—suspected of Nationalist sympathies. The present highway between Toledo and Ciudad Real is studded with granite cenotaphs marking the places where these people were murdered. A typical monument, situated next to an abandoned quarry on a wind-swept hill, reads: "Natalio Rojo, Ruiz Castellanos, Manuel Quintanero, José-Antonio Pérez, Pablo Fernández, Manuel Drake Santiago, and Carlos Martínez Repulles were assassinated by the Red militia of Yébenes in this place, August 13, 1936. R.I.P. Their families beg a prayer for their souls."

another in his pocket; he hovered impatiently around the telephone.

Colonel Soto's fears about the artillery officers were valid. As soon as the Guards arrived in the Alcázar, they were thrown out as reinforcements along the city walls and at key defensive positions in the city, but Moscardó was not quite ready to attempt an occupation of the arms factory. With only a few hundred men under his command, the city was not yet safely under his control; and perhaps the workmen at the arsenal had wired the place with explosives in order to blow it up at the first sign of an attack. However badly its demolition might injure the government, it would also seal the fate of the Nationalists in Toledo. How could the Alcázar withstand a siege with no more than fifty rounds of ammunition for each rifle? Moscardó had to have the supply of cartridges lying in the factory, but he dared not strike until positively assured of success.

Monday evening came on peacefully. Music from unseen guitars floated to the Alcázar from the Corralillo quarter, and in the superintendent's windows, staff officers watched ragged urchins playing football with a knotted rag in the Capuchinos square. Then the Ministry of War telephoned the Alcázar and asked for Moscardó. This time it was General Sebastián Pozas on the line, supreme commander of the Civil Guard. Considering that his organization was, in all but a few places, joining the revolt against the government, Pozas held one of the more ineffectual positions in Spain at that moment.*

"Colonel," said Pozas, "I must warn you that unless you comply with the previous orders immediately, I will send a column against you, and the city will be bombarded."

"But, General," replied Moscardó, feigning surprise, "how am I to send the munitions if there is nothing at my disposal except two trucks, which are very old at that?" He did not add that the east esplanade was littered with vehicles belonging to the Guards who had arrived during the day.

"Only two trucks? I thought that you had more. I will order

---

* Although courted earlier by Franco and other conspirators, Pozas remained an adamant Republican. A capable officer, he was for a short period Minister of the Interior during the early days of the rising and later commanded the Army of the Center, responsible for the defense of Madrid.

the Ministry to send some to the factory in the morning," said Pozas. Earlier in the day workingmen of Madrid, stiffened by cadres of Loyalist officers, had seized the city barracks and the airfield at Getafe, thereby giving control of the capital to the Republicans. For the first time the government could deal with the Toledo situation. Moscardó's delaying game was now transparent. Pozas planned to send more than trucks to Toledo in the morning.

Following this telephone conversation Moscardó grew increasingly nervous. Finally he called a conference of key officers and explained that time was running out. They had to commit themselves publicly, one way or another, while they still had an opportunity to choose without compulsion. The conference, held behind the closed doors of Moscardó's office, was not a long one. Loiterers waiting outside in the courtyard heard a cheer from within, and minutes later the senior officers were hurrying about the Alcázar giving orders in low voices. Soon exterior windows were being removed from their frames, and civilians evacuated from the Gobierno were taking up new quarters in the classrooms and cellars of the Alcázar.

The news filtered down the ranks: in the morning the Alcázar would publish its declaration of war against the Republic. The most elaborate bluff of the war was about to end.

At seven in the morning of July 21, a company of the troop section stood presenting arms beside the statue of Charles V in the courtyard of the Alcázar. When the drum roll ceased, Captain Vela read, in an official monotone, a proclamation stating that the province of Toledo thenceforth was at war with the government in Madrid. On hand to film this historic moment was a Toledo photographer named Rodríguez, a civilian refugee who had brought along his camera and ten rolls of film. His photographs capture the theatrical solemnity of the moment. Vela, though he is in bad need of a shave, is dapper in his immaculate white collar, tasseled cap, and black cavalry boots. The young soldiers stand stiffly, presenting arms, their figures dwarfed by their rifles with fixed bayonets. They look absurdly young and innocent. As Vela marched them down the Cuesta del Alcázar to the Zocodover,

Rodríguez ran ahead to photograph the wobbly column. The soldiers are in step, their free hand snaps upward to shoulder level, but no two rifles have exactly the same alignment.

A crowd of Civil Guards and civilians of the Alcázar gathered at the edge of the north terrace to watch the column descend. One of the Guards remarked contemptuously that they handled their rifles as if they were pitchforks. Bringing up the rear was a truck containing an officer and seven Guards. It mounted a machine gun in case there were Leftists of the city who might mistake the young soldiers of the troop section for cherubs in uniform.

The Zocodover was empty of townspeople. Vela read the proclamation to the upturned chairs in front of the Café Goya, and afterward the soldiers marched back up the Cuesta to the Alcázar. The military ritual having ended, Guards fanned out in pairs through the city to seize known radicals as hostages. According to plan, the civil governor was picked up and brought to the Alcázar and the warden of the provincial prison was seized, but all other dignitaries of the Republic were hiding too skillfully to be found. Meanwhile Vela broadcast the proclamation from the local radio station. There was no longer any possibility of turning back. Madrid let slip the dogs of war with such speed that the Alcázar was caught off balance.

Within three hours the first Republican trimotor circled the fortress and dropped leaflets telling the soldiers that they were being deceived by their officers and assuring them that they would be held guiltless if they deserted. On the previous day these leaflets had been successful in persuading the common soldiers in the Madrid barracks to repudiate their officers and surrender to the armed civilians outside. But outside the Alcázar there was no threatening host, and no soldiers attempted to slip past the hawklike surveillance of their superiors. The appearance of the plane set off sporadic firing from scattered Republicans upon isolated posts of the Civil Guard in the city, and although these attacks were repulsed, the Guards dared not attempt to hunt their enemies in the deathtrap alleyways leading to the working districts. Rodríguez, who had returned home to pick up extra clothing, found himself isolated from the Alcázar. In the

days to come, he had to hide his camera and make his way to
Madrid, where he gained safety but lost his opportunity to become the combat photographer of the Alcázar.*

Leaflets had fallen with no more effect than confetti in a high
wind, but those in the Alcázar knew that the plane would soon be
back with a load of bombs. Without a single anti-aircraft gun in
the Academy, they were defenseless against aerial attack. Worst
of all was the specter of poison gas, a possibility so terrible that
even a mention of it was taboo among the officers. True, the
Geneva Convention outlawed its use in warfare, but this had not
restrained the Italians from gassing Ethiopians. If Republican
planes dropped gas canisters and the fumes seeped down into the
cellars of the Alcázar, what could they do but surrender? Someone remembered that the Academy museum contained a collection
of gas masks, but there proved to be only twenty-five of them—
each one different. Meanwhile Colonel Romero established a
machine-gun pit at the edge of the north terrace for the dual purpose of covering the Zocodover below and harassing Republican
planes above. Further, he placed his best riflemen in the towers,
with orders to shoot down any enemy plane flying near the fortress. He might just as well have armed these men with sports
guns and bird shot, but the order was comforting to civilians and
inexperienced soldiers who did not doubt that airplanes could be
shot down like quail. But Romero knew that even a few bullets
shot into the fuselage of a plane might cause a pilot to make his
second run at a greater height, and the higher the plane the
smaller the target.

It was just past noon when a patrol car posted far out on the
Madrid highway sped back to the Alcázar with a startling report:
a motorized column, led by three armored cars, was bearing
down on Toledo. Moscardó and his staff, conditioned by the
government's procrastination in the past, were stunned by the
alacrity with which the Ministry of War had moved. Pozas was
no fool. Perhaps he had even outfoxed them: it might already be
too late to bring the ammunition at the arms factory into the
Alcázar.

* Thus there were no photographs taken within the Alcázar during the
siege. When it ended, enterprising cameramen posed men at loopholes, but
no such pictures are bona fide.

Sixty men under Major Ricardo Villalba, Moscardó's second-in-command at the Central School, were posted in Tavera Hospital and in the Central School, a hundred yards outside the walls, north of the Bisagra Gate. They would block direct access to the city by the Madrid highway; moreover, Villalba had installed a machine gun in the cupola of Tavera, which would slow down any contingent turning west toward the arms factory a quarter of a mile away. Another machine gun was placed in a second-story window facing the highway, which ran along the walls of the hospital. The men had strict orders not to fire until Villalba gave the signal from the cupola, since the position was a good one for ambushing the enemy but poor for resisting a sustained attack because of the jumbled buildings and maze of alleyways in this quarter. The men were provided with grenades and rifles, but no mortars or artillery. Their greatest danger was that they might be flanked and surrounded before they could retreat back into the city by the Bisagra Gate.

While Villalba was scanning the ridge near the cemetery for his first sight of the Republican column, Lieutenant Angel Delgado of the Civil Guard was dispatched from the Alcázar with twenty men to commandeer the munitions. As he turned into the gate at the factory, Delgado found an incipient riot. The workers had been informed that a column was advancing from Madrid, and they were shouting jubilantly, "Now our men are coming!" It was fortunate that Delgado had brought ten trucks from the Alcázar, for General Pozas had sent none from Madrid. The Guards spread out watchfully over the factory grounds. Since the workers refused to load the trucks, the artillery officers assigned to the summer course stripped off their tunics and began to carry out the cartridge boxes. It was long, hard work under a scorching sun, and the workers lounging near by were amused: few of them had ever seen officers in shirt sleeves, sweating like ordinary mortals. While they were loading, firing broke out in the vicinity of the Bisagra Gate. Major Villalba had made contact with the enemy along the Madrid road.

The Republican column, led by General Manuel Riquelme, comprised approximately three thousand men, most of whom were enthusiastic but inexperienced militia, with a cadre of the

Regular Army which had remained loyal to the government. It approached Toledo cautiously. Near the cemetery Riquelme halted his column and deployed the Army unit toward the arms factory. But he was unable to stop the spontaneous rush of the militia, who, excited by the sight of Toledo below them, ignored his command to regroup. With naïve bravado they set out to liberate the city from the Fascists. These were city dwellers accustomed to paved streets, and instead of spreading out over the fields, they marched down the Madrid road in a cluster, straight toward the Tavera ambush. Out in front an Anarchist waved a red-and-black banner.

Just past the bull ring the militia walked into the sights of the Civil Guard at the hospital. Window glass popped from the cupola as Villalba's machine guns sprayed the road and the Guards delivered point-blank rifle fire. At first the militia were too startled to run, then they bolted for protection behind walls and houses beside the highway. A dozen of their group lay heavily in the road. The Anarchist banner lay across the chest of the leader like a shroud.

To extricate the militia pinned down around the bull ring, Riquelme threw one of his armored cars into the attack. Although a homemade contraption, not much more maneuverable than a steam roller, it mounted a small cannon and two machine guns. While this machine rumbled back and forth under the windows of the hospital—its gun power forcing the Guards away from their parapets—Riquelme launched a direct assault upon Tavera with the militia who had not yet been engaged.

From his post on the second floor Captain José Badenas saw the attack coming, and knew that within minutes the militia would batter down the doors of the hospital and trap them. Seizing a grenade, he raced downstairs and crouched at a basement window, from which he could see the armored car passing back and forth on the road outside. From this point he was able to reach out and place his grenade almost under the wheels. His timing was perfect, and the explosion snapped the steering mechanism. When the smoke cleared, the armored car lay on its side in the ditch across the road. The nearest files of militiamen, now within fifty meters of Tavera, were knocked apart by the fire of the Guards, who had returned to their parapets.

Pulling back his men from the Tavera sector, Riquelme called for artillery support from a 75-mm. gun, which opened fire on the hospital from an olive grove near the cemetery. This shelling produced little effect on the thick granite walls, but it did distract the garrison inside from interfering with a flanking movement toward the arms factory. Sheltered by the eucalyptus trees of the valley, the Asturian regiment dispatched by Riquelme had by this time nearly reached the outer walls of the factory.

Even though the firing around Tavera seemed to be growing heavier and nearer, the artillery officers at the factory continued to pile cartridge boxes into the trucks. The artillerists had decided to proceed to the Alcázar in convoy since individual trucks might be seized by hostile townspeople along the way. However, their work was only half completed when a hatless young man wearing the uniform of an army corporal came through a side gate, waving a white handkerchief on a branch. A pair of Guards brought him to Colonel Soto's office, where he announced that he was General Riquelme's special emissary, sent ahead to accept the surrender of the arms factory. He concluded with an overt threat: "If within a quarter of an hour you do not surrender, the slaughter at the Montaña Barracks will be only a game compared to this." Major Pedro Méndez Parada, senior among the summer-course officers, was outraged—less by the threat than by Riquelme's tactlessness in sending a corporal. On the other hand Soto, who seemed slightly encouraged since the arrival of the corporal, said to Delgado and Méndez, "We must think this over, gentlemen."

"Oh, no," Méndez interrupted. "There is nothing to think about." He turned his back on Soto and walked out to the trucks. To Delgado he said, "Let's be off to the Academy with the transport."

"But I forbid it!" Soto called out after him. When the others ignored him, he turned to the corporal and said chokingly, "Well, as you see, I can do nothing."

Lieutenant Delgado ordered the trucks to roll out. They left so hastily that some of the artillerists left their tunics and hats behind. There was not even enough time to notify the guards that were posted at remote points on the factory grounds, so these were abandoned. On each running board stood an officer with a pistol to make certain that the civilian driver would not attempt to pull out of convoy. As the trucks approached the city, civilian snipers hidden in the town on the bluff above fired sporadically, but their shots were wild. The camions turned into the Bisagra Gate and started up the slow, twisting incline to the Zocodover at about the time the Asturian regiment broke through the gates of the arms factory.

A jubilant crowd massed around the vehicles as they parked on the north terrace of the Alcázar. Eager hands pulled out the crates of ammunition and deposited them in nearly forgotten magazines far underground in the deepest cellars of the building. But the festive mood was shattered by warning shots and shouts from the towers. Those on the terrace looked up and saw three planes bearing down upon the Alcázar from the north, and they barely had time to duck inside the entrance to the courtyard or to throw themselves beneath the vehicles before they heard the bombs exploding around them. Two ammunition trucks exploded in flames. The planes made only one run, dropped twelve bombs, and flew back to the north again before the smoke had cleared. There was only one casualty: dead was a Civil Guard who had been standing by himself on the terrace, gawking in wonder at the falling bombs. The loss of two trucks and a man was of little importance to the Alcázar command. They now had nearly three quarters of a million—seven hundred thousand by rough count —rounds of ammunition. The Alcázar was ready to defy the Republic.

Although most Toledanos stayed indoors and avoided the streets, the proximity of the Republican column and the appearance of the bombers encouraged government snipers to make half-hearted attacks on posts of the Civil Guard. These attacks were beaten back successfully, but it became clear to the Alcázar command that it would be impossible to repulse the Madrid column at the edge of the city and at the same time beat off guerrilla raids inside the walls. The logical step was to order all detachments to fall back to the Academy at once and to prepare for a siege. Moscardó, however, viewed this alternative with repugnance: he could not conceive that a civilian mob, no matter what its size, might force disciplined soldiers into purely defensive positions.

Stubbornly he refused to order the units at Tavera and the Central School to fall back into the city.

Meanwhile Riquelme was exploiting the greatest Nationalist blunder—the failure to destroy the arms factory.* Trucks crammed with munitions were already driving to Madrid arsenals; weapons were being distributed to *milicianos*—militiamen arriving hourly from nearby villages and Madrid to join the Republican column. It was getting dark. Riquelme was in no hurry to dislodge the Nationalists at Tavera: they would still be there in the morning, and his militia would have them surrounded.

Just twelve hours after Captain Vela had read his proclamation of war in the courtyard, General Riquelme telephoned Moscardó and asked for his surrender. The demand was refused.

"Why do you take this attitude of defiance?" asked Riquelme.

"Because I love Spain and have confidence in General Franco," replied Moscardó. "Furthermore, it would be dishonorable to surrender the arms of *caballeros* to your Red rabble."

"Then I will seize them," said Riquelme.

"I am informed, General."

---

* Despite its limited strength, the Alcázar could have acted with greater promptness and force in seizing the arms factory and in destroying it before it fell into Riquelme's hands. But the war was young. Blowing up a national armory may have seemed a more shocking act than revolting against a government. A few months later, when the Nationalists approached Toledo, the Republicans made the same mistake: they failed to demolish the factory, even though they knew it would soon manufacture munitions for the enemy.

3

"THE ALCÁZAR WILL NEVER SURRENDER!"

THROUGHOUT THE NIGHT of July 21 and the morning of the next day, the militia infiltrated the city, bringing with them armloads of pistols and weapons for their supporters; and sensing trouble ahead, small groups of civilians deserted the Alcázar. As they slipped down the Cuesta they passed other small groups, climbing up to ask asylum in the pearl-gray fortress. The officers were willing to allow any of them—except the hostages—to leave and to admit those whose Nationalist sympathies were a matter of public knowledge.

Dawn of July 22 brought a Republican trimotor, which glided down from the north and dropped its load of bombs upon the conspicuous, squat building which would become, in the months to follow, the principal target, navigational aid, and playground of government aviators. At nine o'clock the Republican battery placed in the Dehesa de Pinedo, an olive grove near the cemetery two miles north of the city, began shelling the Alcázar. An hour later the trimotor returned with a fresh load of bombs and succeeded in setting fire to the southeast tower, although this was quickly extinguished. In the afternoon it returned again and left the houses between the Zocodover and the north terrace a blazing heap of debris. Gone was the Posada de Cervantes, a tourist trap associated vaguely with the author of *Don Quixote*. The bombs set fire to this whole area largely populated by the poor, yet left the Alcázar barely touched. No one ventured to put out the fires, which smoldered lugubriously for weeks and were fanned by each breeze into fresh flames. Since these houses could have harbored a large attacking force directly below the Zig Zag, the Alcázar staff was relieved that the bomber had unwittingly cleared a field of fire between the north terrace and the Zocodover.

Much more alarming than the mild bombing and shelling was the ever-increasing *paqueo*, or small-arms fire, which burst out in the city during the second air raid. Unseen snipers were beginning to chip away at the Alcázar from nearby rooftops and windows to the south and west—tangible evidence that the Madrid column was slipping into Toledo and organizing resistance among the workers. The officers of the Academy were infuriated, but it was impossible to attack a whole city pressing in upon them. When the Civil Guards at the Bank of Spain were cut off in the middle of a telephone conversation with Moscardó, he realized that the situation was critical. Abandoning his grandiose plan to hold the city, he sent a heliograph message to Major Villalba, instructing him to withdraw from Tavera and the Central School.

By the afternoon of July 22 the men at Tavera were down to oranges and crackers, and their ammunition was nearly gone. For twenty-four hours these sixty men had kept Riquelme's column at bay, but the bullets smashing against the walls of the hospital were beginning to come from the south as well, indicating that they were gradually being surrounded. Villalba no longer dared retreat through the park which separated Tavera from the Bisagra Gate—the most direct route to the city—because they would have to pass through an area heavily exposed to Republican fire. Instead, he resolved to dash across the Madrid highway and plunge into the Covachuelas slum quarter, where the narrow alleys were so jumbled that the Republicans would find it difficult to seal them off. Although Covachuelas was seething with guerrillas, it seemed preferable to fight them than the militia snipers working toward the Bisagra Gate from the arms factory.

The first group to leave Tavera were civilian refugees, who took the enemy by surprise and crossed the highway without drawing a shot. The soldiers dashed over, five or ten at a time. Then they advanced slowly from doorway to doorway, moving toward the Tagus River under fire from hidden snipers in the quarter. When one lane became blocked by guerrillas, Villalba found another one free. If a man was badly wounded, he had to be left behind. Eighteen were lost along the way, including a military doctor, but whether because of desertion or capture no one ever knew. Although the distance between Tavera and the Alcázar was less than half a mile by road, it took Villalba's force six hours to snake through Covachuelas and to climb to the Academy by the precipitous slope on the eastern edge of Toledo.

Two riflemen defending a remote room at the Central School stayed behind and sniped at the militia until nightfall, when they were dislodged by a grenade. They had covered the retreat of the others without knowing it, for no one had bothered to notify them that Major Villalba was withdrawing to the city.

Lieutenant José Amorena, a nineteen-year-old instructor at the Central School, was the last to leave Tavera. Ordered to bring up the rear, he kept up a covering fire until the others had dashed across the highway, but just as he was preparing to cross over, he saw an armored car flanked by crouching militia approaching from the bull ring. Quickly he ripped off his insignia, stuffed his forage cap into his shirt, and jumped out a back window into a lane hidden by a high wall. When the militia had passed, he dodged onto the highway and nonchalantly walked to the Bisagra Gate. His ruse worked; the militia assumed that he was one of them. He passed through the gate as the armored cars were start-ing up the hill to the Zocodover. At the top he ducked into an alley and hid until nightfall. Under cover of darkness Lieutenant Amorena reached the Alcázar before Villalba and the others.

Nightfall blotted out the Alcázar from the sights of Republi-can aircraft and artillery. A chance shell or bomb during the day had severed the main electric cable, and in the dim rooms of the fortress the blackness was unearthly and terrifying. The burning houses below the Zig Zag cast a lurid glow upon the north façade, but the cellars were like catacombs. Because of the power failure, no radios functioned. There had been comfort in listening to friendly stations like Radio Club Lisbon or Radio Milan, and in knowing that the rising was flourishing in other parts of Spain; now the Alcázar was cut off, deep in the center of Republican-held territory. In less than forty-eight hours the Alcázar had become a solitary White island in the middle of a raging Red sea.

The bombardment had also destroyed the pumping apparatus which brought water to the city from the river. Within hours the latrines of the building were clogged and the odor was nauseating. Laundry tubs were put behind crude screens in the cellar corridors, and rough lettering on the nearest wall indicated *"Caballeros"* or *"Señoras."* There was some consolation in knowing that the city did not have running water, either. By pure chance there was an adequate supply of water for drinking and cooking. The swimming pool in the subcellar had not been drained during the vacation period; moreover, three ancient cisterns in the bowels of the Alcázar were discovered, and the water in them was tested and found potable. There was also a well near the Santiago Barracks, although its site was exposed to shell fire.

Colonel Romero thought that the day had gone badly. The Tavera force had been driven back into the city and had indeed been fortunate in getting back at all. Units of his Guards had been cut off, like the force at the Bank of Spain, and he could guess what their fate would be.* The Alcázar was now faced with a siege, yet no one had made the slightest effort to bring in provisions from the town while there was still an opportunity. On the other hand Colonel Moscardó, who called a meeting of the command late that evening, was in a more complex mood, compounded of nervousness, optimism, and piety. In the superintendent's office, lighted by garish acetylene torches, Moscardó explained that they must be prepared to endure a siege of a few days before being relieved. General Mola was moving his army on Madrid from the north; General Franco would soon be pushing toward Toledo from Estremadura. There was no cause for anxiety. God would provide whatever they needed—as He had

---

* Such fears proved groundless, for these men were well treated. Through the intercession of the manager of the bank, the captured Guards were evacuated as prisoners to Madrid.

provided ammunition and water. Someone asked what they could do about obtaining food, since the provisions in the Academy commissary were known to be in short supply. There was absolutely nothing to worry about, Moscardó assured them; should the necessity arise, they could always counterattack and seize what they needed, from warehouses and stores in the city.

For the first time Moscardó met with opposition from the officers of his junta. But the conference was interrupted by a telephone call. On the line was Francisco Barnés, the Minister of Education, who asked to speak with Moscardó. The Minister's voice was quiet, friendly, relaxed. In contrast to those officials who had called previously, feigning ignorance of Moscardó's treason or threatening him because of it, Barnés was solicitous, even flattering. Moscardó must think of Spain: lives would be lost and the irreplaceable art of Toledo would be destroyed if he persisted in his present course.

"You have acted according to your conscience," Barnés said. "The gesture has been made, but why continue when you do not have the slightest possibility of success? It would be childish, Colonel; admirable in other circumstances, but not in this case. I believe that you ought to stop . . ."

Colonel Moscardó faltered. Was Barnés giving him an opportunity to save his life and salvage his pride—or was this just a subtle invitation to surrender? The faces around him were turned intently toward Moscardó, but he could barely see their individual expressions in the flickering light of the torches. These lives were in his hands, and scattered about the corridors, classrooms, and cellars of the Alcázar were hundreds of others. His stubborn will yielded to the awesome responsibility. Holding his hand over the mouthpiece of the telephone, he asked his junta to vote whether the Alcázar should be defended or surrendered. The majority elected to resist, but this time no one cheered the decision. In a toneless voice Moscardó passed on the information to Barnés.

"Then you will be responsible for the destruction of the Alcázar," said Barnés.

"I can only do my duty to Spain, sir."

"You know we have the artillery prepared and the troops ready. We have the means to annihilate you. This is the last time you have the opportunity to avoid spilling blood. Colonel, if you do not change your mind, I must order the attack immediately." Moscardó paused, then answered heavily, "Then we will receive it. You can begin whenever you want."

This was the last time Madrid called the Alcázar. Henceforth lead and steel replaced the telephone as the link between the Republic and the Toledo Academy. That same night a private of the Civil Guards deserted to the enemy. In making his separate peace with the Republic, Anastasio Prudencio took a step that many others dared not take—until later.

By the morning of July 23 the Republicans held the city. Hour by hour the Alcázar felt the clenched fists tighten over Toledo as the militia crawled into positions close to the fortress and began firing at the windows and walls. Some twenty Civil Guards at the provincial prison set out to fight their way across the city to the Alcázar. At the Plaza de Padilla they were stopped by some *milicianos* who shouted, "Join with us like the Asaltos!" The Guards shot them down and cautiously threaded their way through the sinuous streets leading toward the Academy. A block away from the carriage gate they turned a corner and found a band of militia constructing a barricade of iron bedsteads, sandbags, and sagging mattresses. Just beyond, the Alcázar loomed above the rooftops. At a run the Guards vaulted the barricade, clubbing the thunderstruck militia as they went over, and plunged across the Cuesta del Alcázar. Since the carriage gate was sealed shut, they threw themselves under a truck, parked near by to block access to a path leading up to the north terrace. Soon they were being fired at by both sides, until the sergeant in command put a handkerchief on his rifle muzzle and frantically waved it at the Alcázar windows. *"Viva España! Viva España! Viva España!"* he shouted desperately. Since no Republican ever used this old Monarchist cheer, the men at the Alcázar windows perceived that the figures huddled under the truck were their comrades.* Under covering fire the Guards managed to slip into

* The Nationalists had revived the forbidden *"Viva España!"* of the Monarchists. This, however, was regarded as reactionary by the Falangists, whose *"Arriba, España!"* ("Arise, Spain!") consistently gained currency during the war. Standard among the Republicans was *"Viva la República!"* and *"Viva la Rusia!"* was also used.

the Alcázar. They were the last group to enter, and their *"Viva España!"* was the last to be heard in the streets of Toledo until the siege was lifted.

Although an official census was not taken until a few weeks later, at this time there were 1760 souls in the Alcázar and its dependencies, of which 1205 were military personnel. In defending the place, Moscardó had the following complement under his command:

Unattached and strays	51
Retired officers	17
Central School of Physical Education	45
Academy	261
Asaltos (defectors) and Secret Police	25
Recruiting officers and staff	10
Civil Guard	690
Militarized civilians (including Falangists, Catholic Actionists, Monarchists, and Independents)	106
	1205

There were, in addition, 555 noncombatants, including 5 nuns, 22 drivers of requisitioned vehicles (none of whom were allowed to participate in the defense), and 211 children. Although Toledo had more priests per capita than any other city in Spain, none of them asked for refuge in the Alcázar. Their absence puzzled and distressed everyone, particularly Moscardó, who would gladly have traded, as time wore on, a platoon of combatants (except perhaps the Guards) for a single *sacerdote*.

As soon as the Nationalists were forced back into the restricted perimeter of the Academy, the Republicans were jubilant. "Trapped like so many dogs," they said. Their formula for conducting this siege was a simple one: when the supplies gave out, the Fascists would come out. In the meantime, resistance could be softened by subjecting the Alcázar to aerial bombardment, artillery barrage, and nerve-wracking *paqueo*. No one was foolish enough to propose or encourage a frontal assault. The element of time was now on the side of the Republicans. They knew this and the Nationalists suspected it.

Against the overwhelming Republican resources, in men and matériel, the armament of the Alcázar was pitifully inadequate. True, there were 1400 rifles—and those of the Civil Guard were unusually fine—but the 22 machine guns of the Academy had been a source of cadets' jokes for a generation: worn-out by being stripped down and reassembled in countless classroom demonstrations, more often than not they shook to pieces when fired. In good condition were 16 submachine guns, most of which had been brought by the Civil Guard. The heaviest weaponry consisted of four 50-mm. mortars (with 200 shells) and two 70-mm. mountain guns (with 50 shells), but Moscardó expressly forbade their use, reserving them for a dire emergency. The defense of the Alcázar, therefore, had to be based upon engaging the enemy at close range with small arms. Artillerist Méndez Parada was furious with himself and the other officers who had been at the arms factory: in their anxiety to collect a sufficient number of cartridges, they had forgotten to inquire about shells for the guns. It was now too late. Twenty of the best-trained artillerists in Spain had taken refuge in the Alcázar and had to watch impotently as the Republican guns shelled them.

The supply of food on hand in the Academy proved to be lower than anyone had suspected. Since the cadets had been on leave, no effort had been made to purchase provisions in the summer months. Captain Julián Cuartero, a professor of military history, had been placed in charge of the commissary, and his report was demoralizing. To feed nearly eighteen hundred people, they had the following on hand:

Flour	800 pounds	Tomatoes	275	cans
Beans	2400 "	Dried cod	40	pieces
Rice	1400 "	Salmon	250	pounds
Chick peas	1000 "	Olive oil	1500	quarts
Cauliflower	200 "	Condensed		
Peas	600 "	milk	150	cans
Artichokes	150 "	Cider	125	bottles
Coffee	60 "	Table wine	80	"
Sugar	500 "	Champagne	12	"
Marmalade	275 "	Vermouth	800	small bottles

The captain apologized for the condition of the beans, many of which were rotten, and for the loss of some bottles of cider, smashed by a bomb explosion the previous day. In the stable granaries was a large supply of rough wheat and barley, liberally mixed with mouse nests and common dirt, which, in an emergency, could be baked into a gritty bread. Cuartero explained that this food supply might last a week or ten days, certainly no longer. The store of baked bread was already gone, and the foodstuffs brought in by the refugees were nearly depleted.

There was plenty of food in the city, and Captain Cuartero urged that they act immediately. Colonel Romero brightened at this suggestion. For five frustrating days he had been cooped up in the Alcázar, watching his Civil Guards being forced backward foot by foot by *milicianos*. He was burning for revenge, for an opportunity to unleash his Guards, in force, against this Republican trash. The Alcázar command authorized Romero to plan a counterattack on the city the following day and Cuartero to organize a detail of men who would follow in the wake of the attack and pick the stores clean of food.

Meanwhile the dreaded "Red Terror," nightmare of the middle and upper classes of Spain, made its way into Toledo. By July 23 the trickle of *milicianos* had become an inundation. Bands of them, shod in rope-soled sandals and clad in blue boiler-suits, scoured the streets ferreting out "Fascists" and priests. The former were usually hauled off for interrogation, the latter shot where they were found. The men of units such as "Exterminating Battalion" and "Vengeance Group" seemed to abide by simple rules, the chief one being: kill anyone in a soutane—monks first. Toledo was converted into a noisy *plaza de toros*, but the matador was never in danger of being gored by his victim. Some priests were told that they could escape death by shouting *"Viva el comunismo!"* A few saved themselves by uttering this and anything else the militia demanded, obscenities or blasphemies; most refused. Father Pascual Martín was riddled by bullets in front of San Nicolás' Church as he cried *"Viva Cristo Rey!"* Were his outstretched hands, punctured like Christ's, meant as a final blessing for his assassins, or were they merely raised in an instinctive effort to push the bullets away?

Most Toledanos dared not intercede on behalf of "good priests" because intercession would imply Fascist sympathies, and suspicion alone might lead to execution or imprisonment.* However, popular priests were sometimes hidden by townspeople during the siege. One young girl, for example, succeeded in hiding two priests in her apartment, following a nightmarish pursuit down back alleys by drunken *milicianos*. But these priests still had an ordeal to face—from the window they could see the corpse of the prior of Las Carmelitas lying in the street below them. It remained there untouched for twenty-four hours.

The number of priests killed in Toledo is said to have been 107; most of them were butchered in public thoroughfares during the first hours of the occupation. Women and children hovered around their bodies, cramming pieces of bread or cigarettes between cold lips. Yet the atrocities committed in Toledo were mild compared with those in Ciudad Real, the adjoining province to the south, where the terror brought about the death of *all* the priests. No one in Toledo claimed to have seen *milicianos* dancing in the streets with the corpses of disinterred nuns, a rite which is said to have taken place elsewhere in Spain. Although a crucifix was found in the rectum of a dead priest, it had probably been put there after he died.

A ubiquitous figure at this time was Ranero, a frog peddler, who followed the militia with sadistic glee. He flayed his wares and strung them on a long reed, from which they dangled like miniature naked human beings. For months he had terrified unaccompanied matrons at church doors by pushing his frogs in their faces and chortling, "This is what you and your daughters will look like after we have raped and killed you!" After the militia broke into the town, he trotted behind them like a jackal and spent long hours squatting on his haunches in the streets, feasting upon the spectacle of dead priests.

Many Toledanos seemed to be more shocked by the desecrations than by the assassinations. A band of militia donned blood-stained soutanes, commandeered an open limousine, and drove

* According to the South African poet Roy Campbell, who was living in Toledo at the time, a prominent radical of the city told him that the noble priests deserved death more than the corrupt ones because the latter were good propaganda for the anti-Church factions, while the former were not. Even allowing for the notorious bias of Campbell, the remark sounds credible.

through the streets with a life-sized statue of San Francisco propped up in the seat between them. They had cut off its arms, placed a rifle on its shoulder, and attached a note—scrawled in priest's blood—to its chest: "He is with us." In the square of San Vicente's Church, some of the militia held a mock bullfight with gold-embroidered capes and pointed hats taken from the diocesan museum. Even the newly appointed civil governor, a man named Vega, joined the fun. Dressed in pontifical garments, he led a riotous procession with a crosier in his hand, pretending to be the Archbishop performing the rite of exorcism on the Popular Front. But this show almost had a violent denouement when a drunken *miliciano*, mistaking Vega for the real Archbishop, took a pot shot at him.

Responsible Republican leaders immediately placed guards at the cathedral (appropriately known in Spain as *La Rica*), at the El Greco Museum, and at other principal shrines in the city, but there were so many churches in Toledo that it was impossible to protect them all. San Juan de la Penitencia, San Lorenzo, and others were burned to their bare walls. Yet in the Conception Convent, near the Santa Cruz, a motley band of Anarchists were strangely moved by a *retablo* depicting the flagellation of Christ. After a short discussion among themselves, they decided to smash only the figure representing Christ and to allow the scourgers to remain—after all, they added, the scourgers were early Anarchists! Many peasants sloughed off their traditional Christian piety only temporarily. After a ragged *campesino* had smashed an image of the Virgin in San Vicente's Church, he fell on his knees, and weeping piteously, implored her forgiveness.*

The dogs and cats in Toledo vanished quickly; shooting live targets proved irresistible to militia handling firearms for the first time. Grenade-throwing, too, seemed to intrigue them. In the wealthier quarters they lobbed the grenades through upper-

---

* Similar conflicts between traditional and progressive modes of behavior plagued even the leaders of the Left. Roy Campbell recounts a story about the mayor of Toledo, Guillermo Perezagua, who was trying the case of a young man arrested for saying *"Adiós"*—mention of God being forbidden. The mayor delivered a harangue about the propriety of using *"Salud"* as a greeting instead of *"Adiós,"* and concluded with a warning: "Get out of here and don't let me here of your using that filthy word again!" *"Salud!"* cried the young man, running off as fast as he could. *"Adiós,"* replied the mayor, absent-mindedly reverting to the proscribed word.

story windows for no reason at all, since there were never such Fascist snipers in Toledo as plagued Madrid throughout the war. Those in the Alcázar could chart the course of the militia through the city by the deep-throated sound of the grenade detonations.

In the Zocodover, *milicianos* bellowed curses at the Alcázar, keeping carefully behind cover. From El Cristo de la Vega, a church near the arms factory, they brought a famous wooden image of Christ, and by working it like a puppet, tried to draw fire from the north windows of the fortress. When this failed, they shouted, "Here is El Cristo de la Vega. We are going to burn it. If you are true Catholics, you will come down here and stop us!" There was no reply from the Alcázar. Dismembering the effigy with axes, the militia threw the pieces upon a heap of debris in clear view of the windows. But in igniting the bonfire, two *milicianos* rashly exposed themselves. Rifles cracked, the men dropped into the fire, and the smell of burning flesh mingled with the smoke from El Cristo de la Vega.

From the time the militia began pouring into the city, the family of Colonel Moscardó realized that they were only hours away from captivity—or worse. In the evening of July 21 (the day when the Republican column appeared on the northern horizon), the guards assigned to their home had panicked and retreated to the Alcázar without orders. The wife of Lieutenant Manuel Guadalupe, an Academy officer, knew that the family of the Alcázar commander would be eagerly sought by the militia, so she urged them to hide in her in-laws' apartment, on the Calle de Granada. This they did, although her husband's parents regarded them as dangerous guests whose presence might compromise them and bring about their own execution.

At seven in the morning of July 23, *milicianos* searching for Lieutenant Guadalupe found the Moscardós in the apartment, but as they had destroyed all their papers, their identity was not discovered. Señora Moscardó and Carmelo were not bothered, but since Luis was an able-bodied young man of twenty-four, he was brought for questioning to the Diputación, the provincial delegates' building, where a "cheka" of Anarchists and Socialists had been set up by a local lawyer, Candido Cabello. Cabello could hardly believe his eyes when he recognized the son of Colonel Moscardó. Not entirely convinced of his luck, he sent one of his men back to the Guadalupes' apartment for confirmation, which soon arrived.

Cabello, an obese man with enormously thick glasses, smiled benignly at Luis. He had found the key which would open the gates to the Alcázar. It was now ten o'clock. He picked up the telephone and called the Academy.

Captain José Carvajal, an instructor at the Central School and aide to Colonel Moscardó, answered the telephone and handed it to his superior.

After identifying himself, Cabello said, "You are responsible for all the crimes and everything else that is happening in Toledo. I give you ten minutes to surrender the Alcázar. If you don't, I'll shoot your son Luis who is standing here beside me."

Moscardo's face did not betray his feeling. "I believe you," he said.

"And so that you can see it's true," Cabello continued, "he will speak to you."

Luis was then given the phone. "Papa!" he cried.

"What is happening, my boy?"

"Nothing," Luis answered. "They say they are going to shoot me if the Alcázar does not surrender. But don't worry about me."

"If it is true," replied Moscardó, "commend your soul to God, shout 'Viva España!' and die like a hero. Good-bye, my son, a kiss."

"Good-bye, Father, a very big kiss."

When Cabello was on the phone again, Moscardó said, "You might as well forget the period of grace you gave me. The Alcázar will never surrender!"

In the Diputación, Cabello slammed down the receiver violently and cursed briefly. Then he said to the *milicianos* around him, "Since his father wants it, do whatever you please with him." Luis Moscardó was led out.

In the Alcázar, Colonel Moscardó stood for some moments in stony silence, his staff too stunned even to condole him. Without a word to anyone he walked into his sleeping quarters in the next room and quietly shut the door. Another aide, Major Silvano

Cirujano, went out into the courtyard, where he announced to a hastily assembled crowd that Colonel Moscardó had just sacrificed his own son for a New Spain.*

This was the last telephone call received at the Alcázar. Curiously, Cabello's threat proved to be one of the worst blunders of the siege. He had intended to open the Alcázar with it, but he only succeeded in locking it more tightly. There had been divergent factions within the fortress, who might have exerted enough pressure upon the junta to compel them to open negotiations for surrender. But all alike were electrified by Moscardó's "sacrifice." Before, Moscardó had merely been a colonel commanding what looked like a doomed sector of the insurrection; now he had become a martyr and a symbol of the phoenix spirit of Nationalist Spain. To disobey Moscardó was to share indirectly in the murder of his son. In the weeks to come, what defender would have dared confront Moscardó face to face and plead that the Alcázar had suffered enough and should capitulate?

Although no one in the fortress knew it, Luis Moscardó was still alive, locked in a cell of the provincial prison. But around this time the other son, Pepe, was facing a firing squad in Barcelona, where the rising had been completely quelled by government supporters. Disguised as a hospital orderly, Pepe had successfully eluded the militia for five days, and was about to board a train for

---

* The details of Moscardó's conversation with his son are as well known to present-day Spaniards as Don Quixote's tilt at the windmills. Without question, this is the most widely publicized single episode of the Spanish Civil War. The "sacrifice" was of great use in Nationalist propaganda throughout the war and after. Here was an Abraham-Isaac or a God-Christ analogue in modern dress.

Various efforts to disparage the episode have been met with a convincing marshaling of evidence to prove that the conversation did take place, including the testimonials of witnesses in both the Alcázar and the Diputación (see Manuel Aznar's "The Alcázar Will Not Surrender," a 54-page monograph devoted exclusively to authenticating the episode).

There are, however, more important considerations. Granting that the conversation took place, what does it prove? What colonel, in any army, would surrender his command of nearly two thousand persons simply because his son's life was threatened? Even if his fellow officers allowed him to do so, what guarantee would he have that his son's life would be spared? The point is that while the hostage offer dramatized Moscardó's determination to hold the Alcázar at any cost, it could never have been seriously considered as an alternative.

Toledo when a medal displaying the Virgin slipped out of his pocket and fell to the ground. A bystander noticed it and informed the militia, who took him away to the Montjuich prison for interrogation and execution as a Fascist spy.

4

WAITING FOR MOLA

BY THE MIDDLE of the afternoon on July 23, the Alcázar and its dependencies were surrounded by Republican rifles. The militia were erecting barricades across the mouths of the streets and alleys leading to the Academy, and in some places along the west and south walls, Republicans and Nationalists lay within yards of one another. Militia arrived continually from Madrid and from the villages near by; they were given rifles and led to a barricade, from which they waged their private war upon the open windows of the detested fortress. But much more lethal was the machine-gun post which the Asaltos had mounted and manned in the tower of the Magdalena Church, since this rose above the level of the north terrace only fifty yards away. From the observation post on the terrace, Captain José Badenas (the officer who had knocked out the armored car at Tavera) engaged the Asaltos, although his squad was armed solely with rifles. When the gun began to shatter his temporary barricade, Badenas covered the retreat of his men to the main entrance, but as he sprinted after them, a gun burst from the church tower cut him nearly in half. To retrieve his body took twelve hours and a moonless night. Henceforth the north terrace was swept with gunfire and became useless as a defensive position.

The most vulnerable side of the Alcázar was the north. Here

the hill dropped down so steeply that potential attackers could-crawl up and mass in depth behind the edge of the terrace without being observed by defenders at the northern windows. Thus the defense of the Alcázar depended upon the Gobierno, which squatted at the bottom of the slope and from which the hillside could be observed. Furthermore, the Gobierno blocked access to the only road leading to the eastern dependencies. The wedge-shaped brick building became, as the Republican command soon found out, the keystone of the defense. Across the street from it lay the old Santa Cruz Hospital, which had been converted to the provincial museum, and here the Republicans established their heaviest firing line, behind its filigree Renaissance windows. The distance between the Gobierno and the Santa Cruz was about twenty yards—but these were the longest and most lethal twenty yards in Toledo. Direct attacks against the Gobierno were doubly dangerous because the attackers would come under rifle and machine-gun fire from the northern windows of the Alcázar, which loomed gigantically overhead, as well as from the windows of the Gobierno itself.

No immediate attack was feared from the south or west, for on those sides a maze of streets ran almost to the walls of the Alcázar. No assault column could maneuver in such restricted space and withstand the rifle fire or grenades dropped from the windows above. And since the Academy grounds ran to the brink of the Tagus gorge to the east, it was impossible to launch an attack there. The Republicans did begin to dig trenches and to fortify the brick shanties on the cliffs across the river, but the purpose of these was to cut off daylight communication between the Alcázar and the Gobierno and to harass the defenders in the Santiago Barracks.

After the midday meal the militia forgot the Fascists and remembered the siesta. The fierce morning *paqueo* gradually died away, and by twelve-thirty on July 24 the streets of the city were quiet. At that moment the carriage gate was thrown open and a hundred Civil Guards burst out. They jumped a barricade in the alley opposite the gate, then headed toward a market place several blocks west. At the same time a hundred others dashed out of the Gobierno and ran up the Calle del Carmen past the ruins of the Posada de la Sangre. This wave of Guards poured into the Zocodover and took up firing posts behind the pillars of the arcades along the east side. After them came others carrying laundry baskets in order to bring back food supplies.

The attack was a complete surprise to the militia, but they rallied with such celerity that the Guards were even more surprised. The first column did not reach its objective: it was impossible to advance together in the narrow streets, and from upper windows and rooftops came a barrage of bullets, grenades, roofing tiles, and other missiles, which forced them back to the carriage gate within minutes. Although the second column temporarily cleared the militia from the Zocodover, they had not expected to find an armored car parked at the far corner, out of sight of the Alcázar, which held them back while *milicianos* set up firing posts in the windows facing the square. One Guard, assigned to knock out the armored car, found himself pinned down behind a concrete bench near the bandstand. He emptied four rifle clips at the enemy before being forced back to the arcades with a load of bird shot in his back. This was to be the farthest point of penetration into enemy territory by an Alcázar soldier during the siege. The Guards then fell back to the Gobierno, leaving three of their force dead in the Zocodover. Somehow they had managed to capture three hostages, but their wicker baskets were empty.

Each side thought that it had learned something from the skirmish. At first Colonel Romero refused to believe that civilians, without training or discipline, had routed his professionals in a pitched street fight. The failure of the raid haunted him, and he never again suggested a counterattack. Henceforth he would let Moscardó work out commissary problems with God. The Republicans were also disturbed by the sortie, despite their successful resistance. They assumed that the Nationalists had reached the end of their tether and had tried to fight their way out of Toledo. In order to prevent this, they erected seventeen barricades, blocking every alley near the Alcázar which might be used as an escape route. These barricades were manned night and day in anticipation of the moment when the Fascists would come outside to fight instead of starving within.

To punish the Alcázar for its sortie, a trimotor flew over late in the afternoon and dropped fifteen bombs, most of which fell in the vicinity of the north terrace. The northwest steeple caught fire and burned through the night, since there was no apparatus for extinguishing it, and the north gateway was badly damaged. But there were compensations. A stray bomb fell on the Magdalena Church and destroyed the Asaltos' machine-gun post. However, another was installed and in use the next morning.

Casualties in the Alcázar were mounting: eight men had been killed and thirty-seven wounded. The improvised morgue, a tiny alcove under the central stairway, became noxious in the July heat. In the hours before dawn the bodies were wrapped in mattress covers and carried inside the Picadero, where they were buried in the turf, in the southwest corner. Since there was no priest, the service was limited to a short prayer read by Captain José Sanz de Diego, a young officer dismissed from the Army for his role in the abortive 1932 insurrection against the Republic. The captain became a surrogate priest, officiating at the burials, and at prayers held daily in the Alcázar.

July 25 is the day of Santiago, or St. James, patron saint of the Spanish Army. According to medieval chroniclers, Santiago used to intervene personally in battles between Castilians and Moors. According to a chronicler in the Alcázar, a retired major named Alfredo Martínez Leal, the Apostle did not intervene, however, in the battle between Castilians and Castilians. The day opened with the heaviest artillery barrage that the Alcázar had yet experienced. Major Martínez Leal records the moment: "As soon as the mantle of darkness disappears and the sun shines in all its purity, the bloodthirsty enemy eagerly sends, under the guise of a morning greeting, a hail of projectiles which succeeds in igniting an automobile parked on the north terrace, and the cruel chastisement from the cowardly shelling continues all day." The major was outraged that the Republicans had chosen this particular day to unleash their "barbaric syllogism," but the Republican command was doubtless aware of the grim joke. The day sacred to the Army was fittingly celebrated with pyrotechnics, and the government was delighted to provide them at its own expense.

The Republicans had established two permanent artillery emplacements, one at the Dehesa de Pinedo, the olive grove two miles north, and the other at Alijares, the old camp of the Academy two miles east. The 75-mm. gun had done little damage to the thick walls of the Alcázar, but the addition of nine 105-mm. guns posed a serious threat. Major Méndez Parada concluded that the Republicans handling the guns were inexperienced at range-finding, because many of the shells passed over the Alcázar and exploded beyond, in the city, and furthermore, mixed among the high-explosive shells were dummies used for practice. However, he knew that the Republican gunners would learn and improve in time.

To protect themselves against the shells, Major Méndez Parada introduced a crude but efficient warning system. During a bombardment the courtyard was off limits to everyone except couriers and aides. Observation posts in two towers kept close watch over the Dehesa and Alijares batteries by means of binoculars and periscopes. When they saw the enemy approach their guns, a bugler alerted the fortress by blowing "Attention." When a piece was loaded, an observer called out through a gramophone horn: "Cannon, east!" or "Cannon, north!" When the gun flashed, he yelled *"Fuego!"* ("Fire!"), giving everyone time to dive for cover. The bugler sounded "All Clear" when the observers saw the artillerists leaving their pieces, but on many days the firing was so heavy that this call was not sounded at all.

There were five different barrages during the day. A gap was made in the north entrance, wide enough to allow an armored car or small tank to drive through it. Lieutenant Luis Barber, the engineering officer, had to plug the breach with pillowcases full of dirt. Behind this barricade he buried a small dynamite charge, and behind the mine Méndez Parada positioned one of the 70-mm. guns—in case the mine did not stop an enemy tank. A stray shell smashed the gigantic clock above the south arcade. Eleven men were hurt when a ceiling fell down on them. Someone christened the new Republican guns "the dynasty of the Philips," revamping a stale Academy joke,* but it was difficult to sustain a sense of humor about them.

---

* "Philip" was a traditional nickname for a piece of artillery in the Spanish Army. Many years before, the soldier who fired the sunset salute at the Alcázar was named Philip. When the officer in charge barked the order "Fire, Philip!" the cannon itself seemed to obey the command.

•   •   •

Ever since the electricity was cut off, technicians among the Civil Guards had been trying to find a way to operate their radio by using automobile batteries, but without success. Although they could strip down a machine gun and put it together blind-folded, they were baffled by electrical equipment. Fortunately there were two electricians among the civilian refugees, the Labandera brothers, and they were given the job. By noon of July 25 they succeeded in picking up a weak signal from Unión Radio in Madrid.

Through the static came a news broadcast that astonished everyone: the announcer reported that the Alcázar of Toledo had surrendered! At first this was regarded as a great joke, but soon disquieting implications canceled the jest. If Generals Franco and Mola believed this report, they might abandon their efforts to push toward Toledo and lift the siege. The rumor had to be scotched.

Anxiety increased at nightfall when Republican planes showered leaflets on the Alcázar. Most of the leaflets, printed on red paper, contained the usual propaganda: appeals to the soldiers to kill their tyrannical leaders and promises to respect their lives if they deserted. But among them were pages from a Madrid newspaper article—complete with faked photographs—describing the surrender of the Alcázar. It was like reading one's own obituary.

Moscardó immediately held a meeting of his junta and asked for a volunteer to slip through the lines and convey the truth to General Mola, known to be with his army somewhere in the Guadarrama Mountains northwest of Madrid. He admitted that there was "only one chance in a hundred of the mission being successful." The messenger would have to pass through fifty miles of enemy territory, all of it bristling with *milicianos*. Two captains, both of them instructors at the Central School, stepped forward, and Moscardó chose Captain Luis Alba. A handsome aristocrat, Alba seemed like an ideal choice: he was clear-headed as well as athletic, he was one of the best horsemen in Toledo, and

as an amateur mountaineer he knew the terrain of the Guadarramas. Also, he loved to hunt and fish, and the pursuit of these
sports had brought him into contact with people all over the
countryside, who liked him for his natural and unaffected manner. If anyone could reach General Mola, that man was surely
Captain Alba. All these factors outweighed the only reservation
Moscardó had about choosing him: Alba was married and the father of four children, the last of whom had been born just a week
before.

The night was moonless. After putting on a blue *mono*, Alba
was given the identity card of a hostage, Antonio Gómez, listed
as #173 of the Toledo cell of the Communist party. The card
mentioned no profession, so Alba wrote "fisherman" on it.
Fellow officers gave him a hundred pesetas and a pistol which he
wore on a cord hanging from his neck, hidden underneath his
mono. Friends accompanied him to the east end of the riding
school terrace, where they could hear the Tagus roaring through
the gorge below them. He practiced the clenched-fist salute once
or twice and asked jokingly, "Do I look like the real article?"
Then he swung himself over the railing, and disappeared into the
black void below, while his comrades waited tensely for the
sound of the shot which would announce that he had been discovered.

Since the slope below the Picadero terrace was almost vertical
and since the Santiago dominated this entire sector, Captain Alba
knew that there was little danger of enemy posts lying below.
The real hazards lay in trying to cross the New Bridge a hundred
yards up the river, or walking down river, where working-class
houses clustered all the way down to the edge of the water on
either side. To avoid these dangers, Alba rolled up his clothes and
slipped into the river. The current was as swift as that of a mountain stream. It could have carried him around the entire city to
the shoals by the arms factory, but since there were dams and
other obstructions downstream, he swam to the opposite shore.
He dressed quickly and followed the highway circling the city to
the south, parallel to the river. On the far side of the city where
the Tagus resumed its western course, Alba crossed the river
again near the arms factory, and headed toward open country in
a northwesterly direction. He knew that the farther he got from

Toledo, the better his chance of escaping detection. By dawn Captain Alba, alias Antonio Gómez, was twelve miles out of the city on his mission to Mola.

July 26 was a Sunday. There was no Mass in the chapel of the Alcázar because there was no priest; there was no Mass in the churches of the city because the militia leaders would not allow them. But on this first Sunday of the siege the tourists began to arrive, most of them from Madrid and eager to fire at least one shot at the hated Alcázar. From the Bisagra Gate they climbed up to the barricades around the fortress, where they could peep over the striped mattresses and gape at the walls and windows towering above them less than twenty yards away. They could savor the illusion of being in danger, and were even allowed to pull the trigger of a rifle which some *miliciano* would point for them.* "To fire a bullet at the Alcázar" became, in some circles, the badge of loyalty to the Republic. Many Madrileños came down to Toledo on subsequent Sundays, bringing with them their families, their picnic baskets, and their rifles or pistols. Following a swim in the Tagus, a quiet luncheon *en famille*, and a nap in an olive grove, they would join their comrades at the barricades for a few hours before catching a late bus back to Madrid.

The most popular place from which to watch the siege was the gun emplacements in the Dehesa de Pinedo. The rural people were amused by the roar of the guns and the swirling dust storm that followed the discharge. Unlike the militia, the artillerists were Regulars. Their uniforms drew the women, who in turn attracted cameramen. During the first weeks of the siege, Madrid newspapers often featured photographs of pretty girls posing beside the guns in the Dehesa de Pinedo; and through binoculars, observers in the towers of the Alcázar could pick out the girls

* Usually these were city dwellers of the lowest class. Arturo Barea and other Republicans have expressed their disgust with the carnival atmosphere found on the Toledo front during the early weeks of the siege. Moreover, they have observed that many of the militia here were even shunned by their acquaintances back in Madrid. It was certainly true that one fought against the Alcázar in safer circumstances than against Mola in the Guadarramas or Franco in Estremadura. When a man was referred to as a "Toledo soldier," praise was not intended. As the weeks passed and the Alcázar held out, even dedicated Republicans proudly pointed to their enemies inside and said, "They fight like *Spaniards*."

pulling the lanyards or pressing the firing pins which sent the shells hurtling at them.

In order to save ammunition, Moscardó posted an order that no one was to fire his rifle unless he had a specific target, and the defenders soon found that silence was one of their most effective allies. From the Republican lines the Alcázar looked empty yet ominous. No Fascists passed across window casements; no threatening rifles protruded from loopholes. A *miliciano* might lie for days with his rifle sighted upon a window, yet never see his enemy, but if through carelessness or bravado he exposed himself at his barricade, a rifle cracked at a window. This single shot would set off hundreds of militia rifles in a chain reaction, but no one at the windows deigned to answer them. The Fascists seemed always to be watching, while invisible themselves. Some days the Republicans fired more cartridges than the Nationalists used during the entire siege.

This Sunday was marked in the Alcázar by a slight rise in morale. Neither the sporadic shelling nor the heavy *paqueo* had killed anyone, and the two Republican planes which had flown over had dropped no bombs. The first issue of a mimeographed newspaper, *El Alcázar*, was published in the Academy museum and distributed among the defenders. But most of all they were cheered by the thought that Captain Alba was on his way to Mola. It would not be long, they believed, before a relief column would approach from the west. What none of them knew was that the corpse of Captain Luis Alba lay in a ditch near the 7-kilometer stone on the road to the small town of Torrijos.

Earlier that morning, as he increased the distance between himself and Toledo, Captain Alba must have become increasingly confident. When the sun came up, he left the fields and followed the highway. As he approached Burujón, he was seized with a daring idea. Boldly walking into the village, he presented his identity card to the local militia committee and explained that since he was on a secret mission for the Toledo Defense Committee, he required an automobile and a driver to take him to Arenas de San Pedro, a Republican-held town in the Guadarramas. In the history of Burujón nothing of such consequence had ever happened before; the committee was delighted at this providential opportunity to assist in the war against the Fascists, and a man was dispatched to fetch the only automobile in the village. While they waited, Comrade Gómez was conducted to the local bar so that he could be treated to a *coñac* and could treat them in turn to a first-hand account of the war in Toledo and in Madrid.

News of his arrival had swept through the village, which turned out to welcome the important visitor. Alba grew uneasy, but he dared not show his impatience to leave lest he arouse their suspicion. As he walked into the bar, a friendly voice called out from a dark corner, "Why, Captain Alba! What are you doing here?" The speaker, a lad who had served as a beater on occasional Academy hunts, came forward eagerly to shake his hand. But the militia around him had turned to stone, and the bar was suddenly quiet.

The ominous silence was broken by Alba, who shook the boy's hand and said, "Captain? Who are you calling captain, José? You must think I've come up in the world. How about a drink, eh?" José caught on and tried to pretend he had been joking, but the villagers of Burujón were not to be fooled twice. They dragged Alba outside and were about to shoot him on the spot, but the mayor and another of Alba's hunting companions, Pedro Rodríguez, insisted that he be sent to nearby Torrijos to stand trial. Like José, Rodríguez liked and respected the unaffected young captain.

When the Burujón delegation arrived in Torrijos with Alba, they got an icy reception at the town hall. The local judge had been removed, and the mayor of Torrijos refused to become involved in the petty affairs of Burujón. The consensus was that Alba should have been killed back in Burujón; since that had not been done, he ought to be taken to Toledo. Although vexed by this decision, the delegation dutifully set out for Toledo, eighteen miles away. En route they suffered another humiliation when two Asaltos stopped their car, and after hearing their story, insisted on driving Alba to Toledo in their own car—they were afraid that the captain might be executed without a trial.

As the Asaltos drove off with Alba, the men of Burujón became enraged: in a single day they had been tricked by a wily Fascist captain, rebuked as incompetents by the mayor of Torrijos, and maligned as assassins while attempting to carry out their duty. Starting their automobile again, they sped furiously after the Asaltos.

As the car in which Alba was riding topped a ridge, he saw the Alcázar in the distance for a moment before the vehicle plunged down a long hill. Just before reaching a roadside tavern called Venta de Hoyo, the car struck a pothole and careened out of control into a deep ditch. The Asaltos were stunned. Although his hands were tied, Alba managed to worm out of the car and crawl up to the highway just as the Burujón militia pulled up behind. Aghast at the wreckage and feeling partly responsible for it, one of them cried defensively, "Mother of God! Now see what the *fascista* has done to us!" It was too much to bear. They surrounded Alba and shot him down in the road. Then they pushed his body into the ditch and hurried back to Burujón. Only Pedro Rodríguez had refused to fire a shot.

For two days the body of Alba lay in the ditch. Then it was carried to the arms factory to be claimed by his family. No one of them appeared. His wife and children were in the Alcázar, and his relatives in Toledo feared that they might jeopardize their own lives if they publicized the kinship. Finally the body was taken to Madrid, where it was thrown into a garbage truck and driven through the streets under a placard: THE CORPSE OF AN ALCÁZAR FASCIST.*

In the Alcázar, however, no one knew that the mission to Mola had failed. Each day a special observer in the southwest tower scanned the horizon for a sign of the expected relief column, but the only things he saw in the far west were mountains, plains, and sky. Perhaps the failure of Alba's mission did not matter, so long as those in the fortress did not know the truth. Was it not better to wait for Mola than to wait for nothing?

The flour supply was exhausted by the morning of July 27. In place of the daily bread ration Captain Cuartero distributed a handful of toasted wheat from the granary attached to the Academy stables. This grain was little better than barn sweep-

---

* A friend of Alba's, José Rodrígues Valero, made a detailed investigation of his death several months later. The final burial place is unknown, but a granite monument marks the place where he was killed, on the Torrijos highway, near Venta de Hoyo. In Spanish the word *hoyo* means "ditch"; a secondary meaning is "grave."

ings, but there was enough of it to last for several weeks. Meticulously the captain stored away the remaining foodstuffs for an emergency, keeping out some canned milk for the children and the wounded. It was plain that rations of toasted wheat could not sustain human life; someone pointed out that the horses could be eaten.

From the beginning the Cavalry officers had been worried about how they would be able to feed the ninety-seven horses and twenty-seven mules.* Some of them had already been killed during *paqueos* or bombardments, by direct hits or by kicking one another to death during the uproar. The others had subsequently been brought inside the Alcázar and stabled in the subcellar at the south end of the building. The care of these animals became almost as important as the concern for the women and children: the water in the swimming pool was reserved for their use, and their fodder was carried to them.

Unlike the French, the Spanish have no tradition of eating horseflesh, and the thought of mule meat was loathsome to them. It was decided to eat the horses first and hope that the Alcázar would be relieved before they came to the mules: *El Alcázar* devoted an editorial to allaying misgivings: "The horse is a clean and handsome animal; it eats and drinks only what is in the best condition. . . . All prejudices against it are unfounded." Nowhere is the Spaniard's affinity for rationalization better exemplified than in the concluding sentence: "The nutritive value of the horse is greater than that of the bovine race." Moscardó ordered that the first animal be prepared for the evening meal. Everyone agreed that the victim should be Pistolera, a vicious mare which had thrown or kicked, at one time or another, nearly every rider and groom in the Academy. Many came especially to see her shot, skinned, and butchered. Cajón, on the other hand, was almost a sacred horse, famous throughout Spain as a jumper. The Cavalry officers pledged never to butcher Cajón, but to shoot him if the Reds

---

* While this is the official number according to Nationalist press releases after the siege, other sources list 210 horses and 30 mules. Adding to this confusion, the Alcázar logbook alludes to 199 horses and no mules at all—which is clearly wrong. The probable explanation for this discrepancy is that no one bothered about the specific number of animals on hand until they became a vital source of food.

ever succeeded in fighting their way into the Alcázar. Such a horse must not fall into the hands of the enemy. Since one or two horses each day could not feed eighteen hundred people, a new dish was invented. After the steaks, small chops, liver, and other choice parts had been put aside for the infirmary, the rest was cut into ribbonlike slivers and boiled in kettles with grains of wheat, two quarts of olive oil, and a few beans. In the first days a quarter of a pound of block salt from the stables was added, but this luxury soon gave out. Some of the indigent refugees, for whom any meat was a delicacy, found this stew so savory (and the furnishings of the Alcázar so opulent) that they alluded to their new residence as "Casa Rockefeller." Their enthusiasm was short-lived; they soon learned that it was possible to starve on good fare if one did not receive enough of it.

When the acetylene torches flickered out, fat stripped from the horse carcasses illuminated the Alcázar. One tiny lamp, fashioned from a sardine can and fitted with a rag wick, burned in each cellar room at night. The black fumes and stench were disgusting, but anything was better than darkness—especially during a bombardment. Some officers invited their friends to dine with them on days when their own horses were served, but each guest brought his own ration with him. The horses' bones and entrails were buried in the Picadero, at least during the first weeks. Afterward, when the men became weaker and the barrages heavier, this garbage was thrown, with sewage from the latrines, out of the eastern windows onto the parade ground.

The Alcázar was saved, temporarily, by the horses of the Spanish Cavalry. Captain Cuartero could thank God that the Cavalry had not been mechanized. *El Alcázar* printed an editorial which suggested that the inscription on the statue of Charles V in the patio ought to be changed to conform to the present emergency: it was the horse, not the Emperor, which should be lifted up first. It might then be dragged away and eaten.

Yet only the inexperienced and the naïve believed that the supply would last indefinitely. Moscardó had said that God would provide, but unless He provided something else, it was likely that the Alcázar would quickly be starved into surrender.

Although the Republicans surrounding the Alcázar seemed to hold all the cards, they were reluctant to cut the deck. No one knew the exact number of militia in the city, but it was estimated at seven thousand. General Riquelme was nominally in command, but he had no authority whatever over the individual units of Anarchists, Socialists, and Communists which came and went as the spirit moved them. The Anarchists, in particular, exasperated Riquelme. These were the most numerous—and the most uncooperative. They distrusted everyone else, the Loyalist Army officers most of all. Many of them openly argued that as a first step they should liquidate the Communists and Socialists fighting with them at the barricades, and exterminate the Fascists in the Alcázar afterward. They determined everything by vote: if one of their leaders ordered an attack and they did not care for the idea, they simply demoted him by ballot. Their passion for individual freedom was so consuming that they would not agree to the only measure which might have given them permanent freedom: surrendering a portion of it temporarily.

Even had he possessed undisputed command, Riquelme would not have expected an undisciplined and untrained militia—no matter what their superiority in numbers—to storm the Alcázar by a direct assault. At the barricades the militia showed courage facing the windows of the Alcázar, but this was quite different from dislodging soldiers from protected positions, especially soldiers who were fighting for their lives and, in some cases, the lives of their families in the cellars below. García Lorca had once contemptuously called the Guards "men of patent-leather souls," but the rifles at the loopholes were handled with remarkable skill. Few Guards had ever been dismissed from the corps for cowardice.

Meanwhile Madrid was becoming increasingly angered and embarrassed by the stagnation on the Toledo front. A pocket of Nationalists flaunting rebellion only forty miles from the capital of Spain demonstrated, both at home and abroad, that the civil conflict was a major one. The Republic was seeking promises of aid and intervention from the great neutral nations, who demanded, in return, evidence that the Republican cause was likely to prevail. Rubbing salt into the wound, foreign journalists pointed to the resistance of the Alcázar as proof of the military impotence of the Republic. True, the Republicans were being pushed back in Estremadura and Andalucia, but these defeats took place far away and were therefore easily denied, whereas everyone in Madrid was posted on the conditions existing at Toledo. If anyone doubted that the Alcázar was still holding out, he had only to run down from Madrid for an hour or so and see for himself. The Alcázar was a festering carbuncle on the face of the Republic; it was increasingly difficult to ignore it and to hope that if left alone, it would disappear. Riquelme was given a few more days: if at the end of that time the Academy had not been starved to surrender, some more drastic measure would have to be taken.

Riquelme's belief in the imminent surrender of the Alcázar seemed to be confirmed by the testimony of a soldier of the troop section who deserted during the evening of July 26 and who reported that the flour supply was gone, the vegetables rotten, and the meat nonexistent. Up there the only thing they had to eat was stable fodder. Riquelme was so encouraged by this that he suspended artillery barrages for the rest of the month in order to save ammunition. The deserter had neglected to mention the horses themselves.

Within the Alcázar the five-day lull was interpreted as a sign prefiguring victory. Was a relief column drawing near, or had the enemy learned that the walls of the Alcázar were indestructible? Bullets still sprayed the exterior walls, for the *paqueo* continued, but if a man exposed himself at a window and was hit, he had only himself to blame. The overwhelming fact was that the guns had stopped.

At dusk during these days the giant courtyard resembled the *plaza mayor* of any provincial Spanish town. Seated on folding chairs in the center, the Academy band drowned out the *paqueo* with light-opera selections and military marches. The women were allowed to come up from the cellars, and it was possible for them to collect a little extra water from the pump near the Santiago to wash the faces of their children before strolling with their families along the arcades. Reverting to ancient Spanish custom, bachelor officers sauntered counterclockwise around the courtyard in order to come face to face with the unmarried girls strolling arm in arm in the opposite direction.

On one of these evenings Moscardó arranged a soccer match between the Civil Guard and the Central School—won by the academicians, who got two cigarettes apiece. Even more memorable was the improvised circus, featuring attractions like master juggler Chu-Ling-Kal-Var; a heavyweight wrestling bout (in Greco-Roman style); two magicians, famous from one end of Toledo to the other; and a finale of a fandango—with music by the band. A boy and a girl who had met in the Alcázar requested permission for a civil marriage, but Moscardó flatly rejected their application: marriage ceremonies performed without a priest were little better, in his view, than the barbaric free-love relationships proliferating among the Reds outside.

Clubs were founded. The intelligentsia met in the museum, editorial offices of *El Alcázar*. Falangists and adherents of Nationalist Spain debated politics and refuted Marxist theory in the flag room. A music master played records of Italian opera, although each time his group met, he had to climb the northeast tower to borrow back the gramophone horn from the artillery spotter, who used it as a megaphone. There were two centers of culture, the Cavalry library and the Infantry library, both well stocked with books in shelves reaching to the ceiling. No one foresaw that the time would soon come when these books, many in fine cordovan leather bindings, would be used to barricade these same rooms. Advertising his hours in *El Alcázar*, the Academy barber announced that he would accept payment in pesetas or in kind: customers, however, were kindly requested to bring their own water if they wanted a shave. Since few men could obtain water for shaving, beards and lice flourished.

This period was so peaceful that people forgave Antonio Rivera (nicknamed "the Angel") for his seditious stand. This young man, son of a former mayor of Toledo and secretary of Acción Popular, the Catholic party, had taken refuge in the Alcázar but refused to shoulder a gun or take part in the defense. Hatred was a sin, he claimed, and in order to kill one had to hate. What would happen to them, some of the women screamed at him, if everyone believed as he did? In that case, he told them, they would not be in the Alcázar at all. Since the Alcázar junta had no use for a philosopher, Antonio served on the slop-bucket brigade.

The few secret police who had joined the garrison continued their work. In the first weeks many minor thefts of food and clothing were reported, but the major task of the police was to track down the thief who had stolen the wheat samples from the agricultural display at the museum. Since the booty was eaten, the culprit was never found. It was noted that as the siege wore on, the incidence of theft declined; was this because practicing Christians did not want to die with sins on their consciences? The dozen or so political hostages in the Alcázar were closely guarded only at night; they knew that if they tried to escape in daylight, they would probably be shot down by both sides. They received the same rations as everyone else—on less they would have starved to death.

Trusting in God, Franco, and the Spanish Army, the population of the Alcázar waited, now convinced that the worst was over. The sentence "On this day there were no casualties" appeared twice in the logbook of the Academy, but it would not, in the weeks ahead, appear again. August brought a swift termination to pleasant days in "Casa Rockefeller."

5

BOMBARDMENT

WITHOUT WARNING the stillness was broken on the afternoon of August 1 by an observer crying *"Fuego!"* Seconds later it was followed by the explosion of a shell on the roof of the Picadero, which was empty except for a woman in black, kneeling by the grave of her son. Within minutes, 105-mm. shells were bursting all along the east side of the Alcázar. From their tower windows the observers, who had been completely surprised by the eruption of the Republican guns, watched the unidentified woman scurrying back and forth on the esplanade. Miraculously she was not hit and returned safely to the fortress. For two hours the guns fired on all the dependencies, and they did their destructive work well. At the end of the barrage—140 shell bursts were counted— the Picadero was in flames and the Alcázar was completely enveloped in rolling clouds of black smoke.

At the Gobierno the soldiers clutched their rifles and braced themselves for the expected attack from the Santa Cruz under cover of the smoke screen. But it never came. The Republicans seemed to regard the destruction of the Picadero as sufficient work for one day. This structure was a boxlike affair of brick and mortar with steel girders supporting a roof of sheet metal sheathed by wooden planks; as the planks burned, the sheeting crashed down noisily onto the turf floor. The blaze continued all night, and by morning only the skeleton of the building remained.

After several days of waiting for the Alcázar to surrender, General Riquelme had been ordered by Madrid to blast the fortress apart, stone by stone if necessary, in order to break their will to resist. Their success with the Picadero encouraged the artillerists. The following day they concentrated their fire on the curved passage, at the southeast corner, connecting the Alcázar with the Capuchinos and the dining hall. If this were destroyed, interior communication between the main building and the dependencies would be severed. For three days the passage was shelled, until gaps began to appear in the walls and ceiling. During the barrage, a volunteer team tried to replace the dislodged stones as quickly as they were knocked down, and one man was killed and two were wounded at this work. Although it was still possible to use the curved passage, it was now necessary to run through it, crouching in order to avoid being hit by the rifle fire which played upon the gaps from the shanties across the Tagus.

Two more soldiers of the troop section deserted, during the evening of August 2, by slipping down the cliff to the river and crossing into the Republican lines. They brought encouraging news to General Riquelme: an epidemic of dysentery seemed to be breaking out. *El Alcázar* implored its readers not to evacuate their bowels outside the latrines. People were afraid that the horse fodder was tainted, and had stopped eating it. Bismuth pills were being dispensed with the regular food ration. Horses and mules were the only food left.

In the Alcázar, three meals had been cut back to two. These were ladled out in the dining hall, where Captain Cuartero checked each name on a roster. Everyone brought his own container for the stew ration, and these ranged from plugged flowerpots to enameled bedpans. One prominent Toledano, who claimed that he was a descendant of a Spanish king, ate his horse goulash out of an ornate silver punch bowl embossed with the family crest, but he had to wait in line as all the others. Except for Moscardó and certain key officers of the junta, there was no preferential treatment. Like death, hunger was democratic.

Many Civil Guards saved some of their food so that their children could have more to eat. A line of soldiers waited outside the dining hall after each meal: these men had given away their rations and were allowed to pick over the stew leavings—grease and bones, discarded tail stumps, spleen, or cooked blood. Children received other favors. From time to time Captain Cuartero issued them special desserts: one or two almonds, a spoonful of fruit preserve, and, most prized, a packet of "Postre Ideal," which, if it had been cooked with eggs and milk, would have been caramel pudding.

To demoralize the defenders, the Republican artillerists shelled the dining hall at mealtimes, so that the hours for eating had to be changed from time to time. Smoke in the kitchen chimney always drew a barrage, or at least a *paqueo* from the houses across the Corralillo. There were days when shell bursts in or near the kitchen were so heavy and frequent that the two cooks had to hide behind their cauldrons and work between explosions. It was not uncommon for Eugenio Carrasco, the young, cool-headed chef, to prepare fillets for the infirmary by crouching behind the stove and cooking the meat without looking at it. On one occasion a spatula was shot out of his hand.

Most Alcazareños agreed that Eugenio and his assistant, Gregorio Martínez—a bulletheaded half-wit known locally as "the Dog"—were the real heroes of the siege, and both were several times cited for their comportment under fire. Meals were sometimes delayed; none was ever left unprepared. Fuel for the stove was never a problem. Shell bursts laid kindling at their feet, and damaged furniture provided firewood. In the houses across the Corralillo, militia with megaphones tirelessly bombarded the cooks with insults, obscene recipes, and threats: "Hey, you sons of bitches! We're coming to skin you. We'll cut off 'the Dog's' *cojones* and carry them in procession through the Zocodover." When a shell exploded in the kitchen and blew the quarters of horseflesh into the attic, the pieces were retrieved by "the Dog" and eaten by the Alcazareños. Eugenio pointed out that that stew was particularly rich in iron.

As early as July 29 the Alcázar was buzzing with a rumor that somewhere near the fortress there was a secret warehouse filled with fat sacks of golden wheat. The author of this incredible story was Isidoro Clamagiraud, who owned a bakery in Toledo, although he was actually a French citizen. In the beginning everyone dismissed him as mad, but he besieged Colonel Moscardó's office with such determination that the junta began to put some faith in his report. Don Isidoro insisted that the Bank of Bilbao had leased a small building on the steep slope just beyond the railing of the Picadero terrace, and that in it were tons of wheat, which the bank had collected as payments on loans. The officers recalled several uninhabited sheds thereabout, but none of these had been used for many years; it seemed unlikely that wheat or anything else could have been deposited so near the Academy grounds without someone having heard of it.

With mounting excitement Moscardó and his staff followed the Frenchman up into the northeast tower, from which they could see, barely visible over the terrace railing, the tiled roof of the house he had described. It lay down the hill from the Gobierno, along the Calle del Carmen; across the street from it was a row of decrepit shacks believed to be occupied by militia snipers. Thus the so-called granary was situated in a neutral zone between the lines. Had a miracle occurred, or was the Frenchman a half-crazed liar? To find out, Moscardó ordered a reconnaissance in force to be made after nightfall.

On the evening of August 3, twenty men slipped out of the dining hall, climbed through the charred debris of the Picadero, and began crawling the hundred yards across the terrace. Although the moon was bright, they had some protection from a thin row of acacias by the far railing. They reached the spot directly above the roof of the alleged warehouse, which lay several feet below the terrace railing. While the others held back in the shadows with rifles cocked, the Academy blacksmith lowered himself to the roof and began removing the tiles with a crowbar. Once a tile slid off the roof and clattered onto the road, but if the houses opposite were occupied by the militia, there was no sign. After several minutes of work, the blacksmith had opened a hole large enough to let a man through, and he clambered back up to the terrace.

The job of climbing down into this aperture fell to a soldier named Pérez Molero. After tying a rope to the railing, he lowered himself into the opening. When he reached the floor, he hesitated about lighting a match because he did not know what might be sharing the room with him. Instead, he groped on hands and knees until he bumped into something which he thought was the body of a man. Running his hands over it, he recognized it as a sack. When he slit it with a knife, something poured out, hissing, on the ground. Pérez then risked a single match. Grains of threshed wheat were cascading from the sack, and piled to the ceiling on all sides were hundreds of others.

At once Civil Guards began hauling up sacks through the hole in the roof. When they had collected twenty-three of them— each weighed two hundred pounds—they dragged them across the terrace toward the Alcázar. At one point they were heard or seen by militia across the gorge. A Very light wriggled upward in the darkness and a machine gun sprayed the terrace. The men lay quietly behind their sacks until the firing ceased. It was early in the morning when they reached the dining hall with the last of their burden. Moscardó retired to the chapel of the Academy and gave thanks to the Virgin of the Alcázar. Moscardó was regarded by the garrison with renewed awe: had he not told them that they must not worry, because God would provide? Thus far he had been an accurate prophet. Captain Vela estimated that there were over two thousand sacks of wheat in the warehouse, enough to supply them with bread for an indefinite period—so long as the Republicans did not learn about it.

Converting the wheat kernels into food became a major problem. The first recourse was to cook them with the stew, but stomachs already upset by the bad fodder were not able to digest the grain. Many soldiers were already so weakened by dysentery that they could barely climb up to posts at the upper windows. The raw grain was next distributed so that each person could grind it or do with it whatever he wished. The ingenious and active ones solved the problem. Some employed rocks as pestles with which to beat the kernels into flour on the flagstones of the cellars; others used the casings of exploded shells as mortars, although they complained that their flour tasted like *trilita*—TNT. Few were as lucky as the Civil Guard who filched a neolithic mortar and pestle from the archaeological department of the museum and discovered that the implement was astonishingly efficient. The Alcázar temporarily reverted to the Stone Age. Since many were too weak or too sick to grind their own flour, the junta resolved to process the wheat for everyone.

There was a small mill which had been used to grind animal feed, but there was, of course, no electricity to operate it. The Labandera brothers solved the problem, however, by building a permanent stand for a Harley Davidson motorcycle and running a leather strap from the rear wheel to the roller of the fodder mill. Another strap ran the generator which recharged the batteries used in powering the radio. The policeman who had formerly driven the motorcycle was appointed the official "mill technician" and made responsible for its operation. The gasoline tanks of the trucks and automobiles parked on the terraces had previously been drained, to minimize fires and explosions. There was enough fuel to run the motorcycle for sixty-eight days, since the motor consumed two and a half gallons each day. Every half-hour the motorcycle had to be stopped to cool the motor. Trying to be helpful, a platoon of Civil Guards trotted out to a small car parked on the east esplanade, picked it up, bodily, and carried it into the Alcázar by way of the curved passage. When jacked up, it functioned better than the Harley Davidson, but it consumed so much more fuel that they had to return to the motorcycle. Although the mill produced rough ground wheat rather than real flour, the product proved digestible. Stomach complaints began to disappear.

In the Alcázar there was a large field oven. Like the stew kettles, it was a prime target for the Republican artillerists, who spotted its location by telltale smoke, and had to be moved four times during the siege—from the kitchen to the swimming pool, to the landing of the main stairway, and finally to the subcellar on the south side. One of the first questions which deserters were asked was the present site of the kitchen and oven. Wherever it was, the oven was covered with rubble and dirt for insulation, and in twelve hours of operation baked seventeen hundred cigar-shaped rolls, each about six inches long and two inches wide, and weighing about a quarter of a pound. In shape, color, and texture they suggested dog excrement of several days' standing; one of these and two servings of stew comprised the daily ration in the

Alcázar from August 1 onward. In addition, there were two delicacies which were prepared whenever anyone had accumulated the ingredients: one was toasted wheat cooked dry in a pan after splitting the shells of the kernels; the other was "horse tart" made from a batter of horse grease and crushed wheat. One woman developed a special recipe for her horse tarts and jealously guarded her secret like a master chef. No one ever discovered how she made them, but everyone who sampled them agreed that they were exceptional.

Having discovered the cache of wheat, Moscardó permitted it to remain undisturbed where it was. Rather than transferring the entire supply to the Alcázar on successive nights, he dispatched small groups to bring sacks as they were needed. He must have known that the Republicans would learn of the granary by questioning deserters or by observing unusual movements in that sector at night, but he persisted in his policy of taking only what the garrison required. He did not even attempt to fortify the surrounding houses, although it was plain that should the militia plant a few machine guns across the street, the Alcázar would be cut off from its chief source of food. What was going on in the mind of this curious man? Did he believe that as a gift from God, the granary did not require defense? Perhaps he imagined that if the Republicans seized it, God would provide another, even more conveniently located.

Except for a few private hoards, tobacco had disappeared from the Alcázar. The small stock of cigarettes in the Academy stores had run out, although by way of compensation Captain Cuartero distributed the plain cigarette papers on hand, each soldier receiving two hundred—all of them handsomely decorated with the seal of the Toledo Academy. The smokers whose memories of Havanas remained vivid or who rejected paltry compromise stopped smoking altogether. Those with less fastidious tastes swept the rooms for stray grains of tobacco and dug out crumbs from between flagstones with razor blades. Often, a team of four or five scoured the floors and pooled their booty in order to make a single cigarette, which would then be passed from mouth to mouth.

Men went to fantastic lengths to satisfy their craving for tobacco. Having tried hemp, strips of cloth, and wheat chaff, they finally resorted to the trees on the terraces. They tried them all —acacia, eucalyptus, elm, and mulberry—and acacia became the choice of the connoisseur (and also the daredevil, because these trees were found only at positions swept by enemy fire). Dried rose petals from the superintendent's garden provided a smooth, though very mild smoke; the worst substitute was eucalyptus, which often made the smoker sick. On one occasion a soldier fell out of an acacia tree when a shell exploded near by, but returned triumphantly clutching a sprig of leaves. At least one man lost his life in a standard ambush: the bait was a pack of cigarettes placed in the window of a seemingly abandoned house which was actually crawling with militia. Asked what he thought would help the morale of the garrison, a crusty Guard replied, "Eating less and smoking more"—though if anyone had less to eat, he would probably not be able to smoke at all.

On August 4, observers in the towers counted 170 shells, most of them hammering the curved passage. The next day seven shells were fired at the north entrance; then the guns remained silent for four days. The cease-fire was not planned. It developed because the Republicans had exhausted their supply of shells for the moment, and because artillerists were requesting transfers from the Toledo front. Most of the trained artillerymen were Regular soldiers, and as such they were continually getting into trouble with the Anarchist militia, who controlled operations at Toledo. The Anarchists' long-standing suspicion of the Army erupted into violence as a result of the Durán episode, which seemed to confirm their distrust.

A few days earlier Lieutenant Mercedes Durán had reported to the Defense Committee at the town hall and requested assignment to a gun shelling the Alcázar. Since the militia were in dire need of trained artillerists—which Durán's papers showed him to be —he was driven out to Alijares and put in charge of one of the guns shelling the east façade. The first thing he did was to change the trajectory. When a *miliciano*, looking on in alarm, warned him that the aim was too high, Lieutenant Durán replied coldly, "I know what I'm doing." He was an expert artillerist, as he claimed, but what he had neglected to explain to them was that

he was Nationalist to the bone. Before he was stopped, Durán
fired seven shells: four of them landed on the arms factory, two
on the post office (headquarters of the Defense Committee and its
"cheka"), and one on the seminary, occupied by the Anarchist
militia. Although the damage was slight, the effect was ruinous to
Republican morale. Lieutenant Durán was shot the same day, his
last words being, "I have served my country. *Viva España!*"
Henceforth it could cost an officer his life to miss his target on
the Toledo front. Militia with loaded pistols scrutinized every
movement of "Loyalist" officers directing artillery fire at the
Alcázar.*

From the beginning of the siege, small bands had been stealing
out of the fortress at night to scavenge in the houses near by. The
purpose of these *razzias* was to bring back food for the infirmary,
but each raider had his own personal motive. Since a two-ounce
piece of sausage could be sold for forty pesetas (about four dol-
lars) and a cigar for a hundred, some of the poorer soldiers seized
this opportunity to acquire easy money, even though the risks of
being cut down from ambush were high. Others, chafing under
close confinement, went in order to make believe that they were
striking back at the enemy. For honor rather than for profit,
members of the Falange (most of whom were rich men's sons
anyway) competed with one another to see who could bring
back the greatest trophy. The results were poor. If a *razzia* raked
in half a pound of coffee and a box of salt, it was significant
enough to be written up in *El Alcázar*. Pedro Villaescusa, the
Falange chief, appropriated two chickens and several eggs by slid-
ing down a rope from a window on the west side and raiding a
dwelling near by. Captain Emilio Vela obtained permission from
Moscardó to tap an electric cable in the Republican zone and to

---

* The Durán episode may be a legend concocted after the siege had ended,
although it is part of the "official" story of the Alcázar, as recorded by
several Nationalist historians. That at least one artillerist was killed by the
militia is beyond question. Al Uhl, a correspondent for the Associated Press,
often visited an artillery officer who was directing fire on the Alcázar, but
when Uhl did not see him one day, he made inquiries and was told by a
miliciano, "We had to shoot him. At first he set the guns against the Alcázar
and we made direct hits. Then one day the shells went over the Alcázar into
our ammunition factory on the other side. That could have been an error, but
when the 'error' happened on seven successive days, we knew we had a
traitor, and so we shot him."

run a wire back into the Alcázar so that the range of the radio reception could be increased. Supported by Falangists, Vela crawled through the charred debris of the houses below the Zig Zag, but found that cables and wires had been melted by the fires. Next he tried the houses in the Corralillo quarter, where he was successful in tapping a live cable, but was driven back when a dog betrayed his presence. This was the closest the Alcázar ever came to obtaining current for the Civil Guard transmitter. Only the receiver worked, and feebly at that.

Meanwhile the Republican planes continued their sporadic bombing from their airstrips at Getafe. No matter how many times they were sighted on the northern horizon, winging slowly toward Toledo, someone always raised false hope by shouting, "This time they are ours!" They never were. Those who had doubted that bombers could destroy the Alcázar changed their minds after the attack on August 8. Just before eight in the morning a single trimotor flew over and dropped sixteen 100-lb. bombs. Almost all of them exploded in the Capuchinos and reduced this old convent to a gutted shell. The Academy musicians and Civil Guards defending it were buried beneath bricks, wooden beams, and caved ceilings. Looking down at the Capuchinos from the windows of the Alcázar, Moscardó and his officers saw that the key position of their southern defense had been destroyed. Already the militia were moving through the adjoining houses, aware that if they could occupy the Capuchinos, they would cut off the Alcázar from all its eastern dependencies. Equally alarming was the knowledge that the militia would then have access to the curved passage, which led directly into the vitals of the Alcázar.

Hurriedly Moscardó and Romero massed riflemen at the upper southern windows, from where they could pin down every *miliciano* in the sector. At the same time reinforcements were rushed to the Capuchinos, accompanied by Lieutenant Luis Barber, the engineer, to evacuate the wounded, who were calling for help. Tunneling through the mound of rubble took up the rest of the day. They found that out of a force of thirty, four men had been killed and six badly injured. Two bodies were not found. The August heat quickly made this the most nauseating sector of the defense. Soldiers posted in the ruins tied handkerchiefs across their faces but were still unable to control their vomiting. In time the odor disappeared but the rats remained.

When the building caved in, one of the Civil Guards was pinned by fallen timber. The wall had collapsed outward, leaving him a helpless target for militia in a house several yards away. They saw him, but since they were exposed to withering rifle fire from the Alcázar windows above, they were unable to sight their own rifles and their shots always went wild. After an hour and a half, the Guard was freed by Lieutenant Barber, and returned to the Alcázar unharmed.

While the rescue operations were under way at the Capuchinos, another Republican plane dropped three bombs. Landing squarely in the courtyard, they broke open but did not explode. Thick fumes poured out, and when someone yelled "Gas!" the Alcázar was swept by panic. As the vapor sifted down into the cellars through the ventilators, the people huddled there stampeded up the stairways and tried to break out of the building. Had they succeeded they would have run directly under the rifles of the militia waiting outside. Major Méndez Parada had already prepared for a gas attack, however. At the suggestion of a refugee who was a druggist, he had heaped piles of kindling and light lumber at each corner of the courtyard. These were lit with gasoline, and the sudden draft of hot air swept most of the fumes out of the Alcázar. Panic subsided when the frightened crowd was told that the bombs had only contained tear gas. The attack seemed to indicate that poison gas—the weapon they feared most of all—would not be employed against them.

August 9 was a Sunday, a day on which the militia, reinforced by Madrid tourists, always increased their attacks. First light brought an artillery barrage, an air attack, and a *paqueo* of such ferocity that the defenders were on the alert all day for a general assault from the north. Although the attack did not materialize, the force defending the Gobierno was so buffeted by the fire from the Santa Cruz that nine soldiers waited until nightfall and then slid down ropes to the Calle del Carmen and deserted to the enemy. Some of them, including a Corporal Félix de Ancos, joined the militia and could soon be seen by their former comrades at the windows of the Santa Cruz. Four days later seven others followed them. To stem the tide of desertion, Civil Guards stiffened the detachment at the Gobierno, and the number of officers was doubled. Possession of a rope was henceforth punishable by death.

So that the Alcázar could be battered by night as well as by day, the Republicans began to install powerful searchlights, confiscated from a movie studio in Madrid, at strategic positions. The first one appeared at the Castle of San Servando, across the river near the Alcántara Bridge, and floodlit the whole east façade, making sorties to the granary hazardous. Another was placed at the narrow end of the Calle del Carmen, where this street ran into the Zocodover, and illuminated the windows of the Gobierno so blindingly that it became difficult for a defender to see the Santa Cruz, just a few yards away. In time another searchlight played on the north façade from the Zocodover, and yet another one lit up the south end. Looking from a window, a defender found it difficult to see anything except the light itself; yet he was himself visible and vulnerable. Since it was becoming as dangerous to send relief parties to the Gobierno at night as by day, Lieutenant Barber had a shallow trench dug down the ramp connecting the Gobierno with the dining hall, making it possible to crawl a hundred yards without being detected from across the Tagus.

Perhaps the most spectacular sight of the war was the Alcázar under floodlights, immaculately white above the dim skyline of the darkened city, especially during bombardment. Black puffs sprouted from luminous walls, gray debris and dust dropped down, and a dry crackle reverberated in the gorge. To outsiders it could look beautiful. Those inside watched with horror as the exterior walls were eroded little by little and the searchlights pried farther and farther.

The floodlights were skillfully used in the night attacks on the Gobierno, which commenced on August 14. Late in the evening an officer standing in the little courtyard nearest the Santa Cruz felt a fine spray falling over him. He thought at first that it was drizzling. Then he sniffed. From an unidentified window at the Santa Cruz the militia were spraying the Gobierno with a stream of gasoline. The officer gave the alarm, the defenders scrambled to their loopholes and began firing wildly across the road, but because of the glare it was impossible to determine the location of the hose. Before they had time to consider what should be done, the floodlight was turned off and the doors of the Santa Cruz were thrown open; before their pupils were dilated, *milicianos* ran across the road with flaming rags and threw them into the courtyard. The attack came as a complete surprise, but it was premature. The militia had not allowed for a light wind blowing most of the liquid into the Calle del Carmen. The flames roared in the street but did not damage the Gobierno. The soldiers inside dropped grenades out of the windows, which drove the militia away from the walls and into the sights of the defenders' rifles. The attackers dispersed quickly and escaped down the street toward the river. Hundreds of gallons of gasoline, pumped from a city fire engine, had been wasted in this first frontal attack. The Gobierno reported no casualties, but the garrison realized that they had been lucky.

During the next day, August 15, there was a twelve-hour barrage as the Republicans hurled two hundred projectiles in an effort to sever the line of communication between the Santiago and the dining hall, the two remaining eastern dependencies, and the Alcázar. A trimotor with incendiary bombs joined the attack. Until this day, couriers had carried messages on foot to the outlying buildings, but the terraces were now so swept with shrapnel that runners were delayed. Field telephone lines were therefore strung by Lieutenant Barber, connecting the superintendent's office with both the Santiago and the Gobierno.

Meanwhile the militia in the Santa Cruz were preparing a surprise for the Gobierno. During the day they dug a deep hole in the inner wall at the second-story level, and after dark dislodged a single granite block of the outer wall, leaving a small aperture about a foot square. Through this opening they thrust the nozzle of the hose, which was invisible in the darkness, and sprayed the Gobierno with gasoline. Most of the fluid poured into Stable No. 4, the ground-level basement. Frantically the officer in charge ordered his men out. Then, before the militia attacked across the road, he set fire to the gasoline himself. The stable went up in flames, but with blankets and jackets the defenders beat down the fire spreading to the adjoining rooms, and at the same time riflemen in the windows above and in the Alcázar drove back the militia before they reached halfway across the Calle del Carmen. Although damage was done to some of the rooms, the fire did not weaken the thick stucco walls of the Gobierno, which remained as defensible as ever. For the moment, the Republicans abandoned their gasoline warfare.

With the Picadero and the Capuchinos destroyed and the Gobierno coming under daily attack, the siege appeared to be entering a more serious, even desperate phase. Although only twenty-five defenders had been killed, there were over a hundred who had been wounded or had suffered contusions from falling walls or ceilings; even more alarming, the daily number of casualties increased as the sheltering walls were chipped away by bombs, shells, and bullets. By mid-August the number of deserters stood at twenty-one; there were evidently others who wished to go but lacked the opportunity. Perhaps it required as much courage to desert as it did to resist, for one ran the risk of being shot in the back while crossing the lines or of facing a firing squad when he arrived. On August 11 the Alcázar junta had posted an order absolutely prohibiting conversations with the enemy—including the exchange of obscenities—and three days later followed it with a prohibition of *razzias*, unless previously approved by a higher authority.

In order to fill out the thinning ranks, a delegation of women petitioned Moscardó for permission to join their men at the parapets, as the Republican women were doing. He was horrified. Wives of gentlemen (and the Civil Guards were temporary *caballeros*, at least) must maintain certain standards. It was improper for a lady to kill Republicans. Again and again he had promised that not a single woman or child would become a fatality of the siege. He had pledged his word as a gentleman, and the officers were enjoined to honor this pledge. Thus, when an elderly women died on August 11, she was buried in a wooden coffin (instead of the customary mattress cover), on which was written in conspicuous lettering: "Died of natural causes." The implication was clear: this old lady would have died on that particular day, whether or not she had been in the Alcázar.

The water supply was sinking dangerously low. On August 10 the daily ration for each person had been cut back to one quart. For two hours every morning a "Director of Water" supervised the rationing with a list of the number of quarts allowed to each section, while a captain of the Civil Guards also stood by and supervised the "director." Water was becoming a prominent item on the black market. There was now no possibility of washing one's body or clothes. Ashamed of their dirt, women began to welcome the darkness of the cellars. Some of them scraped plaster off the walls to use as powder (plaster was already being used as a seasoning for the stew). Once when there was a light rain, people surged out of the cellars to stand in the courtyard, their faces lifted skyward, to be washed. The water in the swimming pool was reserved for the horses, though the guards posted there usually turned their backs when children crept up to get a canful of the green, mucous-looking liquid. Men rinsed the dirt from their hands with urine. Aristocrats who traced their lineage back to obscure Spanish kings made their first acquaintance with vermin.

Because the shelling of the east esplanade made it hazardous to go out to the dining hall for their meals, the field oven and big cauldrons were brought into the Alcázar. Along with the Santiago Barracks, the dining hall became a major defensive post against any attack which might come across the Corralillo. Little by little the Nationalists were being forced back into the perimeter of the Alcázar itself. Nearly a month had passed since the Moroccan garrisons had revolted. Where were Mola and Franco? Unión Radio told them nothing. They were sealed off hermetically from the outside world.

Although the Labandera brothers had given up their work on the transmitter as hopeless, they continued to increase the reception range of the receiver. All day long a stenographer sat beside the radio operator, taking down every news broadcast by Unión Radio. This was then taken to the junta, who subjected it to an elaborate "lie analysis," since the Republican censor allowed no broadcast which did not imply that the government forces were gaining ground. They learned almost nothing until the night of August 16, when an announcer spoke of General Queipo de Llano's holding the city of Seville for the Nationalists; here, at least, was proof that the rising was successful in Andalucia. Then, unexpectedly, they picked up Radio Milan. They were able to hear clearly until the announcer commenced his résumé of news from Spain, at which point the reception was drowned by static. Moscardó and Romero, who had rushed to the radio, were bitterly disappointed, but they urged the Labandera brothers to pile on extra batteries and to overhaul the radio once more.

The next morning their pains were rewarded, for over the air came a broadcast from Radio Lisbon, a station friendly to the Nationalists. In the radio room and the corridor outside, Alcazareños relayed the news in tremulous whispers as the stenographer wrote it down: *"The Nationalists hold Seville . . . General Franco has flown to Burgos, the seat of the new Nationalist government . . . The roads between Andalucia and the Pyrenees are open . . . Bilbao has been shelled by the Nationalist cruiser* Almirante Cervera *. . . The Legion and the Moors have taken Mérida and Badajoz, and are now advancing along the road to Madrid . . ."* When the announcer had finished, cheers and *vivas* swept the Alcázar.

Maps were ripped from geography books and were used to decorate the walls of the rooms and corridors, charting the progress of the Army of the South. The fact that Mérida was nearly two hundred miles away and that the motorized columns moving toward Madrid would find stronger Republican resistance the nearer they came to the capital did not distress them. The Madrid press and radio continued to deride the "madmen encircled in the Alcázar" led by the "notorious fool Don José Moscardó de La Mancha." But the defenders began to feel that they had a chance now: if they could hold out long enough, they would be relieved. That the chance was a small one was unimportant—for a Spaniard remote hopes are enough to feed on.

This news was opportune, for it followed on the heels of the most terrifying discovery of the siege—the Republicans were digging a mine under the Alcázar.

6

DISCOVERY

IN THE EARLY HOURS of August 16 a wounded soldier lying in one of the cellar rooms on the west side of the Alcázar began screaming. Half delirious, he said that he had heard the noise of a huge insect scratching deep in the earth below. To humor him, others listened and they heard the sound, too—a faint digging noise, interrupted from time to time by a distant rumble that sounded like horses kicking their stalls. By dawn the peasant families in the cellars were nearly wild with terror; they half believed that the Evil One was digging toward them.

A few hours later Lieutenant Barber, with a stethoscope borrowed from the infirmary, was carefully probing the paving stones and walls of the west cellar. He could hear a pneumatic drill clearly, and the rumbling noise sounded like small dynamite explosions. At first he thought that the Republicans were ripping up cobblestones in the city to make barricades or that they were opening old wells, since the water pipes had been cut long before. But the longer he listened, the more apprehensive he became. The sounds could mean only one thing: the Republicans were digging a mine shaft toward the Alcázar.

Moscardó and his staff, who had anxiously watched Barber's operation, wanted to know what they could do. Would it be possible, for example, to sink a countermine into the tunnel? Barber thought not, because the Alcázar rested squarely on a bed of virgin rock and they had no tools other than picks and shovels. The best they could do would be to establish a listening post in order to determine the direction from which the tunnel was coming and to estimate the time when it would reach the Alcázar. The only way the mine shaft could be destroyed was to locate its mouth in one of the dozens of dwellings which lay across the Cuesta del Alcázar.

Even if the source of the mine could be discovered, it was unlikely that a raiding party would be able to reach it, much less destroy it. All the houses across the Cuesta were infested with militia, and barricades blocked the entrances to all streets and alleyways near the Alcázar. But the attempt had to be made, and Captain Vela volunteered to lead the sortie. He and Barber spent hours together in the upper rooms, studying the intricate maze of houses close to the west façade of the Academy, and in the cellar, attempting to obtain a true bearing on the subterranean noise. Meanwhile Cayetano Rodríguez, a young Civil Guard with experience in the Río Tinto mines, volunteered to assist Barber in detecting and plotting the course of the mine shaft. The garrison noted with satisfaction that his matronymic, Caridad ("Care"), seemed providential.

The Republican mine was the brain child of a woman, Margarita Nelken, a Socialist deputy of the Cortes. When the Alcázar failed to be starved into surrender, she wired twenty-five Asturian miners: I NEED YOU. WE MUST BLOW UP THE ALCÁZAR. Nothing could have pleased them more than this opportunity to destroy the cradle of the Spanish Army, for the military were perhaps hated more by the Asturians than by any other group in Spain. Just two years before, they had had a taste of martial rule when units of the Army led by General Franco had brutally suppressed a revolt of the miners. Better trained and politically more sophisticated than other workers in Spain, they had seized the factories and mines, and demanded that the government live up to its semi-Socialist programs of reform. They could not forget what the troops, especially the Moors, had done to their people, the women in particular. As a result of the Asturian crisis, Franco became an archvillain to the Leftists and a hero to the Rightists.

The Asturians were afraid that the Nationalists might be able to destroy a single tunnel, so they decided to dig two parallel to each other—one to terminate under the southwest tower and the other beneath the west wall, about fifty feet farther north. Once these tunnels reached the walls of the Alcázar, the Asturians would hollow out cavities, deposit several tons of TNT, and detonate them. As the entrances of their tunnels they picked out two houses on the Calle de Juan Labrador, a street running parallel to the Cuesta two blocks west. Each house had a good-sized patio, where the rubble could be deposited unseen from the street. The distance between the mouths of the mine shafts and the Alcázar was about seventy yards—no distance at all for these Asturians, who were tough, cheerful workmen.

They figured that the noise from two tunnels being worked at the same time would throw off the calculations of the Nationalists, and to add to the deception, they located their compressors farther down the hill and kept moving them around, so that the sound of the machines always appeared to be coming from a different place. The Republicans increased their riflemen throughout this sector of Toledo, and a special militia unit which called itself "Eagles of Liberty" was given the job of defending the houses where the shafts commenced. The miners worked around the clock in four shifts. No one was permitted to come near these houses unless he gave the countersign, which was changed twice each day. Progress was rapid in the beginning, since the miners made use of an old Moorish drainage system beneath the houses, but it was not long before they had to resort to dynamite to dislodge the solid rock. These were the explosions which sounded, in the Alcázar, like the distant kicking of horses.

When Captain Vela and Lieutenant Barber thought they had located the mine entrance, the "Death Squad," consisting of Falangist volunteers led by Vela, slipped out of the windows near the carriage gate at 11 P.M. on August 19, and crept across the Cuesta. (Because the slope of the hill curved, the floodlight in the Zocodover illuminated only the upper windows of the Alcázar.) They climbed over the rooftops of the low dwellings and cut through deserted rooms wherever they dared, until they reached the designated house. They quickly doused it with gasoline, and fell back while Captain Bela wired two grenades together and lobbed them through a window. The resultant explosion set off every rifle in the vicinity as the militia came alive, but Vela and his raiders retraced their route hurriedly and got back safely before the militia were able to cordon the area. The house was reported destroyed, and Moscardó brought out one of the last bottles of Academy champagne to drink the health of the "Death Squad."

But the following morning the delirious soldier began raving again. Corporal Rodríguez Caridad and Lieutenant Barber went with Colonel Moscardó to the cellar, where they heard the sound of digging. They had destroyed the wrong house. The militia seemed to be enraged, for their *paqueo* was heavy. During a lull in the firing the soldiers by the western windows heard a taunting voice from across the Cuesta, "Come on, you Fascist bastards, try it again! Just try it again!" And that night a searchlight in the tower of the Magdalena Church flooded the Cuesta. It was not feasible to send the "Death Squad" across the light-drenched road. They would have to wait for a more propitious moment.

Everyone had a single question for Lieutenant Barber and Corporal Rodríguez, who had established a twenty-four-hour listening post in the west cellar: How much damage will the mine do? On Moscardó's specific orders they minimized the dangers, but few were fooled. All realized that soon they would be sitting on a volcano. Reactions varied. Some ignored it or trusted in Providence. The weaker ones cursed their luck. Older men lamented that they would leave their families; younger men, that they had no families to leave. Time dragged. People began to welcome the sound of Republican *paqueo*, since it drowned out the faint, terrifying sounds of the encroaching mine.

Mortar fire against the Alcázar began on August 19, and against this hidden weapon the warning system was useless. Shells began falling in the courtyards of the Academy and the Gobierno, and the observers in the towers were unable to determine exactly where the mortars were placed, although the patio of the Santa Cruz seemed the logical answer. On the same day the supply of condensed milk ebbed so low that what was left was reserved for the wounded. The children had to go without their daily ration: three ounces ladled from a pot in which three cans of condensed milk had been mixed with ten gallons of water. To encourage morale, Moscardó assured the readers of El Alcázar that a relief column was pushing rapidly toward Toledo, and placed large canvas panels in the courtyard and on the east esplanade for the benefit of Nationalist planes (none of which had been sighted yet). Written on the panels were the words "We are resisting," followed by arrows and numbers indicating the direction and distance of the Republican batteries. The worst news came from the artillery observers, who reported that big 155-mm. guns were being established at the Dehesa de Pinedo and at Alijares.

The following morning the Alcázar was alerted to prepare itself for a barrage from the 155's, and the observers scanned the enemy emplacements for the slightest sign of activity. Nerves were on edge, for the 75's and 105's had already done great damage. What the 155's were capable of doing was all too apparent.

The courtyard was filled with people who wanted a last deep breath of fresh air before the cannonade forced them down into the cellars. Two Civil Guards named Garrido and Carrión had been working on the radio antenna. Garrido was standing in the upper arcade with the antenna wire in his hand, but Carrión, who was supposed to make the connection in the courtyard below, had disappeared. Garrido called down to the people below, asking if they had seen Carrión, but no one paid any attention. Ruffled by this, he shouted at the top of his lungs, "Carrión! Caaaarrión!" The hubbub in the patio stopped at once, and startled faces jerked skyward. Someone yelled *"Avión!"* and the crowd scrambled for the stairways to the cellars. The courtyard was emptied. After minutes had passed with no sound of a plane, an officer poked his head out of a doorway and saw Garrido and Carrión completing the wiring. Enraged at what he thought had been a practical joke, he asked Garrido, "Did you see a plane?"

"No, sir."

"Then why the devil did you call out '*Avión!*'?"

"I didn't say that," Garrido protested. "I was only calling out to my comrade, 'Caaarión!' "

The officer was amused at Garrido's explanation. Turning to Carrión, he asked, "What is your mother's family name?"

"Morales, sir."

"All right, Carrión, for the rest of this siege you are Private Morales."

Moscardó was not entertained by the episode, however. And a few days later when a nearly identical event occurred (this time the soldier's name was Cienfuego), he had to issue an order prohibiting anyone except officials from shouting in the courtyard.

The barrage of the new 155's came a few hours after Garrido had cleared the courtyard. Their target was the main entrance on the north terrace and the damage done was alarming. Even though the guns fired only twenty-five times, pieces of the Renaissance veneer dropped from the Alcázar like chunks of icing from a wedding cake. By nightfall it was clear to the junta that the enemy intended to batter a hole in the north wall so that a tank could lead an attack past the Gobierno, up the Zig Zag, and into the courtyard of the Alcázar. Other than holding the Gobierno, there was, of course, no defense against this plan.

Having verified the range, the 155's pounded the north wall deliberately on the following day, throwing sixty-eight shells. As they hurtled through the air, these shells produced a sound like ripping silk, magnified a thousand times. During the next ten days over three hundred of them exploded near the main gate, until the entrance itself was buried completely by fallen masonry. In the middle of the north wall the interior rooms became exposed to machine-gun fire from the tower of the Magdalena Church, so that the shells tore these apart, too. Third-story rooms vanished; first-floor rooms were buried. From the north terrace an immense mound of rubble reached up to the second-story windows and sloped down into the courtyard. Here was a perfect pathway for a tank attack.

Pressure against the Gobierno increased; gasoline attacks occurred almost every other night, and mortars pounded the building daily. The interior was a wreck: inflammable objects—tables, furniture, loose flooring, and chemicals from the military stores—were heaped in the courtyards and burned in order to reduce the menace of a general conflagration. Rifle and machine-gun fire from the Santa Cruz was incessant, day and night; the defenders spent more time repairing sandbags on the parapets than they did shooting at the enemy. The men strung chicken wire across the lower windows so that grenades thrown from the street would bounce back on the militia. One hundred men held the Gobierno —now called "Death Corner"—and these were relieved every four days.

Then came August 22, a day which no one in the Alcázar would ever forget. Daybreak coincided with a strange incident. Observers in the towers heard an airplane engine, although the northern sky was empty. They gave the alarm to the crowds below in the courtyard, but the words were still on their lips when a plane skimmed over a hill to the southwest of Toledo and roared over the building at less than five hundred feet. Many did not even have time to throw themselves on the ground; the observers steeled themselves for an explosion. Nothing happened. The airplane, which had burst upon them so quickly that no one had noticed its markings, made a complete turn and flew back toward the southwest. As far as they knew, there were no Republican airfields in that direction; gradually it dawned on them that the plane might have been a Nationalist scout, dispatched by Franco to determine if the Alcázar was still holding out. The Army of Africa was known to be out there somewhere.

Rising morale was momentarily dampened a few hours later when two Republican planes came from the north dropping twelve bombs and some immense milk cans filled with gasoline, but the gasoline splashed out without being ignited by the bombs. Throughout the day the *paqueo* coming from San Servando, across the Tagus, was heavier than usual. Colonel Romero ordered his Civil Guards to the eastern windows, and at five o'clock they opened fire on the castle. For fifteen minutes they emptied their rifle clips at the Republican stronghold and succeeded in silencing it altogether. For the moment the enemy seemed to have had enough, and the Guards returned to their regular posts, elated with their day's work.

During the evening meal, at six-thirty, a sniper in the southwest tower spotted another plane coming toward the Alcázar so low that it seemed barely to be clearing the rooftops. Before he had time to alert his commanding officer, it swept over the building with a shattering roar at less than a hundred feet. Large containers were tossed out; they smashed but did not explode. Seconds later, as the plane flew over San Servando, it dropped three bombs. Although these missed the castle, the explosions touched off wild jubilation in the Alcázar. Everyone shouted the news: "Our planes have come!" Embracing and thumping one another, men ran through the corridors and cellars shouting *vivas* until they were hoarse.

Four aluminum containers, each of foot-locker size, had fallen in a straight line between the carriage gate and the east esplanade, where they split open like ripe melons and spewed forth cans of milk, sardines, potted ham, preserves, and cocoa. One fell in the courtyard, the others outside. Captain Cuartero shouldered his way through the excited crowd to claim the supplies for his commissary, but he was too late to prevent people from scooping up the marmalade and grains of coffee which had spilled on the ground. Children were scooping up chocolate dust with the zest of miners in a gold rush. Considering that the Alcázar held about eighteen hundred people, the supplies were infinitesimal, but the airdrop was tangible proof that they had not been forgotten by friends beyond the walls.

Some wanted to have nothing to do with this manna from heaven. They maintained that it was really a Republican plane dropping poisoned food to kill them and bombing San Servando to deceive them the more completely. Fantastic as this theory was, it threw a chill on the celebration. Moscardó felt compelled to ask the druggist to analyze the food in the Academy laboratory. It is very doubtful that he had the training or the equipment to make such an analysis, but after several hours behind closed doors he came out and announced that nothing was contaminated.

Meanwhile the Republican heavy guns were retaliating against the Nationalist airdrop. They threw seventy-four shells at the north façade, making it impossible to send a search party outside to look for the remaining containers. But if few slept that night, it was not the shells that kept them awake but hope, which many of them had nearly given up. Some even claimed that when the airplane had flashed over the building, they had seen Captain Luis Alba in the cockpit.

At daybreak the next morning there was a service in the chapel, in which they prayed to the Virgin for victory to come soon. Then Major Ricardo Villalba led a detail out to the east esplanade to retrieve two of the aluminum chests, which were carried to the superintendent's office and opened. In one, wrapped in a Monarchist flag of red and yellow, was a letter. Moscardó read it aloud, his lips quivering and his eyes brimming:

"GENERAL OF THE ARMY OF
AFRICA AND SOUTH

"A greeting from this army to the brave defenders of the Alcázar! We are approaching; we shall relieve you. In the meantime, resist. Until this time comes, we will be able to help you little. Surmounting all obstacles, our columns are advancing, destroying resistance. *Viva España!* Long live the brave defenders of the Alcázar!

"General Fr. Franco Bahamonde
"August 22, 1936"

The effect of this short, vague message was electric. The officers wept. The news swept into the courtyard, up the stairways, and down into the nightmarish regions of the cellars. The letter was tacked up in the courtyard for all to read, to marvel at, to touch. A single thought surged through everyone: "We are saved!" It did not matter that Franco's army was no closer than Trujillo, a hundred and fifty miles southwest, nor that it was meeting increasing opposition with every mile that it advanced along the Madrid road. If they held out long enough, Franco would save them.

The Monarchist banner told them that this symbol had been adopted by the Nationalists. Moscardó put the women to work making buttonhole rosettes of red and yellow. At sunset the flag was arranged in the courtyard, and to an accompaniment of rolling drums, soldiers representing each section filed past, knelt, and kissed it, after which it was raised above the crumbling north wall in the last rays of the setting sun. Each man was given a rosette—made out of old Navarre-style berets which cadets of the Academy had worn a quarter-century before. A "banquet" followed. In addition to the horse stew and bread ration, everyone received part of a sardine, a morsel of *chorizo* (Spanish sausage), and a teaspoon of marmalade. It was little enough, but many of them recalled the miracle of the loaves and fishes.

But they were also reminded that the siege was far from ended when the Republicans battered the Alcázar mercilessly throughout the day. Mortar shells pounded the troops in the dining hall and in the Santiago Barracks; a trimotor flew over and dropped bombs and cans of gasoline; fifty 155-mm. shells caused so much damage to the room just above the north entrance that it had to be abandoned permanently. Militia from the Santa Cruz dashed across the road and hurled grenades into the gaps in the walls of the Gobierno. And below them, there was the relentless digging of the tunnel. Yet, soldiers standing at their loopholes often prefaced their remarks with "When I get out of here . . ." *When* had replaced *if*.

The defense of the Gobierno was becoming untenable. Since the Santa Cruz lay on slightly higher ground, the militia were able to stand on the roof and lob grenades. The Asturian *dinamiteros* rigged a crude petard, fashioned of dynamite cartridges and scrap iron, which they placed in a pouch, with two ropes tied to it, each about three feet long. Grabbing the ends of the ropes, the *miliciano* swung it around his head, his body swinging with it, until he got sufficient momentum. Then, in the manner of a hammer thrower, he flung the petard at the Gobierno. Their primary target was the iron gate, a flimsy affair blocking access to the Zig Zag. This was located in the ditchlike lane on the far side of the Gobierno (called the "stable approach" because it also led to the Picadero). A few yards beyond the iron gate a truck had been parked across the lane to form a second carrier. Since the iron grille provided no more protection against bullets than the bars of a cage, the defenders had thrown up a fence of loose bricks behind the gate, but the post was the most dangerous one at the Academy. On August 23, for example, a young Civil Guard was struck by eleven separate bullets from the Santa Cruz. He died, hysterically screaming "*Viva España!*" at the militia across the way.

The most incredible episode in the defense of the Gobierno

occurred on August 29. A narrow alleyway ran into the Calle del Carmen opposite the Gobierno; on the northwest corner was the Santa Cruz. During the hostilities the house across the alley from the Santa Cruz, on the southeast corner, was destroyed, so that the Conception Convent, lying right behind these ruins, down the alley, had an unobstructed view of the Gobierno. Unbeknown to the Nationalists, the Republicans had placed a 75-mm. gun behind the wooden door of the convent facing Stable No. 4; the distance was about seventy yards. After knocking out a panel in the door, the artillerymen shoved the muzzle of their piece through it and began a rapid shelling of the Gobierno.

Private José Palomares of the Civil Guard was posted by a window of Stable No. 4 when the gun opened point-blank fire. The first shell smashed against the wall with such a wallop that for a moment Palomares thought someone had clubbed him from behind. The gun was so near that its report and the explosion of the shell were almost simultaneous. Dazed, he peered out the window, saw dust and smoke in the alley leading down to the convent, and just had time to throw himself on the floor before a second shell ripped out a two-foot segment of the wall. A third opened a wider hole and sprinkled the stable with shrapnel. Those who could bolted out of the room. Unless something were done quickly, the militia would soon have an immense opening, at street level, through which to enter. Clutching his Mauser, Palomares resolved to do something about it.

The next explosion caved in part of the wall on top of Palomares, but he dug himself out, crawled up to the window, and began firing at the convent door. Three times the concussions of the shells exploding on the outer wall knocked him off the pile of debris on which he was lying. His sense of hearing was gone, but he continued to clamber up the mound of rubble, blazing away. Fellow soldiers tossed him fresh rifle clips, but none volunteered to take his place. The stable was filled with yellow smoke, the hole was large enough to drive a motorcycle through, but the rate of shell fire was slacking. After a total of twelve salvos, the 75-mm. gun was silent. An officer ordered Palomares to cease his fire, but he did not hear, or ignored the command. Like a madman he lay on the rubble, his teeth clenched and his face caked with brick dust and black powder, and poured shot after shot at the doorway of the convent. Finally he had to be restrained by force and dragged, fighting and cursing, from the opening in the wall. José Palomares was later promoted to corporal by special order of Moscardó. He never fully regained his hearing, but he was otherwise unhurt. Four militiamen had been wounded while manning the 75-mm. gun, and the piece was never used again from this position. David had defeated Goliath.

Two days later the attack on the Gobierno was so intense that for a time there was fear that the building might have to be abandoned. From the roof of the Santa Cruz the militia used their slings to hurl petards of dynamite on the military pharmacy (the wedge-shaped corner of the Gobierno nearest the Zocodover) and the iron gate. At the same time other militia ducked out the front door of the Santa Cruz and took up firing posts behind the pillars supporting the iron fence of the yard. Then, while their comrades in the windows behind them peppered the windows of the Gobierno, they were able to run across the road and sling cans of gasoline into the upper windows or on the iron gate. If they reached the walls of the Gobierno they were hidden from the forces inside, who would have been able to repel them with grenades, were it not for the fact that grenades were reserved for last-ditch emergencies. Defenders let big slabs of masonry fall out of the windows to discourage *milicianos* from hugging the walls of the building.

On August 31 it was feared that the militia might enter the Gobierno through the gap in the wall of Stable No. 4. Major Méndez Parada got permission to set up a 75-mm. mortar in the courtyard and was given six of the carefully hoarded mortar shells to repel attacks across the Calle del Carmen. None was wasted. At the height of an attack the mortar shells exploded almost in the doorway of the Santa Cruz. This was the first time during the siege that the militia had faced any weapon larger than a .50-caliber machine gun, and they were chastened—for a while.

During one of these attacks the militia sloshed a bucket of gasoline over the wooden door of the pharmacy and lit it. Flames began to lick through the cracks until Lieutenant José Espiga, a cavalry instructor, grabbed a machine gun and put out the fire with a single gun burst, which cut away the burning wood as neatly as a scalpel removing gangrened flesh. But everyone knew that the defense of the Gobierno was tottering. Every dull-throated explosion of the petards slung from the rooftops across the road ate away a little more at the building and made the defenders a little more vulnerable. Much of the roof nearest the Santa Cruz had been opened, and before long the corridors of the building might serve as bowling alleys for Republicans with grenades. Lieutenant Colonel Manuel Tuero, responsible for this sector, told his men not to let the militia get across the Calle del Carmen—troubles multiplied when they did. The advice was well intentioned, but like the colonel's patrician admonitions not to destroy the fine Renaissance moldings above the windows of the Santa Cruz, impossible to follow.

Colonel Tuero, an infantry instructor at the Academy, inhabited a world totally baffling to the rougher-grained Civil Guards and six-month conscripts he commanded. This white-haired, gaunt officer in shiny black boots flourished his tasseled dress sword like some incongruous ghost out of the pages of Cervantes, and exhorted his men with flamboyant classroom rhetoric which few of them could even understand. They could never decide whether he was utterly fearless or partially crazy—or a little of both. Absent-minded and near-sighted, sometimes confusing these grimy men with *caballeros cadetes*, he seemed to regard the defense of the Gobierno as a theoretical tactical problem. Tuero peered out of each window, poked each sandbag with the point of his sword, and seldom stopped talking:

"Take care of the *paqueo*, young man. Don't expose yourself unnecessarily. And be sure not to hit that molding on the Santa Cruz. It's priceless, you know. Remember, we are civilized and respect art, whatever the Rebels may do. And don't become discouraged. Soon we will take part in the victory march in Madrid. We will march down the Calle de Alcalá in our rags and our beards—and be proud of them. On that day Spain will be what it used to be in the days of the empire and the kings. You will see. By the way, repair this barricade as soon as you can. I see that sand is running out of one of your sacks."

Sand was running out of the hourglass as well. As Colonel Tuero hovered over the shoulders of his men in the Gobierno he might have seemed as detached as a professor squinting into his student's microscope, but no one better understood the vulnerability of the crumbling building. And furthermore, he knew that they had to hold on to this corner of the defense, no matter what it cost.

A visitor to the Santa Cruz during the last week in August was Louis Delaprée, war correspondent for the *Paris-Soir*. The Santa Cruz remained a museum even in the midst of the battle raging across the narrow Calle del Carmen, but it was a weird jumble of empty food tins and minor masterpieces. Most of the windows were stuffed with mattresses, from which the militia, with large straw hats in Pancho Villa-style, fired at the Gobierno. Each time the mortar went off, Arab jewels, ceramics, Flemish retables—all shook in their glass cases.

"Why don't you put all these treasures under protection while there is still time?" Delaprée asked a captain, after a quick dash up the four steps of the stairway, which a Nationalist sniper had a bead on.

"We can't carry off all of Toledo," the captain replied.

Delaprée obtained special permission to see some canvases of El Greco, for these had been carefully stored away. He was profoundly moved by the "long-bearded visages of a phosphorescent pallor" and idly wondered why El Greco had painted faces in such an extraordinary manner. But returning to the Zocodover by a back alley he found a group of people looking at something lying on the pavement. It was a corpse. A bullet had hit the victim's eye, and the face was green and phosphorescent. It was a face he already knew.

As a result of the barrages on August 27, 28, and 29, most of the north façade of the Alcázar had vanished. Portions of the wall clung to the towers, but the rest of it had been ground to rubble and powder, and shells began to roar through the breach and explode in the courtyard. Without exaggeration the Minister of War could announce over Unión Radio: "There is no longer a façade to the Alcázar." The press was also told that a 240-mm. gun was being installed on a concrete platform (some zealous correspondents reported that the gun was of 420-mm. size) and would soon open fire on the Alcázar.

The damage wrought by the 155's was so extensive and so

demoralizing that Moscardó felt compelled to deny it in print. In *El Alcázar* he wrote that although the bombardments of the last few days had produced some gaps in the walls, there was no real danger to their security; further, he stated that the morale in the fortress was higher than during the first days of the siege. It was obvious to anyone that the closer the relief columns came to Toledo, the more strongly the Reds attacked; "easy" days worried him most.

To deny what was, to affirm what was not—such was the logic of Colonel Moscardó. It was the argument of a fool, but a wiser man would have surrendered long before.

7

"FLIES" AND "ABYSSINIANS"

THE SIEGE OF THE ALCÁZAR differed from most other sieges in history in one striking way: here the combatants were separated not by miles but a few yards. It was, as one correspondent remarked, difficult to tell the besiegers from the besieged. When the *paqueo* was light and the guns silent, it was possible to lie behind a parapet and listen to the conversation of the enemy. It was not uncommon for an Alcazareño to spy a brother or a cousin on an adjacent rooftop, and nearly everyone, at one time or another, spotted a former acquaintance among the enemy forces. Civil war had warped relationships, reducing them to simple forms: that man at an opposite window was the enemy—no longer Spaniard, townsman, or neighbor.

The "rules" of killing varied from sector to sector. Between the soldiers in the dining hall and the militia in the houses bordering the Corralillo, for example, was a gentlemen's agreement that it was bad manners to shoot to kill. Obscenity was the most common weapon employed here. Green militia, if they had luck, were assigned to this sector to learn the finer arts of gunnery and invective. However, a few yards to the west the front was manned by men with a particular score to settle with the enemy, for the windows along the south wall harbored the Toledo Falangists, whose hatred of the Republicans was only matched by the Republicans' hatred of them. This was the sector for a man with a grudge, and sometimes personal duels between opposing windows raged for weeks at a time.

In contrast, those who defended the northern front rarely saw the enemy face to face. In this sector, war became an anonymous and depersonalized struggle in which survival depended upon developing a sixth sense about falling shells. The enemy was not a man with a rifle but a caving ceiling or a tottering wall.

Everyone agreed that the worst place to be assigned was the Gobierno. From the Alcázar there were only two ways of getting there: one was quick and extremely dangerous, and the other was slow but less dangerous. One could dash out of the door beside the northeast tower on the east esplanade (the swimming pool door), and in full view of the militia across the Tagus and in the tower of the Magdalena Church, cross the narrow footbridge above the stable approach, and enter the Gobierno by a door on the upper floor. Or else one could leave by the door at the curved passage (by the southeast tower), slip down to the ramp, and crawl down to the Gobierno through Lieutenant Barber's trench. Down there, however, the dangers were compounded: not only was the fighting relentless but there was the gnawing fear that the building would be cut off from the Alcázar. Yet even here, during the first weeks of the siege, there were informal rules. Twice each day there was a cease-fire to allow a blind beggar to tap his way up the Calle del Carmen in the morning and to return in the evening. It must have been a curious sight—this hesitating cripple creating silence for a moment as he passed. Later he was perhaps informed that his presence was a grave inconvenience to the *señores* trying to kill one another, for he was seen no more.

Mosca is the Spanish word for "fly." Making a pun on Moscardó's name, the Republicans called the defenders of the Alcázar "Flies." The nickname soon became gruesomely appropriate, in view of the millions of flies which bred and flourished in the filth and stench of the Academy. The Castilian heat stewed the rancid heaps of refuse and offal dumped out of the eastern windows, and the slightest breeze fanned the toxic smell until that part of the city was infected with it. One did not need eyes to determine where the Alcázar was. Militia posted near the walls were able to comfort themselves by comparing their misery with that of the "Flies" inside; and visitors to the city made their tours dabbing their nostrils with handkerchiefs.*

Admiration for the Italian victory in Ethiopia led the Alcazareños to dub the Republicans *"abisinios."* ** Just as *Il Duce* was pressing for the restoration of the Roman empire, so General Franco wished to revive the spirit of Spanish nationalism which had been lost since the time of Charles V. The *"abisinios"* besieging them were the flotsam of history—mere barbarians destined to fall before the superbly blooded professionals of the Army of Africa. That the vanguard of this army, the Moors, were Africans themselves did not seem to trouble them, if indeed they thought of it at all. Admiration for the Italian brand of nationalism was reflected even in the style of the beards they cultivated, the bushy spade of the Italian aviators being the favorite.

In mid-August a new weapon of untested potency was set up by the Republicans in the Zocodover, and it was soon the most hated machine of all. It was a sound truck, parked beyond the range of Alcázar rifles. When additional amplifiers had been installed behind obstructions only a few feet away from windows along the west wall, "Radio Cigarral" began its broadcasts to the Alcázar. The daily program usually consisted of a dozen scratched recordings of popular songs, interspersed with lectures on Marxism and strident demands for surrender.

At daybreak the "Flies" were aroused by a voice amplified twenty times—a voice so loud that individual words were often drowned in sheer noise: "Attention! Attention! This is 'Radio Cigarral' with its early-morning broadcast to the idiots of the Alcázar. Greetings, Fascist swine. How is that son-of-a-bitch Moscardó? Does he manage to stay alive without his daily ration of whore's milk? Listen, soldiers, you are our comrades. You are not to blame. The Republic authorizes you to disobey your offi-

---

* According to Peter Kemp, an English writer who revisited the Alcázar in 1951 after an absence of fifteen years, the offensive odor remained.

** Since in Spain an *abisinio* is also a kind of cream puff, the Nationalists may have intended an insult to the Republicans' courage as well.

cers. Kill them all. Bring them to us, dead or alive. Kill Moscardó first, then the others. There are only a few of them against so many of you. Come over to us. There is no reason why you should die for their crimes. Soldiers, long live the Republic!"

These appeals were not without effect, for in the course of the siege a total of thirty-five soldiers deserted to the enemy. Few succumbed to the broadcasts on Stalinism or collectivization; generally they were swayed by announcements which probed more basic areas—particularly food and family. The most effective advertisement for desertion was himself a deserter, Corporal Félix de Ancos, who was used by the Republicans as tangible proof of their kind disposition toward the rank and file of the Alcázar.

"Fascists!" blared the amplifier. "What have you eaten today? Horse? What are you drinking? Horse piss? Your friend, Corporal de Ancos is now waiting for you in the Zocodover with kegs of cool beer. We have a fillet of beef, and ham, and fresh bread. Why don't you come down and join us? You have no tobacco? A pity. Here comes a smoke for you." (A 155-mm. shell would explode on the Alcázar.)

An even greater torture was the individual taunt. "Ventas, hey, Ventas! Are you still alive up there? You're a dirty coward for hiding up there, Ventas. If you only knew what a great time we had with your wife and daughters—before we shot them."

At times the militia displayed the family of an Alcázar soldier at the doorway of the Santa Cruz, and announced that this was the last time he would ever see his relatives. Some defenders watched helplessly; others snatched a rifle and fired desperately at the enemy lines. A few of them stored the picture in their minds and later, during a quiet evening, slipped away to the Republican lines to discover for themselves whether the militia had been bluffing. The wife of one local soldier was made to stand in the middle of the Cuesta near the northwest tower, and beg her husband to come out and save his family from starvation. She repeated her lines obediently, but those in the Alcázar windows were able to see that at the same time she was signaling with her fingertips that he must stay where he was.

A young girl forced by her parents to take refuge in the Alcázar was able to speak occasionally with her fiancé—a *miliciano*—from a barred window on the west side. The young man lay behind his barricade and strummed his guitar for his sweetheart. But when Moscardó prohibited all unauthorized communication across the lines (in order to minimize the possibility of desertion), the love affair perished. The fighting assumed a character in which the traditional Spanish courtship—boy, girl, guitar, and grated window—had no place.

Meanwhile "Radio Cigarral" continued its deafening broadcasts. The two most frequent recordings were "The Ride of the Valkyries" and "The Music Goes Round and Round." Neither was ever forgotten by those who survived.

The women of the Alcázar, cooped up night and day in cellar rooms lighted only by horse-grease lamps, had little to do beyond caring for their children and assisting the wounded. Since the quart of water which they received each day was insufficient for washing, many of them refused to show themselves above ground even on those comparatively quiet days when the junta allowed civilians in the courtyard. They preferred to huddle together in the dim rooms, humiliated by the dresses that were falling to pieces on their bodies and ashamed of the dirt which caked them. Their men visited them, but as the weeks wore on, sexual desire disappeared—the flesh had become repugnant. The women were allowed to mend uniforms and sew machine-gun belts and stanch minor wounds. Only one woman, Teresa González, the wife of an Academy musician, demanded and took the status of the men. She was put in charge of the detail which cut special steaks for the wounded in the infirmary, and was once cited for distinguished conduct under fire.

A little over two hundred children roamed the cellars. Some learned to take their first steps in the Alcázar. Two were born there, and the first sounds they heard were the explosions of shells overhead and the rattle of the *paqueo* outside. After a few weeks some of the younger ones forgot that other world beyond the caves of the fortress, and their mothers tried to explain what was meant by sunlight, trees, and silence. One small boy had brought his tricycle with him: there was not room enough to ride it, but he guarded it as if the war was being fought to take it from him. The son of a Falangist, a boy of four, wore a tailor-made blue uniform—complete with Sam Browne belt, riding breeches, and tiny black boots—just like his father; his open-hand salute was nearly perfect, and he spoke contemptuously of the "Reds." During lulls in the firing the Republicans outside could hear the younger children crying in the cellars. Many of them dreaded this sound: children could scarcely be Fascists.

Older children amused themselves with toys made from empty bullet casings or shrapnel. Although there were plenty of rags, none of them could be used to fashion dolls, since they were assiduously collected and used as bandages. A seven-year-old girl kept a diary. In it she recorded her experiences during a single day: "We do not want to play with María Luisa, who was very stupid and did not want to go up for seats on the patio when we wanted to kill those bad people. We played with empty cartridges of the soldiers and a little girl sang a song about the Virgin, which was very pretty. We put pieces of paper in our shoes and in our hair. Some of the children sneaked up into the tower. I was afraid only when the roof fell in."

They had a dog and a cat to play with. Zoradida was an aloof tomcat, which might easily have deserted but chose instead to remain, and displayed remarkable coolness during barrages. On the other hand, battle was a serious matter to Jalifa, the wolf-hound mascot of the Academy. Eyewitnesses reported that he had better intuition of approaching trouble than anyone in the Alcázar. Almost before the bugler had given warning of bombardment or enemy planes, Jalifa was taking the stairway to the cellars.

Six weeks of siege had passed. Classrooms which in June had been immaculate were now filled with junk. Desks and tables from the upper rooms had been hurled into the courtyard for use as firewood for the stove and oven. Maps and charts dangled from the walls. Every window sill was piled high with stones, pillowcases stuffed with dirt, or books and encyclopedias from the libraries. Bound copies of the *Illustrated London News* and *L'Illustration* were in great demand: four hundred pages would not only stop a bullet or shrapnel without splintering like a brick but torn-out individual pages also provided a wealth of reading matter. The alcoves of the windows were ankle-deep in empty

A view of the Alcázar in Toledo, taken from the northeast across the river, showing its commanding position. In one of the last photographs taken inside the fortress before the siege, Captain Vela (BELOW) reads the Proclamation of War in the courtyard.

From barricades set up all around the Alcázar, heavy fire from rifles, machine guns, mortars, flame throwers and cannons blasted the defenders. People came from all over Spain to "shoot" at the fortress.

After dark, the Alcázar was floodlit, and bombardment continued even at night. Here one of its towers has been gutted and another is blazing.

This dramatic photograph shows the moment the tremendous charge of dynamite exploded under the Alcázar. The defenders were powerless to stop the mine from being planted, but incredibly, they withstood the massed attacks that followed.

RODRÍGUEZ

The courtyard of the fortress showing destruction (FAR RIGHT) *by both shells and the mine. In the rubble is the statue of Charles V, knocked from its pedestal. A view of Toledo* (BELOW) *as seen from the western windows of the Alcázar. The mine leveled nearby houses, but snipers continued their withering fire from those just beyond.*

RODRÍGUEZ

The shattered ruin of the northern front of the Alcázar after the siege. Above the rubble can be seen the blasted remnant of the courtyard façade. On the extreme right is the breach in the west wall, blown out by the mine.

The office from which Moscardó directed the siege has been preserved as it was. The portraits of the colonel and his son Luis have been added. The telephone on the right is the one Moscardó used when he told Luis to prepare to die because he could not surrender to save his son's life.

This remarkable photograph purports to show three Nationalist soldiers, after relieving the Alcázar, pursuing a Loyalist through the Cuesta del Alcázar in their mop-up of the city. (BELOW) *Colonel Moscardó and defenders after the ten-week siege had been lifted.*

bullet casings, and soldiers lay upon them as if they were piles of wheat. These windows were manned around the clock, the men sleeping in protected corners when off duty and one of them going down for meals and water. In their leisure time many of them fashioned grenades by hand according to a design of Major Méndez Parada. The best kind was made by packing dynamite into two hemispheric doorknobs and tying them together with baling wire or hemp. It was detonated by lighting a fuse and proved to be a lethal weapon, although the timing mechanism was so crude that it was dangerous to handle.

El Alcázar met every deadline except on two occasions when the editor's typewriter was damaged by a shell. It continued to bolster morale by promising prompt relief by the Army of Africa and charting the advance of the relief columns as reports came in over the radio. Its Lost and Found section featured such announcements as "Lost: Slightly used pince-nez. Please return to the Editor's office." Moscardó's lists of those "distinguished" and "very distinguished" in the day's action were interlarded with heavy-handed attempts at humor ("It is absolutely forbidden to pick up enemy shells before they explode; it would be a pity not to permit them to fulfill their mission"). Any left-over space was usually filled with fancy calligraphy featuring time-tested morale builders: "Viva Spain! Viva the Army! Viva the Civil Guard! Viva the Worthy Civilians! Viva the Legion! Viva the Moors!" For the Nationalists, always vague about specific goals, it seemed to take a great many "vivas" to make a war.

If the dominant mood of the defenders was somber, they nevertheless appreciated a joke when they found one. When a shell missed the Alcázar and exploded in the houses beyond, somebody would sing a few lines of the popular song "Adiós, Granada," punning on the word for "grenade." A never-failing source of amusement was to poke a hat on a stick above a parapet and counting the number of bullets fired at it. When the Republican bomber failed to appear one day, the editor of the newspaper published a notice in the Lost and Found column: "Lost: A little bird that for the past two days has flown in the vicinity of the New Numancia.* It answers to the name of Trimotorcito. If

* After a siege of many years, the Iberian village of Numancia was captured and destroyed by Roman legions in 133 B.C. It is a byword for Spanish

anyone sees it, please notify us immediately." On several occasions a soldier in the Gobierno stopped enemy attacks on the iron gate by blowing the Republican signal for cease-fire on a whistle.

Dust, sweat, and wear combined to disintegrate uniforms and shoes. Trousers bore multiple patches like crazy quilts; boots were held together by twine. Civil Guards along the west side helped themselves to the exotic uniforms in the Academy museum, and it must have been a strange experience for a Republican rifleman to train his weapon upon some dim figure in an upper window sporting a Hussar uniform dating from the Napoleonic period or an iron helmet such as Charles V himself might have worn. (These helmets, the defenders learned, were easily pierced by a .30-caliber bullet.) One evening in late August, Captain Vela conducted a *razzia* to a tailor shop near by and returned with armfuls of masquerade costumes. A few days later a harlequin and a circus clown took their places in the firing lines; the men who wore them claimed that their absurd-looking clothes were at least more comfortable than the rags they had exchanged for them. One soldier ended the siege dressed in a soccer outfit—striped shirt and shorts.

Major Alfredo Martínez Leal, the chronicler with literary ambitions, composed a military anthem entitled "The Siege of the Alcázar of Toledo" (dedicated to "the heroic General, His Excellency Don Francisco Franco"), which the conductor of the Academy band set to music. After a first stanza alluding to the Red traitors, who denied the Religion, the major wrote:

> *These bombs and grenades*
> *That incessantly strike us,*
> *Bursting in our Alcázar,*
> *Can never destroy it.*

But after its publication in *El Alcázar*, the hymn came under attack. His critics argued that the shells *were* knocking the fortress to pieces, stone by stone; the major's patriotism transcended

---

tenacity in battle. Unbeknown to the defenders, other Nationalist newspapers were at the same time making the same reference to the Alcázar siege, and this comparison is now commonly made by Spaniards.

his fidelity to facts. Little daunted, he again took pen in hand and revised the stanza to read:

> *These bombs and grenades*
> *That incessantly strike us,*
> *Never can defeat us*
> *Nor even frighten us.*

This point remained to be proved, but the revision was universally admired. Martínez wanted the Academy band to assemble in the courtyard and play the anthem so that the Red hordes outside could hear it. But this suggestion was turned down on the ground that such a performance would draw enemy shellfire, and as Moscardó pointed out, the band already had enough to do defending gutted Capuchinos. Major Martínez Leal proudly claimed that both the words and the music were written within a forty-eight-hour period, a claim that critics of poetry and music have not disputed.

No one was more apprehensive about conditions in the Alcázar than the medical staff, and with good reason. They were inadequately trained for battle responsibilities, and their medical supplies consisted solely of items found in the Academy infirmary. The senior physician, Dr. Manuel Pelayo, had been accustomd to sending seriously ill cadets to Madrid for treatment. Assisting him was Dr. Pelayo Lozano, a dermatologist by training but by experience mainly a consultant on athlete's foot and acne, through his several years of duty with the cadets. The surgery fell to Lozano, who prepared for operations which he had never seen, by studying textbooks in the library. From his first amputation he had emerged as bloody as a butcher's apprentice, with trembling hands, but after cutting off five legs and four arms, he had acquired a working knowledge of surgery. He boasted that none of his amputees died while in his care (although at least two died in a Toledo hospital after the siege had ended). A third doctor, Daniel Ortega, was an oculist, and he became skillful in extracting metal.

Their greatest fear was that an epidemic would break out. There were too many people crowded into too small an area. The place was filthy. It was a serious offense to be caught relieving oneself in a public area, but in the isolated rooms above or in the dark corners below, there was no one to see. Preparing for the worst, the doctors studied medical encylopedias and speculated as to what kind of plague was most likely to break out.

The infirmary originally held eighteen cots. This number was doubled, then tripled, until finally the wounded overflowed into the cellars, where the women helped care for them. As soon as a patient could walk, his bed was taken from him. Leg amputees were given a blessing and a pair of broomsticks to hobble around on. The five nuns who had taken refuge in the Alcázar were placed in charge of the infirmary, which was constantly moved from room to room due to newly created demands for space and out of fear that the Republican gunners might discover its whereabouts.

As the siege wore on, medical supplies were depleted, particularly chloroform, the only anaesthetic in the Academy dispensary. The doctors used it sparingly, reserving it for the most serious cases. If a bullet or shrapnel was not lodged too deeply, it was extracted under medieval conditions: the patient was given a stone or a rag to clamp his jaws on while the forceps probed. The rococo desk of a professor served as an operating table, and following an operation the orderly mopped up the blood with a swab in order to save water. During the last weeks of the siege, operations took place in near darkness, since the grease lamps gave off little light and the upper rooms were untenable because of nearly continual shellfire. When the surgical saw broke, Dr. Lozano had to borrow the meat saw from the chef and return it to the kitchen afterward.

For those with mental disturbances, God was the only psychiatrist available. One of the most carefully guarded secrets of the Alcázar has to do with the number of people who went permanently insane.

By way of contrast, life among the *"abisinios"* was leisurely, even festive. The militia ate well, and each barricade had its wicker chairs and overstuffed sofa from which they shot desultorily and sometimes violently at the thick walls of the Alcázar. Russian observers, shocked to see *milicianos* shading themselves with parasols in the blazing sun, ridiculed "the war of lace ruffles," but parasols were a necessity, not a luxury. The sun killed, too. There were cases of militia left wounded on tiled rooftops and actually being broiled by the sun. The besiegers observed their ritual of siesta as religiously as they did during times of peace. Besides, there was no hurry—they knew that they were the hunters, not the hunted.

On paper, General Riquelme commanded the Republican forces in Toledo, but in actual fact he could do nothing without the co-operation of individual militia leaders, who, in turn, could do nothing without the consent of the men they represented. "Orders" arriving from the Ministry of War were, in the province of Toledo, little more than recommendations, and the result was military incompetence and general confusion. Unlike the Nationalists, whose acceptance of military caste and ecclesiastical hierarchy had conditioned them to accept command unquestioningly, the Republicans were victims of their jealously guarded autonomy. Although the officers gingerly tried to establish a chain of command, the average militia captain cheerfully went his own way and waited patiently for the Fascists of the Alcázar to be forced to come out into the streets and fight.

The only Republican in Toledo who understood the mystique of power was Major Luis Barceló,* who headed the awesome Militia Defense Committee of Toledo, which had its headquarters in the post office. In July, Barceló had been in charge of the executions of the Nationalist officers taken prisoner at the Carabanchel Barracks near Madrid, where he had acquired a reputation for ruthless efficiency. Shortly thereafter he made his way to Toledo, where he organized the committee in order to draw the different militia groups into a loose confederation, with himself at its head. In Toledo he wielded his power like a czar. Sentences imposed by his "cheka," or informal tribunal, were final and not subject to appeal; his police force served also as firing squad when

---

* During the last days of the Republic, in 1939, Barceló headed the revolt of the Communist soldiers in the Army of the Center, whose commander was Colonel Seigismundo Casado. Casado had arranged to surrender Madrid to the Nationalist army, since the Republic was doomed; but Barceló seized the central areas where the ministries were located. Thus began the civil war within the ranks of the Republican army. The fighting lasted for several days, during which Casado overpowered Barceló and had him executed. Madrid was then handed over to Franco's army.

the need arose. Without Barceló's co-operation, General Riquelme could do nothing; without his permission, the general was not allowed inside the city walls.

The butchery of the first days had been a spontaneous and unauthorized demonstration largely directed against the clergy, most of whom were killed in the streets while the militia were entering Toledo. After this, executions assumed a quasi-legal form, the accused standing trial at the post office and being judged by the committee. Anyone suspected of harboring Nationalist sympathies—and in this city of Church and Army there were many—was in danger of losing his life. In doubtful cases a rule of thumb applied: if the prisoner employed one servant in his household or two workers in his business, then he was a Fascist. One might be killed outright, like the eighty-year-old proprietor of the famous Venta de Aires restaurant, who was hauled off to a rubbish heap behind his house and shot in front of his wife, or one might be killed indirectly by being refused a ration book, which meant death by starvation if charity failed.

On the western edge of Toledo, in what was once the Jewish quarter, stands the old synagogue of El Tránsito. Across the street is a shady little park called the Paseo del Tránsito, in the middle of which is a monument to El Greco, who once lived in a house near by. Under these trees most of the mass executions ordered by the committee took place. During the summer of 1936 the phrase "to take a stroll through El Tránsito" meant "to be taken away and shot." A gypsy living in the vicinity was an eyewitness to one of these executions, and even allowing for obvious exaggerations in his account, his report is typical of others: "There were hundreds of them, including women and priests. They either prayed over their rosaries or gave praise to God. There were pools of blood which I could not step across. They were shot in the afternoon and left all night. Then in the morning a truck came for them. Some of them were still alive, because I saw movement among the bodies."

Another favorite place of execution was the Matadero—the municipal slaughterhouse—just down the hill. As the siege progressed and the militia became more sensitive to public opinion, the Matadero displaced the Paseo de Tránsito as an execution ground because no prying journalist would be able to tell the difference between the blood of human beings and that of cattle. Bodies were dumped by the cemetery wall outside of town for the custodian to dispose of as best he could.

Armed search parties routed suspected Nationalists out of their homes and led them to the tribunal for interrogation. The treatment of the prisoner depended upon his own attitude and the particular mood of his guards. Candido Cabello, the lawyer who had tried to trade the life of Luis Moscardó for the surrender of the Alcázar, was regarded as humane and even hospitable by some captives. On one occasion he comforted a priest by saying, "I am an atheist, but I don't understand why they have to kill somebody for being a priest." And once when a mob outside tried to enter by force and seize the prisoners, Cabello grabbed a pistol and drove them away, shouting, "If you enter here, it will be over my dead body!"

One frightened captive was handed a bowl of coffee by a burly Anarchist. Fearing it was poisoned, he said meekly, "I don't care for coffee." Enraged at this suspicion of his perfectly good intentions, the Anarchist whisked a pistol out of his pocket and jammed the muzzle into the prisoner's forehead. "Drink that coffee, you Fascist pig, or I'll blow your rotten head off!" he roared. The man drained the cup and admitted that it was indeed excellent coffee.

Isidoro Clamagiraud, the baker who had pointed out the granary to Moscardó, was picked up by the militia sometime in August while he was on a raid collecting flour from the family bakery. The committee sentenced him to death and ordered him to be taken to the Paseo del Tránsito. In the meantime, however, one of his workmen notified the French consul, M. Garrustu, who was in Toledo at the time, arranging for the safe-conduct of several French families to Madrid. Garrustu hatched a bold plan. With the flag of France flying from his windshield, he stayed in his car in front of the post office until Isidoro and his guards emerged. Then he jumped out, and in a short speech in French, which the militia did not understand, claimed the captive in the name of the French Republic. While the militia watched openmouthed, Garrustu drove away calmly with Isidoro to the Madrid highway, and when the city was behind them, raced to the capital. The next day the committee sent an indignant envoy to Madrid to re-claim the prisoner from the embassy, but this demand was rejected. Eventually Isidoro Clamagiraud made his way safely to France.

Such luck was rare. Self-appointed guides did a good business leading thrill-seekers through streets nauseous with filth (not once during the siege were these streets swept) to the main tourist attraction, the Paseo del Tránsito, where bloodstains on the far wall were a memorial to those who did not manage to escape. Nationalist authorities later claimed that eight hundred had been executed.

Many Toledanos owed their lives to the Spaniard's hatred of authority, a trait he seems almost to be born with. The committee's order that all Fascist sympathizers be reported was often disobeyed because it was an order. One waiter spent his days at a barricade, loyally firing at the Alcázar, and his evenings transporting certain friends on the "wanted" list to places of safety, because he believed that this was a duty as well. Had the committee discovered what he was doing, he would of course have been shot for treason.

The Asaltos, in particular, refused to support the committee's policy of executing private citizens, and since they were the best fighting unit, the committee dared not move against them. A Sergeant Vila, who commanded the armored car in the Zocodover, was universally regarded as the boldest Republican in Toledo. He was the only man in the city who dared cross the Zocodover, in full range of Alcázar rifles, at a slow walk, and on one occasion he sat down in the middle of the square and calmly ate a melon while bullets spattered the cobblestones around him. One of Vila's best friends, Lieutenant Celestino Vicente, was inside the Alcázar and Vila had a plan to save him when the fortress was taken. He kept a *mono* of Vicente's size in his armored car. When the Asaltos fought their way into the Alcázar, he intended to look for his friend and make him put on the disguise so that he could escape in the confusion. What he did not know was that Vicente had been killed by an Asalto bullet during the second week of the siege.

At times even the fearsome FAI, the Anarchist secret society, could be swayed by an unexpected inducement. One of their patrols ferreted out a major in his home and prepared to take him to headquarters. Before he left, the major's wife handed him a holy medal which he had worn in the Moroccan wars, but one of the FAI men grabbed it and jeered, "Look at this trash she gives him." "Yes," blazed the woman, "and perhaps your own mother has a medal for you as well." The Anarchists were embarrassed. Then one of them broke in gruffly, "Let him keep it. We respect all beliefs, even his." These men would burn a church or kill a priest without remorse, but they still retained a certain awe when confronted with a religious amulet. The story confirms what Unamuno said. "In Spain, all are Catholics—even the atheists."

One of the most notorious mass killings occurred on August 23. At noon a Republican trimotor flew over Toledo and dropped twenty-four bombs, but some of these fell in the Zocodover and injured many of the Sunday tourists who were gathered there. Although the pilot was responsible, he was inaccessible, and the crowd sought revenge elsewhere. That night the mob, stiffened by angry militia, swarmed around the provincial prison and demanded the captives inside. Without consulting the authorities, the jailor let them take fifteen Nationalist prisoners, including the dean of the cathedral, the commandant of the Infantry Orphans' School, and the two Moscardó brothers.

Luis Moscardó had been in this prison since July 23, the day when Candido Cabello telephoned Colonel Moscardó, but Carmelo and his mother had been staying with the wife of Colonel Tuero until August 13, when the militia net pulled all of them in, Carmelo sharing a cell with his elder brother. The wives of the two Alcázar colonels were locked up together in a distant corner of the prison and were not disturbed by the lynch mob which broke in on August 23.

The instigators of this mob violence were a band which called itself "the Archangels," led by a militiaman nicknamed El Verdugo ("the Hangman"), because he had been serving a sentence for murder before the insurrection broke out. They tied the victims' wrists and linked the prisoners together, in groups of two, to a long rope. Luis and Carmelo were side by side, but as they were being pulled to the door, an Anarchist called El

Granadino spotted Carmelo and asked his age. When he learned that Carmelo was only sixteen, El Granadino asked his comrades, "Do you mind if I take this kid and make a good revolutionary out of him?"

"Take him. We don't care," they told him.

Carmelo's rope was cut and his place was taken by the dean of the cathedral. El Granadino then ordered Carmelo to say good-bye to his brother. As the procession moved toward the door, one of the prisoners complained that he had left his blanket behind, but was interrupted by a roar of laughter from the mob. "Don't worry about blankets," someone said. "You won't need them where you're going." Carmelo was locked up again.

A few hours later El Granadino returned, and Carmelo was brought into the interrogation room. When he begged to know what they had done with Luis, the militiaman said, "Justice was done, just as it's going to be done now." A priest who had been overlooked in the earlier roundup of prisoners was now brought in for questioning. El Granadino debated with him for several minutes about the existence of God. When the priest won the argument, the Anarchist lost his temper. Picking up a rifle by the barrel, he said, "This is how to end such discussions." As Carmelo looked on in horror, El Granadino swung the rifle like a sledge hammer and smashed the priest's skull with a single blow. Carmelo was again locked up by himself.

The following morning El Granadino came again. He told Carmelo that although the rest of the militia wanted his hide, he could join the CNT, the Anarchist trade union, and be spared. The boy chose to join. He was taken to the Anarchist headquarters, where they poured a bottle of red wine over his head and baptized him a "child of Marx." El Granadino, who had developed a bearlike affection for him, now appointed Carmelo his deputy. Two days later Carmelo got permission for his mother to be released from prison and to join him at headquarters. Two days later, Carmelo asked to be dropped from the CNT and to be returned to prison. El Granadino was very disappointed, but he arranged to have Carmelo and his mother placed in the chapel of the Toledo insane asylum where they would be safe. Here they remained for the rest of the siege. El Granadino allegedly sent them parcels of food and other gifts from time to time. Luis had

been executed at the Matadero with the others, but Carmelo
owed his life to the strange caprice of the Anarchist implicated in
his brother's murder.

For a foreign journalist in Madrid a trip to Toledo was easily
arranged, provided that he was listed as a *bueno* or a *muy bueno*
by the Ministry of War—which simply meant that his reporting
had favored the Republican cause. One such was the Englishman
John Langdon-Davies, who was assigned an automobile, a driver,
and an armed guard, and was driven down to Toledo in the fifth
week of the siege. He found the city expectant and tense. The
"Army of Overalls" had fortified the Bisagra Gate with machine
guns pointing inward to prevent the "Flies" from fighting their
way out of the city. As his guard led him through narrow alleys
to the Anarchist headquarters in the former seminary, Langdon-
Davies occasionally caught a glimpse of the Alcázar looming
above the low buildings. Tiny puffs of smoke whiffed out through
its narrow windows.

Independent of the Militia Defense Committee, the Anarchists
had their own "cheka" in the seminary. Above the door to this
inquisitorial chamber an inappropriately small sign read: EN-
TRANCE PROHIBITED. While talking with his guide, Langdon-Davies
saw the door open and two prisoners being led out into the patio
to urinate. Their collars had been cut off their shirts—collars
being a hated class symbol to the Anarchists—and their shoelaces
had been removed. Both were unshaven, heavy-eyed, and gray-
looking. In due time they would no doubt be shot, but Langdon-
Davies saw no sign of maltreatment.

Before climbing to the roof of the seminary, Langdon-Davies'
guide tucked his forage cap into his pocket, explaining that
snipers were less likely to shoot at bare-headed targets. From the
rooftop Langdon-Davies had a broadside view of the Alcázar
across the vermilion roofs of the thick-set city. The battle raging
below was a contest between the Republic of the future and "the
last fragments of age-long despotisms starving to death," as he
put it. The Anarchists regaled him with fanciful anecdotes about
the Alcázar. Rebel officers, they said, propped machine guns
against the shoulders of their hostages, so that the militia dared
not return the fire; the garrison was down to a sliver of horse

meat and a half-pint of water per day. Everyone was convinced that the fortress would surrender at any moment, and after studying the siege, Langdon-Davies agreed with them.

Davies' guide led him closer to the Alcázar. The Calle del Arzobispal, which dropped down to the cathedral, had been re-named the Calle de Carlos Marx. On the wall of the Archbishop's Palace was a stenciled sign: POST NO BILLS. But directly below it there were three: ENLIST IN THE FIFTH REGIMENT (the Fifth was a crack Communist-controlled outfit), GIVE TO THE SPANISH RED CROSS, and FASCIST CANAILLE!

As they moved in closer the *paqueo* became louder. The cross streets which were exposed to Alcázar rifles had been roped off to prevent people from wandering accidentally into a line of fire, but in some places the rope had been carried off by someone who apparently thought he had a better use for it. The guide pointed out a place where a nine-year-old girl had chased a ball beyond the danger line and been instantly shot by a sniper, the bullet passing through her cheeks and ripping out her upper teeth. Al-though they were less than a hundred yards from the west wall of the fortress, Langdon-Davies was chiefly impressed by the ap-parent normality of life in this zone. Oblivious to the battle being fought a few streets away, women bargained with the milkman as they had always done, a small boy played with an empty sardine can on the cobblestones, and from a balcony festooned with geraniums an old woman pitched a pot of foul-looking liquid into the middle of the street.

At one intersection the Englishman noted that his guide took pride in running across a twenty-foot space directly within the sights of an Alcázar sniper. There was a ritual of bravado at this dangerous corner. One was supposed to gaze contemptuously at the enemy window as one ran across at a speed slow enough to demonstrate courage but fast enough to avoid being hit by the bullet smashing into the wall beyond. Langdon-Davies suggested that they ought to drape sheets across this intersection so that the sniper would not know when to fire, but the militia were scorn-ful. Such screens were all right for *extranjeros*, not for Spaniards. If there was no way of showing one's contempt for death, a man could not be considered truly brave. This ritual of courage and insolence seemed to be borrowed from the bullfight.

At the most advanced barricades Langdon-Davies found a dozen or so *milicianos* waiting for the counterattack which all of them believed was inevitable. Three or four men squinted through peepholes or fired at the gray walls of the doomed fortress, while others rested on mattresses or lounged in wicker chairs. In the most protected corner lay a big wineskin. At one barricade Langdon-Davies met four German anti-Fascists, one of them a girl in blue overalls, who had come to Spain to fight for the Republic.

Beyond the sandbags and heaped furniture of the barricades was the blighted waste of no man's land. It was littered with hundreds of empty tin cans, a kind of crude warning system in case the Fascists attempted a sortie after sundown. Such posts as these were the frontier of the Spanish Republic. Beyond was the Alcázar, which occasionally emitted a tiny cloud of smoke from a window like "the splashes of raindrops on a misty lake."

As the sun was setting, Langdon-Davies heard the roar of an airplane above the rooftops. It seemed to come out of nowhere, and seconds later, to have vanished again. This was the Nationalist plane which dropped supplies and Franco's letter on the Alcázar. An urchin in his early teens darted into a house near by, and returned with an unloaded revolver, and clicked it angrily at the already empty sky.

A few hours later Langdon-Davies returned to Madrid. The thing which impressed him most, and which he could not get out of his mind, was the absolute refusal of the militia to stretch a sheet across that intersection.

While Republican artillery peeled away the outer husk of the Alcázar, the Army of Africa inched along the Estremadura highway toward Toledo. When it approached Talavera de la Reina, a city fifty miles west of Toledo, a ripple of alarm swept through the Republic. Would Franco's relief columns reach the Alcázar before it was captured? Just back in Madrid from a tour of the Estremadura front, the President and the Minister of War assured the people that the Nationalist advance would be permanently halted at Talavera—"our Verdun"—by impregnable fortifications, but at the same time they urged the militia besieging the Alcázar to finish their work as quickly as possible so that they could buttress the Talavera line. The President and the Minister always received the same reply: "Give us a few days more."

Arturo Barea, a Republican press censor, viewed the optimistic prognostications of his superiors with increasing gloom. He decided to find out for himself how things stood in Toledo, so, with his inventor-friend Fausto, whose design for a new type of grenade had been sent to the arms factory months before, he drove down from Madrid. At the factory a workers' committee had taken charge of the plant, but the grenade was not being manufactured because no one had been willing to make the decision to go ahead. An atmosphere of general distrust pervaded the place.

"We had to shoot the explosives expert," the *responsable*, or man in charge, told them. "For sabotage. He absolutely refused to give us powder for rifle cartridges, so we confiscated his whole stock. But then the cartridges exploded. So we had to shoot him."

Fausto examined the explosive in question and said, "But if you put mitramite, which is what was in stock here, into a rifle cartridge, it blows up the whole rifle."

The *responsable* shrugged. "I tell you, the cartridges exploded in the rifle, and that's sabotage."

Before Barea and Fausto left the arms factory, the *responsable* surreptitiously showed them a switchboard in the corner of his office. "If the Fascists come here, we've prepared a nice surprise for them. If you pushed down this lever now, not one of the workshops would be left. They're all mined, with a dynamite charge underneath." Then, in a whisper, he added, "But that's a secret!"

Leaving the factory, they walked up the hill to watch the battle. It was even more depressing. In the Zocodover every windowpane was broken and the square was littered with scraps of paper and dirty pieces of discarded uniform. From doorways and corners, militia and Asaltos were firing at the inscrutable façade of the Alcázar. Crouched in awkward positions, yelling and gesticulating, the besiegers shouted orders to one another, fired their rifles, and blew shrill whistles. Occasionally a puff of smoke came from an Alcázar window, as though from an indifferent smoker across a room, but the sound of the shot was drowned by the fusillade from the crowd milling at the base of the Alcázar. The scene reminded Barea of a film when the synchronization of sound and picture goes haywire.

Fausto was disgusted. "Let's get out of here," he growled. Later he added, "We're going to lose the war if this is a symbol."

Between the Santiago Barracks and the Tagus gorge, a steep road, rocky and potholed, runs along the edge of the cliff from the Alcántara Bridge to the Corralillo. More suited for mules than vehicles, this track was never feared by the defenders as an attack route, since the windows of the Santiago commanded it. But one afternoon late in August a sentry posted at a window was startled to see a black Peugeot sedan with a Madrid license bouncing wildly up this road with a huge red banner fluttering from its window. The sentry thought it was the vanguard of a Republican column and shouted for assistance, but by the time reinforcements joined him the vehicle had passed by below the Santiago and had nearly reached the Corralillo. When they poured a volley into the rear of the automobile, it jerked to a stop. A few seconds later the door on the driver's side was flung open and a man jumped out so quickly that no one had a chance to shoot before he plunged over the embankment and disappeared from view. Almost at the same time the other front door opened and an attractive woman stepped out into the road. She swung the red banner arrogantly before bullets cut her down. For a while she lay twitching beside the car, and then she was still. When the soldiers in the Santiago tried to fetch her body for burial, they were driven back by a heavy *paqueo* from militia across the river. That night there was a full moon, and they saw small objects moving cautiously toward the girl's body. They were rats. Revolted, they drove them back by firing short bursts with a machine gun, but the creatures kept creeping back toward the outstretched hands. A Falangist crawled out with a can of gasoline and doused the corpse with it, but when he lit it, the flames succeeded only in enveloping the automobile and bringing down a renewed *paqueo* from across the Tagus.

Throughout the following day, in the blazing sun, the body of the young woman lay sprawled on the road. The smell of smoldering rubber gave way to something worse. There had been

a corpse lying in full view on the Alcántara Bridge since the first
days of the siege, but for the garrison in the Santiago this one was
infinitely worse: not only was it a stone's throw away, but also, it
was a woman. However, it would have been suicide for any of
them to have attempted to remove it. The next night was cloudy,
and the men were grateful that the body could not be seen. At
daybreak they looked out of their windows in disbelief—the
Peugeot was still there, but the body was gone. The mystery remained. No one ever knew why the automobile had been driven
up that road (was it a stunt by some youth eager to prove his
fearlessness to a girl friend?), and no one ever found out who recovered the body of the girl.

September arrived, and Major Barceló announced that the
Asturians had pushed their mine shafts to the Cuesta del Alcázar.
It would not be long, he announced confidently, before the walls
of the Alcázar came tumbling down.

8

THE THREE EMISSARIES

UNDER THE REPEATED artillery barrages the Alcázar was falling to pieces like a wet lump of sugar. Although the publicized 240-mm. gun did not appear on the Toledo front, the nine 155's, eight 105's, and seven 75's in the Dehesa de Pinedo and Alijares had converted the sculptured north façade into an amorphous heap of rubble. Troops defending this side of the Alcázar no longer concealed themselves behind windows; instead, they scooped out rifle pits along the crest of this huge mound of loose stone and dust. Having caved in the north wall, Republican artillerists began on September 2 to concentrate on the northeast tower, doubtless hoping to topple it backward into the courtyard. The following day a steady bombardment loosened the hard outer shell of the tower and began to tear out chunks of the softer inner lining as easily as a knife cutting cheese. By the end of the day there was a gap in the tower as large as a railway tunnel some eighty feet above the east esplanade, leaving the steeple hanging in the air as if the force of gravity had been suspended.

Dawn of September 4 found the rooftops of nearby buildings packed with militia eagerly waiting for the huge tower to topple. It did not take long. After a few more 155-mm. shells had exploded in the gap, the tower broke loose from the wall. It fell a hundred feet to the esplanade, where it was writhing for a moment like a living thing until the steel girders inside it relaxed. The spike pointed eastward to the Alijares battery like an accusing finger.

The crash was heard all over Toledo and was followed by cheering and bell-ringing, as the myth of the indestructibility of the Alcázar disappeared in the rumble of broken masonry. Militia, ignoring the bullets fired at them from other parts of the Alcázar, stood up in barricades or on rooftops and shook their rifles in frenzied excitement. Those in the cellars of the Alcázar felt the ground shake as in an earthquake. Fine dust sifted down over them through cracks in the vaulted ceiling, but there were no cave-ins. They could thank God that the tower had fallen outward, onto the solid earth of the esplanade.

Minutes later the militia were pouring a withering fire upon upper rooms laid open by the destruction of the tower, for the northeast corner of the Alcázar now resembled a doll's house with a segment lifted out. Defenders scurried like rats to find new rifle pits in the rubble of the upper stories, since wholly new avenues of fire had been opened up for the Republican militia.

The Alcázar junta was aghast at the damage and the threat to their plan of defense. The enemy artillery could now pick apart the east side, room by room, with enfilading shots. The four massive towers had braced the walls like the legs of a squat table; with one tower gone the structure of the fortress was endangered. In desperation, Moscardó even consulted with Romero about a possible counterattack to the outside, preparatory to evacuating the building. Then something happened which they attributed to the intercession of God: the enemy artillerists began firing on the other tower, at the northwest corner. For them the excitement of knocking down towers apparently outweighed the more important business of widening the gap at the northeast angle. The arrogant-looking towers of the Alcázar seemed to have bewitched the artillerists, because in the weeks ahead they remained the principal targets of the 155's.

On this same day, September 4, attackers from the Santa Cruz succeeded in setting fire to the Gobierno, and the blaze spread unchecked throughout the building. Demoralized, the men fled from the holocaust, ran up the ramp to the east esplanade, and took refuge in the dining hall. The chemical laboratory, a small stucco building on the north edge of the east esplanade, caught fire and exploded in green flame and smoke. The militia had at last driven the Nationalists from the Gobierno, but they could not occupy the building themselves until the fire died down. Moreover, in the smoke and confusion the retreating had not been discovered; as far as the militia knew, the Nationalists were hiding somewhere in the building, waiting to spring an ambush as they had done in the past.

In the evening the junta planned a counterattack to reoccupy the Gobierno, but they could no nothing, either, until the building burned itself out. Meanwhile Moscardó dispatched fifty-three men to the granary to bring in sacks of wheat, for if the Gobierno were not retaken, this supply would be completely cut off.

At dawn a furious shellfire played upon all the dependencies of the Alcázar and bottled up the counterattack. It was not until five-thirty in the afternoon that Captain Vela with a band of Falangists was able to steal out of the fortress and take up positions in the ruins of the chemical laboratory. At the same time Lieutenant José Espiga led the troop section down the ramp and into the stable approach, just beneath the rifles of the Falangists. While Vela's force fired at the militia who had occupied the Gobierno, Espiga's men, mostly armed with pistols and machetes, kicked open the doors of the still smoking building and burst in. Instructed to make as much noise as possible, the attackers howled, "Kill the Reds!" and bore in upon the militia already pinned down by the rifle fire of Vela's men on the terrace a few yards above them. Completely taken by surprise, the militia did not wait to see who or what was coming toward them through the smoke. They dropped their rifles and bolted from the building, some of them jumping from the windows next to the Calle del Carmen. Without a single casualty the Nationalists had recovered the Gobierno.

During the next two days the 155's retaliated. Over two hundred shells battered the Gobierno, but the troops who crouched inside had learned their lesson: retreating held more dangers than holding fast. As their officers said—was it not better to defend the building rather than lose it and be forced to recapture it? It was now perfectly clear to them that Moscardó and his junta had no intention of allowing the Republicans to occupy this protruding salient of the defense.

Sounds of the mining were becoming more audible. During the first week of September, Captain Vela led two sorties after nightfall, but once again he had guessed incorrectly and bombed the wrong house. Lieutenant Barber, entrusted with charting the progress of the tunnel, no longer believed that these sorties served much purpose: the miners might be using any of several dozen houses near by, and the Alcázar did not possess the means, or the time, to destroy them all. As an engineer, he wanted to study the mine so that he could devise some way of minimizing its effect or at least predict the maximum degree of damage. Therefore, on September 6, he crawled out into the Cuesta del Alcázar with his borrowed stethoscope, and passed an hour listening patiently to the dull heartbeat of the digging under the road. Searchlights played on the Alcázar windows above him, but Barber hugged the shadows in the shell-pocked street and crept back safely. After scribbling a few notes on a scrap of paper, he asked for an interview with Moscardó and his staff.

The Republicans, he announced, were digging two mine shafts—not one, as they had thought. One was working toward the southwest tower, and the other toward the carriage gate. He thought that the miners would place their explosives in such a way that the wall would be blown inward to bury much of the Alcázar under rubble. Both mines would, of course, be detonated simultaneously. Could the whole fortress be blown up? Barber thought not, though it was possible that the shock wave might dislodge foundation stones and bring portions of the building down. Passageways might be blocked by falling stones, in which case the Alcazareños would be buried alive, or sealed off long enough to allow the Republican assault columns to occupy parts of the building and to pick them off one by one as they dug out from below. There was one encouraging detail, however: in their impatience to complete the work, the miners were using larger blasting charges in the tunnels than they ought to, and this might confuse their sense of direction. If they burrowed even a few feet beyond the center of the wall, for instance, the exploding mines would hurl tons of rubble outside the perimeter of the Alcázar.

The same question occurred to every officer listening to Barber's report: how much time did they have? The lieutenant estimated that it would take eight more days for the tunnels to reach the walls, for the miners were now digging through solid rock. Moreover, additional time would be required to place their explosives, a day or two at the outside. The conference then ended, but to keep morale high, Moscardó enjoined the officers not to talk in public about the mines, even though he knew that they probably would.

Lieutenant Barber's predictions brought a wave of gloom into the Alcázar. September 6, which had opened so well, ended on a despairing note. At dawn a Nationalist airplane had flown over the building and dropped three more aluminum chests. These were not from Franco but from General Mola. Two of the chests fell within the Republican lines, and the delicacies inside—goose liver, sardines, chocolate—were eaten by the militia. ("Radio Cigarral" asked Moscardó to thank Mola for them when the two officers met in hell.) But in the third chest there was a brief note from Mola to the "brave defenders of the Alcázar," saying that the Nationalist forces were advancing on all fronts (although Mola himself had been tied down in the Guadarramas for the past six weeks) and that Talavera de la Reina had been taken by the Army of Africa. Mola's note was something of an anticlimax. Franco's message had arrived at a time when the garrison regarded itself as hopelessly surrounded and abandoned, and they now regarded him as their savior. Mola, the principal rival of Franco for supreme command of the Nationalist armies, had been outfoxed.

Moscardó was so little impressed by the second airdrop that he omitted all mention of it in his operational log, even though this was a book so meticulously kept that it recorded every sack of wheat retrieved from the granary, and every shell—with its size—that struck the Alcázar. If Mola wished to help them, he would have to send more than rhetoric and goose liver.

The food situation was becoming intolerable. Food had replaced sex as the main subject of conversation among the soldiers. Moscardó was deeply depressed to discover that some of the

Civil Guards had been sneaking off at night to comb the bone yards on the east esplanade for refuse from the horse carcasses. Others had broken into the Academy medical store and devoured every tablet and pill that tasted of sugar; fortunately none had been poisoned. Moscardó himself had been having the same dream repeatedly during the past week: he was sitting in front of a couple of fried eggs, dripping with grease and encircled by fried potatoes. Yet he never ate them in his dream; he put them aside for the future. He was dimly haunted by a fear that if he succumbed to hunger and ate those eggs, his dream would signify that the Alcázar would surrender.

One of the officers, a notorious complainer, confronted Colonel Moscardó openly and insisted that he be given more to eat than the wretched daily ration. The colonel rummaged through his pockets, pulled out a fifty-peseta bill and said, "Take this. Go outside and buy something, if you like. It's the best I can do for you."

Despite the strict prohibition against raids, small groups of the Falange continued to slip out of the windows on the south side, justifying themselves with the time-worn excuses that they were looking for food for the infirmary or for an electric cable to tap current. Although their *razzias* seldom netted more than a small pile of rotten figs or a few cans of condensed milk, plunder was not their motive: they were eager to prove that despite their civilian status, they could fight like trained professionals. The professionals, on the other hand, granted the Falangists their courage but thought that they went to ridiculous lengths to prove it. "All guts, no brains," they said. It was sometimes difficult to tell where courage left off and foolishness began, as the raid on September 7 showed.

During the morning barrage, six Falangists led by Maximiliano Fink, who had previously been cited for bravery in the Gobierno fighting, darted out of the door on the south side. Since the militia posted in the houses facing the Plaza de Capuchinos ducked out of sight during barrages to avoid being hit by shrapnel, Fink figured that he could jump a barricade without being detected. He was wrong. Halfway across the square the Falangists ran into a cross fire from two barricades. Only when the others had taken cover behind a low wall near the Alcázar did they become aware that Fink's body lay crumpled in the square, some fifteen yards away. At first they thought that he was writhing, but it was the militia's pumping bullets into the body that created the illusion. This was more than Godofredo Bravo, Fink's best friend, could bear. Dropping his rifle, he vaulted the wall and ran out into the square to retrieve the body, but he was also killed.

By this time the Plaza de Capuchinos was developing into a shooting gallery as militia rushed into the sector to determine the reason for the excitement and Nationalists crowded into the high windows of the south façade. As soon as the superior marksmanship of the Alcazareños began to dominate the scene, a third Falangist, José Canosa, dashed out to Fink's body with a rope and succeeded in looping it under the arms. But as he ran back toward the low wall, a bullet whined past his ear, and ducking, he lost his hold on the rope. When a fourth man started to go after the rope, a bullet hit him in the shoulder and he plumped docilely behind the wall again. At this point another Falangist, José Berzosa, ran out, grabbed Bravo's body, and using it as a shield, dragged it back into the Alcázar. Miraculously he escaped injury, although the corpse was struck twice. Fink still lay in the square.

Since a Falangist—even a dead one—was a trophy for the militia, they made several attempts to recover the corpse. An intrepid Anarchist managed to grab the rope and drag Fink a few feet before he, too, was shot dead. For the rest of the day a savage vendetta raged in the Plaza de Capuchinos. Republicans abandoned their barricades in other sectors to join in the fun along the south wall, alternately trying to lasso the body and shooting bullets into it. Inside the building the Falangists were livid. Moscardó finally had to dispatch Captain Vela and other officers to the south door to prevent them from making a sortie *en masse*. Grizzled veterans of the Civil Guard incredulously gathered around, astonished that a shot-up corpse in the road could be the real cause of this hullabaloo.

After dark the Falangists were able to bring back the body of Maximiliano Fink; it was so punctured with bullets that it nearly fell apart as his comrades carried it inside. A big Germanic-looking blond, Fink had been regarded as one of the boldest Nationalist fighters. A few hours later, militia near the southern windows heard a weird chant, the burial service for a Falangist killed in action,* coming from the dark upper rooms of the Alcázar:

"Camarada Maximiliano Fink!"

"*Presente!*" boomed the chorus.

"Camarada Godofredo Bravo!"

"*Presente!*"

"*Arriba, España!*"

Despite their loss, the Falange were proud of the day's action. Some of their critics conceded that they were glad to see the young *fanáticos* fighting with the Army and not against it. Others, like Colonel Romero, regarded the episode as a presumptuous bit of foolishness that had endangered the security of the fortress. He demanded, and the junta approved, that members of the Falange be absolutely prohibited from making further raids and from participating in skirmishes with the militia unless there was an all-out attack. The Falangists were indignant when they learned about this veto, but were somewhat mollified when Moscardó promised that he would use them in the most hazardous assignments to come.

The Republican artillery had been pounding the northwest tower for four days, registering 272 hits with their 155's alone. From the Zocodover the tower looked like a monstrous face: under two eyelike windows there was a huge hole shaped like a yawning mouth, which belched smoke and dust whenever the tower was struck. The steeple, stripped of its roofing slates, resembled an absurd bird cage, and the complexion of the monster was pockmarked and pitted. On September 8 the 155's fired twenty-nine more shells at the tower, which shuddered convulsively, sagged slowly westward, and fell with a crash across the Cuesta del Alcázar. All over Toledo, klaxons celebrated the fall of the second tower while further shells exploded in the breach, for good measure. The defenders braced themselves for an infantry assault, but none came. The fog-thick layer of dust

---

* Immediately following these obsequies, the Falange voted a posthumous Silver Palm for Bravo and proposed the names of six others for this prized badge of their organization. Fink, though as dead as Bravo, was awarded nothing.

from the collapsed tower momentarily obscured the sun and coated the statue of the Virgin in the chapel, but there were no cave-ins below.

When the barrage ceased at noon, Moscardó and his aides clambered through the wreckage. They observed with some satisfaction that the fallen tower blocked the Cuesta to vehicles or tanks. If attackers advanced up this street from the Zocodover, they would have to come on foot, and the men would have to scale an uneven mound of loose rubbish thirty feet high in order to reach those areas where the mines were expected, farther up the Cuesta. Some of the officers felt that the obstruction improved the defensive position of the Alcázar, but Lieutenant Barber was worried. Since the tower had carried with it the northwest stairwell, the upper rooms along the west wall could now be reached only by the stairway in the southwest tower, which would in turn be destroyed when the mine under it was exploded. It would then be impossible for anyone in the Alcázar to reach these upper rooms. Barber feared that the Republicans might be able to climb up into these rooms from the outside, but none of the others agreed—the Civil Guards entrenched along the northern crest would prevent this, they said.

At sundown an eerie silence fell over Toledo. The militia stopped their *paqueo* entirely. When the Falangists hurled insults and obscenities, they failed to raise a shot in reply. The city seemed asleep, even dead. A ripple of uneasiness passed through the Alcázar. Was the city being evacuated for the explosion of the mine? Utterly impossible, Lieutenant Barber said. Perhaps the Republicans were preparing a night attack? Moscardó ordered every able-bodied man to his emergency position. The garrison waited tensely.

At ten-thirty in the evening a megaphone in one of the ruined houses bordering on the Plaza de Capuchinos sharply broke the silence: "Academy! El Comandante Rojo wishes to speak with either Colonel Moscardó or Captain Alamán."

Since *El Comandante Rojo* means "the Red major," the retort was a burst of rifle fire from the men in the southern windows, who assumed that "Radio Cigarral" was about to begin a nocturnal broadcast. The fire was not returned. The voice called out again: "No! You misunderstand me. I am El Comandante

Vicente Rojo, and I must speak with your commander immediately."

Inside the Alcázar the officers were stunned. Major Vicente Rojo, a former professor of military history at the Academy, was known personally to most of them. Widely recognized as the best military strategist in the Army, Rojo had dropped out of sight when the rebellion broke out. No one in the Alcázar was certain whether his sympathies were Republican or Nationalist, but everyone who knew him agreed that the voice of the megaphone was his.

While orderlies alerted all posts to the possibility of a trick, Moscardó hurried down to a lower window, where he cupped his hands over his mouth and called out, "This is Colonel Moscardó speaking. What do you want?"

"This is Major Vicente Rojo—"

"I know who you are," Moscardó broke in. "What do you want?"

"I have an urgent communication from the government. Will you permit an hour's cease-fire tomorrow morning at nine o'clock so that I can enter the Alcázar?"

For the next five minutes there was complete silence while Moscardó consulted with his staff. Then he called out, "All right. You may have it."

"And my personal safety—do you guarantee it?"

Moscardó was incensed at this note of distrust. "We are gentlemen here," he snapped, "not like your Republican trash. You may have an hour."

The rest of the night passed without a shot being fired on either side, but it was a sleepless night for most of those in the Alcázar. A rumor was circulating that because of the breakthrough at Talavera de la Reina, the Republic wished to arrange for an armistice. Others, however, contended that Rojo was merely bringing a demand for their surrender.

The events of the first week in September had caused major changes in the government. The rapid advance of the Army of Africa toward Madrid had brought down Prime Minister José Giral's coalition government, which had never conducted the war vigorously, and brought into power the popular Socialist

Largo Caballero, who promised to unite the country and make Spain "the grave of Fascism." One of Caballero's first acts of office had been the appointment of Colonel José Asensio Torrado to command the forces besieging the Alcázar. The forty-four-year-old officer, regarded as one of the most brilliant of the Loyalists, had been instructed that "once and for all the Toledan nightmare must be ended." He had arrived in Toledo on September 7, made a tour of inspection, and quickly won the confidence of most representatives of the seven thousand militia there. He had brought with him thousands of forage caps, each with a bright red tassel, which were distributed to the men. Since they were Regular Army issue, the Anarchists, of course, refused to wear them, but the others willingly accepted this token of assimilation into the Army. The disorderly mob began to succumb to military discipline. Asensio Torrado made it clear that the Toledo front was no longer the place for sluggards and assassins.

While the colonel tightened the siege, Caballero grappled with another problem: what to do about the women and children in the basements of the Alcázar. It would be inhuman to blow them up with the garrison; besides, it would be bad publicity. The government was being bombarded with demands that the non-combatants be set free before the fortress was leveled, and even journalists sympathetic to the government's cause balked at the prospect of innocents being slaughtered. Many correspondents, following a natural impulse to side with the underdog, were now writing stories slanted in favor of the defenders.* The best course therefore was to obtain an outright surrender, or if this could not be achieved, to arrange for the evacuation of the women and children. This done, the Republic could reduce the Alcázar to ashes without outraging world opinion. Whether he realized it or not, Colonel Moscardó's most powerful defensive weapon consisted of the women and children huddled in the cellars; to wrest this weapon from him, the government had sent Major Vicente

---

* Sympathy for the defenders was rapidly spreading among otherwise loyal Republicans, especially among those engaged in the fighting. Later, when it was rumored that the Alcázar had been relieved by General Franco, Olaff de Wet, a foreign-born pilot who had flown many missions against the Alcázar, wrote in his diary: "I hope it is true. . . . I admire immensely the heroic defenders of the old fortress. There are many amongst even the most rabid who think as I."

Rojo down to Toledo to negotiate with his former colleagues of the Academy.

At nine in the morning of September 9, a megaphone announced that Major Rojo was coming across the lines. A moment later a figure in blue overalls, with a tan forage cap on his head and a service belt strapped around his waist, stepped out of a bullet-flecked doorway on the Plaza de Capuchinos. Under the major's star, pinned to his pocket, Rojo wore the red, yellow, and purple colors of the Republic. The Alcázar officers recognized Vicente Rojo at once by his short build, his thin brown mustache, and the scholarly face behind moon-shaped, horn-rimmed spectacles. As he picked his way through the clutter of the square he glanced up at the seemingly vacant windows of the Alcázar and must have noticed the muzzle of a heavy machine gun noiselessly following his course. But he walked confidently and briskly to the middle of the square, when a voice from the fortress told him to halt. Binoculars popped above window sills and examined him with microscopic attention. Then the voice commanded him to walk down the Cuesta del Alcázar to the carriage gate, where he was kept waiting in the roadway. Finally the door swung open slowly and two officers, Major Blas Piñar and Captain Emilio Alamán, stepped out, both squinting and shielding their eyes in the dazzling sunshine. They were as white as chalk. As they beckoned Rojo to climb up to them, a *miliciano* across the street muttered, "That's the end of that fellow."

The Alcázar officers blindfolded Rojo, as prescribed in field regulations, and led him through the door, which was then slammed shut and bolted. Everyone in the fortress had been commanded to maintain absolute silence during Rojo's visit lest he form any conception of their number or their condition. When his guides, trying to confuse him, led him in circles on their route to the superintendent's office, Rojo must have been amused, since he knew the layout of the Academy as well as they. Several times his hand involuntarily went to his nose, but he checked himself. When they finally stopped, he heard faint whisperings around him. The blindfold was whisked off and he found himself blinking at a tall, vaguely familiar colonel who stood stiffly in front of him, looking at him sternly. He immediately recognized the office around him, which was almost unchanged except for a thick film of dust and piles of bricks at the window, but the identity of the colonel evaded him for a moment. The face was hidden behind a full gray beard, the uniform was baggy and stained, the form within was more suggestive of a scarecrow than a man. When he recognized Moscardó, Rojo stepped forward and extended his hand, but turning aside abruptly, Moscardó ignored it. The colonel asked that all officers leave the room except Lieutenant Barber, who was retained as the official witness to the parley.

Without further ceremony Rojo said, "I have a document from the Defense Committee of Toledo." He handed Moscardó a typewritten paper, which the latter read, his lips moving with the words, his hands shaking, while Lieutenant Barber looked over his shoulder. The paper outlined the terms of surrender: safe-conduct for all occupants; immediate freedom for women, children, and combatants under sixteen years of age; and delivery of all other combatants to the Republican tribunals, which would determine the extent of their guilt. There were ten signatures, some of which were illegible scrawls obviously written by hands not accustomed to holding pens. The last name on the list was that of El Comandante Vicente Rojo.

When he had finished reading the document, Moscardó excitedly slapped it with the back of his hand, and passed it to Lieutenant Barber. Then he said to Rojo, "We are willing to let the Alcázar become a cemetery, but not a dung heap."

Sitting down at the superintendent's desk, Moscardó penned on a scrap of paper: "Concerning the conditions for the surrender of the Alcázar presented by the committee, it gives me great pleasure to inform you that from the last soldier to the commander they reject said conditions and will continue to defend the Alcázar and the dignity of Spain until the end." He rose, handed this to Rojo, and walked to the door. Rojo asked if there was anything he could do for them.

"Yes," Moscardó replied. "You can send us a priest. We want nothing else from you." He then left the room.

As soon as Moscardó had gone, the office filled with Nationalist officers, who surrounded Rojo and eagerly fired questions at him. The atmosphere was as relaxed and as cordial as that of an officers' club. Most questions concerned the mines—how big would they be? Where were the tunnels located? When would they be ready? Rojo said he had no idea where they were but that he had been told they would be ready for detonation in about a week. Asked about the Nationalist advance on Madrid, he said the Mola had been stopped completely in the Guadarrama Mountains, and that although Franco was still advancing, his progress was slowing down. He added with a smile, "The enemy is very short of ammunition." When someone asked why he did not remain with them in the Alcázar, Rojo became pensive. "If I did, this very night my wife and children in Madrid would be killed," he said. Not until afterward did anyone note that Rojo had avoided telling them whether he wanted to stay with them or not.

Before being blindfolded again, Rojo dumped the contents of his tobacco pouch on the desk and said, "This is the best memento I can give you." As the bandage was tightened around his eyes, he suddenly cried out "*Viva España!*" as a soldier might do if he were facing a Republican firing squad. Though this was a Monarchist cheer, it was ambiguous—which Spain was Major Rojo alluding to? Major Piñar and Captain Alamán guided him back to the carriage gate, the other officers following them quietly. As the door was being opened and the blindfold removed, Rojo muttered to Captain Alamán, "For the love of God, keep hunting for the entrance to the mines." Then the door slammed and Rojo was standing outside, listening to them piling rubble against the wooden panels inside. It was only five minutes to ten. Major Rojo had not even used up the hour which had been given him. As Rojo passed through the Republican lines on his way to hand over Moscardó's scrap of paper, the men in blue uniform, noticing that his eyes were moist, stepped back and let him through without asking any questions.

Inside the Alcázar, Moscardó paced a dim corridor with an aide at his side. For a long time he did not speak. Then he stopped and said, "I just can't understand why a man of Major Rojo's integrity did not remain with us." After more pacing back and forth he turned to his aide and asked, "Do you think it would have been proper if I had shaken his hand? I wanted to do it, but I couldn't."

At the post office Rojo handed the piece of paper to Barceló and said simply, "They have refused."

"But the women, the children . . . ?" Barceló asked.

"One of them said to me, 'Our families will perish with us. If we could, we would carry the whole world with us to death.' "

The head of the committee angrily picked up the telephone. "Artillery batteries? Good. This is Major Barceló. Fire night and day on the Alcázar! Erase it! Leave no stone larger than my little finger."

At a quarter to eleven the twelve-hour silence in Toledo ended suddenly as the Republican guns erupted again. At the same time the wife of a cadet gave birth to her first child on a table in the electrician's workshop, a foul hole in the north cellar. He was named Restituto Alcázar Valero and was made an "honorary cadet" of the Academy.

His mission accomplished, Major Rojo returned to Madrid.* On the same evening the French correspondent Louis Delaprée came down from the capital to Toledo in order to write a story about the surrender of the Alcázar. Heavy red clouds hung low over the city, reflecting the fires burning in the fortress. He met Red Cross ambulances driving toward Madrid with wounded militia. The interior of the city was a dark network of gorges, destitute of people, and filled with choking fumes.

Delaprée found Major Barceló surrounded by his committee at the post office and asked what happened to the negotiations for rescuing the women and children.

"I don't know you! Get out of this city!" roared Barceló.

Delaprée protested, saying that this was his sixth trip to Toledo and that everyone had talked with him freely before.

"I know no one!" shouted the major. "And it is my duty to suspect everyone."

Four *milicianos* then escorted the correspondent to the edge of town, where they waited to make certain that he left for Madrid. The Alcázar still flamed above the low rooftops of the

* Several months later Rojo became Chief of Staff of the Army of the Center, and by the end of the war was a distinguished Republican general, said to have masterminded the Brunete and Ebro offensives. After Franco's final victory in 1939 he went into exile; however, in the 1950's he was one of the few Republican commanders allowed to return to Spain, where he now lives quietly in retirement, still highly respected by his former enemies.

city, and artillery shells kept dropping at the rate of one every other minute. It seemed impossible that human beings could survive there, but the shellfire and Barceló's tantrum proved to Delaprée that they were indeed there and that they had refused to surrender.

Even the Republican artillerists at the Dehesa de Pinedo batteries were stirred by the refusal to surrender. Nodding at the fortress, a shirt-sleeved gunner told another foreign correspondent, "If we had a few—just a few—like that on our side, this war would soon be over."

Each day the number of shells exploding on the Alcázar increased, although each day there remained less of the building to shell. More searchlights were installed in the Zocodover to assist the artillerists, and trimotors bombed from five thousand feet, safe from pistols and rifles below them. One bomb fell upon the southwest tower, slithered down two flights of iron stairway, and landed, without exploding, among a group of Falangists on the ground floor. Major Méndez Parada found that the fuse had not been set. "Does this mean our sympathizers have penetrated the Republican air force?" the Falangists asked him. "Not necessarily," replied the major. "Just that they're incompetent."

The Dehesa artillerists did not lack skill. Their shells roared through the great breach along the north and exploded in the courtyard, bringing down portions of the arcades—the great courtyard where King Alfonso XIII had once reviewed the cadets. Massive pieces of marble columns and escutcheons carved in stone lay scattered among less distinguished rubble, as though awaiting the appearance of an archaeolgist. The bronze statue of Charles V had been knocked from its pedestal, but it landed upright and unbroken. The long-jawed Habsburg still stood with his foot on the writhing infidel, even though pieces of his detachable breastplate were scattered far and wide.

Acting upon Major Rojo's advice that they continue to search for the entrances to the mine shafts, Captain Vela led a force of Civil Guards and Falangists into the Capuchinos quarter at four o'clock in the morning of September 10. Daubed with mud and shod in rope-soled sandals, they thought they had escaped detection when they reached the first parallel street to the south. Suddenly they walked into an ambush: the firing was so heavy that the dark street was illuminated by rifle flashes and grenade explosions. Vela's men dropped to the ground; he expected a counterattack, but it did not materialize. When the force returned to the Alcázar with one man dead and thirteen wounded, Moscardó abandoned the attempt to destroy the tunnels.

The barrage of September 10 was nearly as heavy as that of the preceding day, a total of 149 shells exploding on the Alcázar. But at dusk there was an abrupt cessation of firing. Then, at ten o'clock, the posts along the south wall were surprised to hear a voice calling to them across the Plaza de Capuchinos. *"Academia! We grant your request. Canon Vázquez Camarasa will visit you at nine o'clock in the morning for a three-hour period. We send you your priest."* Wild hooting among the militia accompanied the announcement. Someone in the shadows yelled, "Damn your souls! A few days more and you'll be able to use every priest in Spain."

Moscardó, who had hoped they would send a priest sentenced to death by the Republic, learned to his disappointment that Camarasa had been selected for the mission. In his judgment Camarasa, reputed to be one of the most liberal clergymen in Spain, was little better than a Marxist; nevertheless, a bad priest was better than none at all. The colonel was distressed that the priest would not be allowed to remain permanently with them, but he pledged his word that Canon Camarasa would be permitted to leave the fortress at the end of his three-hour visitation. The Republican's obviously suspected that they might attempt to use the priest as a hostage.

It was the second quiet but sleepless night for most inhabitants of the Alcázar; the thought of their visitor in the morning kept them awake. Many of them waited for Camarasa as fervently as if he were a liberating angel. Others saw him as an angel of death, for a disquieting thought passed through their minds: the Republicans had permitted a priest to come to them because the end of the Alcázar was at hand. Camarasa would be administering the rites of extreme unction.

Shortly after eight o'clock in the morning of September 11 a touring car stopped outside the Bisagra Gate, and five armed *milicianos* stepped out. With them, in an ill-fitting blue suit, was a tall man with gray hair, his puffy face covered with gray stubble. Canon Vázquez Camarasa, formerly of the Cathedral of Madrid, had arrived in Toledo with his secular escort.*

Slinging their rifles over their shoulders, the *milicianos* filed through narrow streets leading into the center of the city, Camarasa between them. A spectator could not have determined whether the escort was protecting the canon or preventing him from getting away. By the time they reached the post office, the morning barrage had lifted and the crackle of small-arms fire around the Alcázar had ceased. Here Major Barceló met them, and they threaded their way toward the Academy through a labyrinth of alleyways. News of Camarasa's arrival had swept through Toledo, and throngs of people turned out to watch the procession. Someone made the clenched-fist salute, crying *"Viva la República!"* and Camarasa acknowledged this by making the same gesture, but he said nothing. As they walked past the Carmelitas Church, perhaps Camarasa recalled that he had preached the Lenten sermon there, and although no one alluded to the butchery which had occurred in the church less than two months before, doubtless Camarasa had heard about it. They turned a corner, and directly ahead of them lay the towering south wall of the Alcázar, appearing slightly blue through the smoke which drifted down in wisps.

Carrying a white flag the size of a sheet, Major Barceló and a militia captain went forward by themselves into the middle of the Plaza de Capuchinos, where they stopped and waited. A door squeaked somewhere in the fortress, and a uniformed figure stepped out. This was Captain Sanz de Diego. He looked like an apparition from another world. His uniform, though carefully brushed, was badly stained and torn; the gaunt face behind the beard was the color of old plaster. A dirty bandage hung down over one eye, for Captain Sanz, who had performed some of the

* In *Man's Hope*, André Malraux says that the militia plucked Camarasa out of a beer cellar in Madrid to bring him to Toledo and that he was regarded by them as a "faker" because he used ten minutes to say what could be said in half a minute; moreover, that Camarasa had refused to take the assignment unless he was promised safe-conduct. Although it is a work of fiction, *Man's Hope* remains true to the spirit of the siege and accurately reflects the low opinion the Republicans had of this clergyman.

functions of a priest in the Alcázar since the beginning of the siege, had been struck in the face by shrapnel while conducting a funeral service in the Picadero a few weeks before. Unlike Barceló, he did not carry a white flag—Moscardó refused to give the militia this small satisfaction. Barceló opened the conversation. "You must swear to vouchsafe Canon Vázquez Camarasa's life and not try to detain him." "Colonel Moscardó gives his word," replied the captain.

Across the rubble came Camarasa. In his left hand he carried a soiled white cloth and a drawstring sack containing his religious implements, and in his right hand he clutched a cumbersome crucifix of tarnished brass. Scurrying around in the background were several newsmen who wanted to get a closer view of the Alcázar, but Captain Sanz raised his hand, palm up as in the Fascist salute, and cried out, "Keep back. No one else." The newsmen turned back, as if they had confronted Lazarus. The captain then blindfolded Camarasa with something that looked like a fine silk scarf, and the two men were swallowed up by the Alcázar.

Once inside the building Sanz grabbed Camarasa by his lapels and asked hoarsely, "Can you say Mass?" and held on tightly until the priest replied, without enthusiasm, "All right, if you wish." While another officer checked the blindfold, Camarasa's shoulders twitched. The men around him laughed and someone said, "Don't worry. It's only the crowd out there that murders priests." Without further delay he was guided to Moscardó's office to be closeted with the commander, who darkly suspected that the canon had been sent not to preside over their souls, but to frighten them into surrender.

Meanwhile in the streets outside the truce began to be felt as a palpable quality. *Milicianos* climbed out of their barricades and strolled self-consciously along the southern edge of the Plaza de Capuchinos. Riflemen popped their heads gingerly above the window sills of the Alcázar, half expecting to be fired at; then they stood up, and finally leaned outside to inhale the fresh warm air. Several Nationalist officers, led by Captain Emilio Vela, came out of the fortress and walked together in the square. Men on both sides wanted to open conversations across the lines, but none of them seemed to know how to begin. They were separated by a wall of embarrassment. Breaking through that wall, a zealous *miliciano* called out, "Surrender! You are being deceived by the Fascist trash. Save yourselves!"

But his admonition was at once drowned by voices from his own lines: "Oh, shut up!" "Leave the poor bastards alone!"

The Alcázar officers, however, were ready to accept the challenge. One of them shouted, "You bandits! You are the ones who are deceived. We stand for God and the people."

"God? That's a joke. The churches are fat and the people are starving."

"Liar! We're the ones who are starving. You bastards are living on the fat of the land, while we don't even have tobacco."

"What's that?" said a *miliciano*, an Anarchist with a tattoo on his arm. "No tobacco?" He walked over to the officers, carrying a pack of cigarettes in his hand as if he intended to hurl it at them, and distributed them one by one. When the Alcazareños in the windows above saw what had happened, they raised a hullabaloo. "Hey, cigarettes! Hey, *hombre*, give us cigarettes, too!"

Another *miliciano* called out, "Wait a minute!" He ducked around a corner and returned a few minutes later carrying a sheet of newspaper piled with cigarettes. The men in the windows broke into cheers as Captain Vela accepted the gift and passed it into the Alcázar. Yet the bitterness of two months was not to be canceled by a single gesture, for the Nationalists were as ashamed of accepting as the Republicans were of giving. The gibes continued:

"You've sent for a priest? It looks like it's all over for you."

"That's what you think. Our troops will be here soon enough, then we'll show you what's what."

"You might as well wait for the Second Coming as for Franco."

"You're wrong. We won't have long to wait—since your men are running away like rabbits."

"A pack of lies! Why are you letting your beards grow? Getting ready for paradise?"

"What do you expect me to shave with? My sword?"

At this, another *miliciano* pulled a packet of razor blades out of his pocket and started to throw them to the officers as one might throw peanuts to a monkey, but then with an ugly look he handed the packet to the nearest officer and walked away, swearing to himself. When the officers crowded around the packet, some *milicianos* across the street laughed, but Captain Vela gruffly ordered the officers to disperse.

Suddenly a single rifle shot snapped the brittle truce. Captain Vela crouched like a boxer preparing to ward off a blow, while the militia dived behind their barricades. No other shots followed, and it was several seconds before anyone realized what had happened. Then some of the men pointed up to a second-story window of the Alcázar, where a body was lying slumped over the sill. Nicolas Hernández, a young Falangist, had been leaning from this window, trying to glimpse his parents' house not far away, and the target had been too tempting for an anonymous *miliciano*. The two men had probably been feuding with each other for several weeks.

Furious cursing broke out on both sides, all of it heaped upon the assassin. Militia called across to the Alcázar that they would apprehend him and kill him. In the midst of this hubbub, Vela ordered his officers back into the fortress and brought up the rear, carefully facing the enemy across the square as if to imply that no *miliciano* would find an opportunity to shoot *him* in the back. He stopped for a moment in the doorway, glaring contemptuously at the crestfallen Republicans. Without uttering a word, he snapped his arm outward in the Fascist salute as if daring them to shoot at him, then wheeled around and disappeared. No other shot was fired during the rest of the three-hour truce.

Meanwhile, in the superintendent's office, Camarasa was painting a glowing picture of conditions in Madrid: the churches, although closed, were not being desecrated; his own quarters were protected by an Anarchist guard; food was plentiful. Then, in a casual manner, as if unaware of the military importance of the question, he asked Moscardó how many people there were in the Alcázar. Moscardó said that while he respected the canon as a clergyman, he could give him no information on purely military matters. Camarasa blushed and apologized profusely for his indiscretion. Moscardó had turned to ice. "Did you come prepared to confess us and celebrate Holy Mass? That's all we want." The canon nodded meekly and followed Colonel Moscardó down the cellar corridor to the southeast corner, where worshipers were already kneeling on the flagstones.

The next scene suggested something from the annals of early Christian history—the ragged devout huddled together in a catacomb greasy with the smoke of wick lamps. But one detail was entirely inappropriate in this squalid setting: the altar platform was resplendent with an immense, thick carpet on which the royal arms of King Alfonso XIII were stitched in purple and gold.

In his sermon Camarasa spoke movingly of doom and damnation. Warming to his work, he addressed his congregation as if they were already dead souls confronting the Supreme Judge. He warned them that when the Alcázar was pulverized, the responsibility would rest as much with those who had defended as with those who had attacked. They, too, would be judged as murderers of the innocent children among them. An elderly officer kneeling near the front clasped his hands and muttered over and over, "For Spain, for Spain, for Spain." Others began to sob; a few women became hysterical. Even Colonel Romero was shaken by this fearful sermon; later he admitted that Camarasa's words had brought a chill to his heart. Other officers were angry. Was Camarasa speaking for God or for Largo Caballero?

Since there was no time for individual confessions, general absolution had to suffice. Restituto Alcázar Valero was baptized, and the Sacred Host was carried to those who were lying seriously wounded in the infirmary. After these ceremonies Camarasa asked Moscardó for a private conference, and when they were alone, he broached the subject of surrender. The mines, he said, would destroy everyone, and the weight of the responsibility rested squarely upon Moscardó. Even though it was right for soldiers to give their lives in the line of duty, it was wrong that innocent women and children should be made to suffer—and perhaps be eternally damned—to satisfy Moscardó's personal vanity. Even if he refused to surrender the Alcázar, the innocent ones ought to be released. Officers outside the door heard Moscardó's replies to the priest: "No, señor . . . no, señor . . . no, señor!," each time a little louder.

When Camarasa insinuated that the women and children were being held against their will, Moscardó, indignantly summoned a young woman, Señora Carmen Romero de Salamanca, daughter of Colonel Romero and wife of a lieutenant in the Civil Guard. He said to her, "The Reverend Canon says that in Madrid they believe the women do not leave the Alcázar because the officers will not let them go. Will you tell the priest about this?"

Carmen turned upon Camarasa. *"Held here?* That's a lie! I have talked with every woman in the Alcázar and all of them think as I do. Either we will leave here free, with our men and children, or else we will die with them in the ruins."

It was useless for the canon to argue that her own particular case might differ from that of the other women not married or related to officers, so he said nothing more. He was defeated, and he knew it. Though his three hours had not yet expired, Moscardó called one of his aides and announced, "The Reverend Canon will leave the Alcázar. Kindly escort him outside."

Out in the hallway some of the officers milled around Camarasa, asking him to do some favors for them when he reached Madrid. A former policeman asked him to carry an emerald- and diamond-studded ring to a local shrine, which the canon promised to do. Others wanted him to take messages to their families, but as Camarasa reached for these notes, Moscardó pushed the officers back. "Give no addresses to Republicans. You know what they might do to your families!"

Camarasa started, as though slapped in the face. "But—you must know I am a gentleman . . ." he stammered.

"I don't deny that," replied Moscardó, "but the people you associate with are not. The addresses will remain here."

Unlike Major Rojo, Camarasa left no memento behind. He was blindfolded and led out of the Alcázar by a single escort, Captain Sanz, who called out across the empty square, "Attention! The Reverend Camarasa is coming out!" It was lunchtime, and the only people waiting for him in the Republican lines were two newsmen, who later reported that his lips were trembling and that he would not tell them what he had seen. In the blaze of noon the canon was shivering, and he stopped in the middle of the road to tie the white cloth over his head. A short time later he was driven out of Toledo in the black touring car. Not until he was far along the Madrid road did Canon Vázquez Camarasa escape the sound of the artillery which was once again battering the Alcázar.*

That night Madrid newspapers declared that the Facists of the Alcázar had lost their last chance to save the lives of their women and children. Now they would all die together.

On September 11, the day of Camarasa's visit, 74 heavy shells burst on the Alcázar; on September 12 there were 159; and on September 13 there were 100. Ever since the fall of the northwest tower, the Republican batteries had concentrated their fire on the east side in order to sever completely the line of communication between the Gobierno and the Alcázar. Subterranean explosions in the mine tunnels continued at regular intervals, and drew closer. Many of the families occupying cellars along the west wall were transferred to the already teeming dungeons to the east and north. Casualties now stood at 38 dead and 208 wounded; it was becoming increasingly difficult for riflemen posted in the upper stories to protect themselves against shrapnel and cave-ins because of the erosion of the outer walls and inner partitions.**

During these days, as the world press publicized the imminent explosion of the mines, the diplomatic corps in Madrid was trying to avert the tragedy. As the head of a committee, Núñez Morgado, the Chilean ambassador and doyen of the corps, finally obtained permission to visit Toledo in order to beg Moscardó to let the women, children, and old people be evacuated. The Ministry of War provided him with an automobile and an escort, and Morgado arrived on September 13, accompanied by the Rumanian chargé. After a five-hour conference with Major Barceló and the Defense Committee, the diplomats succeeded in extract-

---

* Two weeks later Camarasa crossed into France, a most unusual feat for a priest within the Republican lines. He told an interviewer from *Le Figaro* that he had never interfered in Spanish politics and that "ecclesiastics should be like stars, which shine above the clouds." Six month later, still in Paris, he wrote an article stating that the proposition to Moscardó that the women and children should be evacuated was entirely his own idea. Moreover, he admired "the sacrifice and heroism within those walls." Camarasa died in exile, scorned by both sides.

** The official log of the Alcázar distinguishes between *muerto* (killed), *fallecido* (death by natural causes), *herido* (wounded), and *contuso* (injured by falling materials). These records were kept as meticulously as the scoresheet indicating the exact number of shells fired at the Alcázar. When I allude to "wounded," both *heridos* and *contusos* are included.

ing a guarantee that the lives of those who left the fortress would be spared. Further, asylum for them was to be arranged in two abandoned convents, where they would be protected under the flag of Chile until their transfer to embassies in Madrid.

The two diplomats and their escort reached the barricades next to the Plaza de Capuchinos at seven o'clock in the evening. Using a megaphone, Barceló shouted to the Alcázar, "Attention! The ambassador of the Republic of Chile wants to speak to you. Our forces will suspend firing. If you agree, raise a white flag on the nearest tower."

Five minutes passed, but no white flag appeared. Barceló repeated his message. The diplomats expressed doubts as to whether there was really anyone inside the silent building. A machine gun sputtered from a window farther down the west wall. Barceló repeated his message.

Finally they heard a voice from the Alcázar. "If these gentlemen are sincere in their proposal, they should direct themselves to the government at Burgos, the only one recognized by the Alcázar." When *milicianos* heard the word Burgos, they peppered the window where the voice seemed to be coming from. After that there was only silence. For a long time the two diplomats squatted behind the barricade, debating as to how they might converse with Moscardó. "Why don't you try walking across the square and knocking on the door," said a *miliciano* dryly. In the end they did nothing, because there was nothing they could do. It was clear to both of them that the Geneva Convention and the "rules of war" meant nothing to these men locked in their savage, no-quarter combat. By midnight they gave up and returned to Madrid.

"This is a brave country," Morgado said sadly, "but the women are braver than the men."

Colonel Moscardó had noticed that his parleys with the Republicans were demoralizing the garrison, some of whom had begun to yearn for peace at any price, so he announced to the junta that no further discussions with the enemy were to be tolerated. The doors of the Alcázar were henceforth hermetically sealed, and would be opened again only to General Franco's relief columns. Nerves were so frayed that it was necessary to post an order prohibiting anyone from spreading news that might be considered alarming. The population was told that they should trust in God and in their officers. To lift morale, Moscardó instructed Captain Cuartero to distribute extra rations of wheat, but this did little good. Fear of the mines seemed to have canceled interest in food.

There were several suicides. On the day of Camarasa's visit, a middle-aged soldier had climbed up into the southwest tower and told the sentries that he wanted to look out over the city in the twilight. When they allowed him to pass, he stepped calmly out of the window and fell three flights without uttering a cry. The next day a Civil Guard committed suicide by blowing out his brains. Among the women lurked the fear: if the mines failed to kill them, what would the militia do to them? The wife of Eustasio Gómez, a Civil Guard, told her husband, "If you see the Reds enter, come down to the cellars, kill me and our son, and return to your parapet until they kill you."

A new wave of desertion swept through the garrison. On the day after Ambassador Morgado's abortive effort to mediate, four Civil Guards escaped down the northern slope and surrendered. They knew that they could expect to be executed as war criminals, but perhaps the firing squad held fewer terrors for them than the thought of what might happen when the mines exploded. Usually deserters left all their equipment behind, but Corporal Fidel Gutíerrez, a corpulent soldier of the Recruiting Service, was an exception. After strapping rifle, ammunition, and mess gear to his body, he tied a rope to a dead horse in the Gobierno and slid out of a window on the night of September 12. When the rope broke and he fell clattering onto the Calle del Carmen, he had the cheek to hurl invectives at his sergeant, who he was sure had cut the rope, before limping to safety across the roadway. He was not seen again.

Half-crazed creatures prowled the fortress buttonholing anyone willing to humor them. Despite Moscardó's injunction they told depressing tales: "More guns are being installed at Alijares . . . Today I found out that the Reds are digging another tunnel into the courtyard so that they can pop up out of ground when our backs are turned." These harbingers of doom were usually avoided, for they put into words the agonizing fears that everyone felt. The worst was the Toledo mathematics teacher who ceaselessly mumbled numbers: he was keeping a record of the seconds they had spent in the Alcázar.

On the other hand, in some instances adversity totally changed a person's character. Antonio Rivera, who earlier had been dubbed "the Angel" because of his piety and pacifism, underwent a transformation. For reasons known only to himself, he asked to be placed in the firing line. "Perhaps it is right that I should kill —so long as I do not kill in hatred," he said. Since he scarcely knew which was the killing end of a rifle, he was assigned to the northern slope as loader of a heavy machine gun.

Lieutenant Barber made it clear that so long as the militia remained in the barricades and the artillery kept firing at the Alcázar, the mines would not be set off. By a strange inversion, the defenders were now comforted by the clatter of the *paqueo* and the explosion of shells. The sight of a boiler-suit in the streets or windows near by no longer provoked feelings of hatred. What they now feared was the moment when the militia would drift away from the walls of the Alcázar and vanish from sight, for in that void the mines would speak.

9

EXPLOSION

As LIEUTENANT BARBER had predicted, the two mine tunnels reached the west wall of the Alcázar on September 14. Just after dawn the compressors stopped, and a new, more chilling noise was heard—the sound of hand shovels scraping gravel directly beneath them. To prevent the sappers from fixing their position by listening from below, Barber enforced absolute silence throughout the southwest corner of the building. The tunnels appeared to terminate under two classrooms, one of them next to the foot of the tower and the other about fifty feet to the north. Lieutenant Barber and his assistant, Corporal Rodríguez Caridad, both of them barefoot, moved about noiselessly, like birds listening for the sounds of insects under the ground, and they communicated by strange gesticulations. Lying flat on his stomach and probing the flagstones with his stethoscope, Barber could hear human voices underground, although he was unable to determine what they said or how far away they were. The miners seemed not to know whether they had penetrated far enough, because from time to time their drill would hammer for a few minutes and then stop. The Asturians knew that they were in a ticklish situation: if they dug too close to the surface, the enemy might sink a countermine, but if they remained too deep, the force of the explosion might be suppressed by the intervening rock layer.

Having located as best they could the probable sites of the two tunnel endings, Barber and Rodríguez strung a line of barbed wire along the perimeter of the area. Thereafter no one was permitted to go beyond this fragile barricade, which drew crowds of Alcazareños who seemed to take comfort in the lieutenant's "science." It was Moscardó, however, who made the decision to buttress science with religion. One of the cellar rooms in the demolition zone had been used as an additional infimary, but the wounded had had to be moved to safer areas, in the north cellars. This room was now converted into the chapel of the Alcázar, and the plaster statue of the Holy Virgin was placed just outside the line of barbed wire. Moscardó reasoned that here would be an excellent test of respective power: the Holy Virgin would be pitted against the infernal mines. Even if Santa María could not prevent the explosion, she might at least cushion it.

Beneath the Alcázar, approximately in the center, lay the ancient cisterns. The explosion might either crack their walls or bury them altogether, in which case there would be no water except the limited amount in the swimming pool. Therefore they began cranking up bucketfuls and transferring them to a nearly empty cistern of the same type in the northeast corner. Lines of men sweated all day at this backbreaking labor, until they began to drop from exhaustion. Since they no longer had the strength for such heavy work, as much water was spilled as transferred, and the idea had to be abandoned. If the cisterns were destroyed, the blast would more than likely be great enough to demolish most of the Alcázar, too—in which event water would no longer be necessary.

Throughout the day the *paqueo* was unusually heavy, and after nightfall the enemy slingers lobbed petards against the iron and carriage gates, but the junta reasoned that having expended so much effort in digging the tunnels, the Republicans probably had no intention of launching a serious frontal attack. A junior officer even suggested that it might be a good idea to allow the militia to establish a foothold inside the fortress, since then they would not be about to set off the explosion without destroying a contingent of their own men. But, Major Méndez Parada objected, "how could we dislodge the contingent if they decided *not* to blow up the mines?" The red-faced subaltern confessed that he had not thought about that.

At night the firing slackened, and those on duty at the Santiago Barracks and the Gobierno heard a singsong coming from the Republican positions across the Tagus. At first they thought the militia were drunk, but then they picked out the words of an improvised chant, repeated monotonously:

> "Send out the women.
> *It will soon be too late!*
> Send out the children.
> *It will soon be too late!*"

Eight weeks before, the soldiers would have answered with a volley of rifle shots, but now they just listened and tried to think of something else. The siege was making stoics out of them; besides, they were too weary to fire unnecessarily. Perhaps some of them preferred to think about the order of the day, which appeared in *El Alcázar.* "The worst is over. . . ," Moscardó had written. "The enemy continues to destroy our precious Alcázar, but do not worry. . . . The Reds have no discipline and the masses refuse to obey their officers. . . . Trust in God and your officers. . . . The relief columns are converging upon Toledo. . . ."

Relief columns—this was the magic phrase repeated so often and with so little justification that the men must have wondered whether these columns existed outside the colonel's imagination. In fact, the Army of Africa was pushing along the Estremadura highway toward Madrid, but it was still far away. Fatigued by two months of steady fighting, its momentum was slowing down. The advance troops had not yet reached the pueblo of Maqueda, the junction at which one road, the main highway, led directly to Madrid, twenty-five miles away, and the other branched off toward Toledo, twenty-four miles to the southeast. No one, except perhaps God and General Franco, knew whether the Army of Africa would swerve from its main objective, Madrid, in order to come to the aid of the Alcázar. Such a deflection would give Madrid additional time to prepare its defenses, and this time might prove fatal to the Nationalist plan to seize the capital and end the war. No detached observer would have considered the relief of the Alcázar worth the risk.

In the meantime, along the Tagus, the Republican militia continued to chant: "Send out the women. *It will soon be too late!*"

September 15. Daylight brought a four-hour bombardment. Shells from the Dehesa batteries roared through the northern branch and exploded in the south arcades, while those from Alijares hammered at the southeast tower. Though the east walls were ten feet thick in places, at the end of the day's bombardment a long vertical split could be traced from the esplanade to the roof. Since most of the Civil Guards were quartered in the upper rooms on this side, the shells took a heavy toll, killing five and wounding four others.

Within the mine tunnels there were periodic explosions, followed by the sound of scraping shovels. Concluding that the Asturians were in the process of enlarging the cavities, Lieutenant Barber assembled a ten-man squad of the huskiest men he could find, and began to dig a countermine. After removing the stone flooring of the cellar classroom, the men hammered with picks at the granite ledge underneath. After a few hours' work they learned how weak they really were: they relieved one another every five or ten minutes but penetrated less than half a foot, and the work had to be abandoned.

September 16. An hour after daybreak the artillery battered the same targets again. The Cavalry library lay open and raw. Although it was thirty feet above the esplanade, the rubble on the ground below was accumulating so rapidly that it was possible for someone to climb the mound and enter the Alcázar through the library gap. In the cellars below, a riot broke out among the civilians unable to tolerate the shell bursts just above their heads. Officers ran in and restored order, removing the most frightened ones into the already jammed cellars to the north.

There were seven minor detonations in the mine cavity nearest the southwest tower, but since no sounds came from the other tunnel, Lieutenant Barber concluded that the Asturians had completed work on it and were loading it with explosives.

Just before noon three light bombers with Nationalist markings buzzed the Alcázar and dropped bombs on the city. Although they did little damage, their presence implied that General Franco had not forgotten them and was encouraging them to hang on for a few days more. Minutes later Republican fighters circled over the Alijares batteries, doubtless waiting for the bombers to return, but they had vanished toward the west. This was the first time that the Nationalists had displayed any aviation strength over Toledo.* Observers in the Alcázar were gratified to see the Republican artillerists make frantic efforts to camouflage their guns, which until this time had been standing in the open.

After nightfall forty sacks of wheat were gathered from the storehouse. Since no one had the strength to drag, much less to carry the 190-lb. sacks to the Alcázar, the wheat was poured into pillowcases. Men who had lifted the sacks only six weeks before found themselves staggering under the weight of a load one-fourth as heavy. Much of the wheat was stored in the Gobierno, which would continue the defense if the Alcázar were destroyed by the mines or occupied by the militia.

Following this sortie for wheat the officers discovered that one of their caste had deserted. Lieutenant Fernando Barrientos, a young staff officer from the Central School of Physical Education, had left the fortress with the others but had slipped off in the darkness. A veteran of the Moroccan fighting a decade before, Barrientos had welcomed a fight in open country during the first weeks of the siege, but since that time had become increasingly depressed by the claustrophobic conditions of the Alcázar, which he dubbed "the sarcophagus." His close friends remembered that he had expressed morbid fears of being buried alive and that his attitude was: "I'll support the side that lets me live. I'll be dead long enough." For several days he had been wearing a blue boiler-suit which he had picked up somewhere, but since motley uniforms were commonplace around the garrison, it had aroused no suspicion. Lieutenant Barrientos was the only combatant of officer's rank to desert from the Alcázar, and his fellow officers were deeply affronted by his defection.**

* It is a little strange to find Malraux, in *Man's Hope*, writing about dangerous missions against the Alcázar, as if the fortress were a kind of minor Gibraltar. During the siege no Republican aircraft were shot down, no airmen were killed or, so far as is known, even wounded.

** Lieutenant Barrientos was picked up by the militia the same night and

September 17. No sounds came from the mine chambers. The entire west side had been evacuated except for a handful of select riflemen, who were relieved every hour because the explosion was expected from minute to minute. The militia outside seemed sparser, and their *paqueo* was more noisy than accurate. It seemed evident that the Republicans were drawing back in order to explode the mines. Even though the miners operated their compressors from time to time, Lieutenant Barber knew that this was done only to deceive them.

At five o'clock there was a brief barrage aimed at the cellars along the east wall. Officers bitterly called this "the Barrientos barrage," since they assumed that their Judas had told the Defense Committee that most of the people in the Alcázar were concentrated in the cellars on that side.

The evening was black and moonless. In the electrician's workshop the wife of a Civil Guard went into labor. *El Alcázar* came out on schedule, as if all were normal. Colonel Moscardó reminded his officers that in just a few hours "the Crusade" would be exactly two months old. But for most Alcazareños there was only one thought: Will the mines be exploded tonight or tomorrow?

Like Moscardó, Major Barceló was well aware that the evening of September 17 marked the end of the second month of the war. Five tons of TNT were already placed in the two cavities hollowed out beneath the west wall, and Barceló intended to inaugurate the third month by utterly destroying the Alcázar. One hour before midnight he ordered the city to be evacuated. *Milicianos* ran from house to house, banging on doors and shouting "Toledo is going to be blown up! Get out of town fast!" While Barceló knew quite well that most parts of the city would not be harmed by the explosion, he used this ruse to flush concealed Nationalists out of their hiding places.

taken to the Defense Committee. He pleaded "not guilty" to the charges against him, arguing that during his period in the Alcázar he had never fired a shot at a Republican; but when another Alcázar deserter, an enlisted man, swore that he had seen Barrientos manning a machine gun, the lieutenant broke down and confessed that this was true. He was executed by a *miliciano* on the day the relief column approached the outskirts of Toledo.

Soon streams of townspeople and animals were flooding down the hill toward the city gates, where militia scrutinized their identification papers. Those not passing this inspection were escorted to the *plaza de toros,* just north of Tavera Hospital, to await a more leisurely interrogation. There they were packed into the ring while their guards, occupying the seats above, told them that in the morning the bulls would be turned loose on them: the fall of the Alcázar would be celebrated in the old Roman style. "You'll probably enjoy it. You Christians believe in martyrdom, don't you?"

Many Toledanos, however, refused to leave their homes. Some even doubted that the mines existed; they thought it was a trick by the *Rojos* to pillage their belongings in their absence. An eighty-year-old water carrier who lived with his wife not far from the Alcázar stubbornly refused to go, contending that he did not like "the country," but since the old couple were inside the danger zone, two Anarchists carried them down to the Bisagra Gate in their arms. Patients in hospitals were driven out of the city in automobiles, ambulances, and trucks.

Front pages of newspapers all over the world prepared their readers for the terrible explosion. VAST BLAST OF TNT TO RAZE ALCAZAR, announced the *New York Times.* In Madrid, newsmen bargained and fought over vehicles road-worthy enough to carry them down to Toledo. Throughout the evening of September 17, caravans of journalists, cameramen, government officials, and thrill-seekers pressed along the highway. Two miles from the city they were waved off the road and parked in olive groves. Most of them slept under the trees fringing the dirt track that serviced the Dehesa de Pinedo batteries. A few, including a Paramount cameraman, carried their gear down to the Bisagra Gate and wangled a place among the shock force which would be thrown upon the ruins after the mines had done their work.

For fear that the demolition of the Alcázar with its noncombatant population would shatter the benign image of the Republic, authorities in Madrid, hoping to keep the public away from Toledo, denied that the mines would be exploded in the morning. Journalists were told that the "terrible decision" had been postponed for a few days, but few were misled. In Toledo, Major

Barceló told newsmen that he knew nothing about Madrid decisions and cared less. The mines would be set off early in the morning. Asked what would be done with the survivors, if there were any, Barceló said that the women and children would be taken prisoners, "if they surrender." And the men? The major shook his head. "Oh, no. The men will all be killed."

When his press conference was over, Major Barceló briefed the two Republican commanders, Majors Madronero and Torres, who would be responsible for leading the assault. The mines would be detonated by an electric switch in the town hall at six-thirty. As soon as all the debris had fallen to the ground, twenty-five hundred men, divided into two equal columns, would move in to attack, supported by two armored cars and one tank. Six hundred Asaltos, a tough, well-disciplined force, would be out in front; they would be followed by units of the Regular Army and ordinary militia (over one thousand of whom were from the province of Toledo). The attacking force did not include the hundreds of militia who would vacate their barricades next to the building minutes before the blast and who would be held in reserve, firing from rooftops and windows.

Major Madronero was in command of the column which would strike at the Alcázar from the north. His point of departure was the Paseo del Miradero, a public park below the Santa Cruz, about halfway down the hill between the Zocodover and the Bisagra Gate. After the explosion he would lead his men into the Zocodover, where the column would be split: half the force would climb up the Zig Zag behind a tank, the others would dash up the Cuesta del Alcázar and enter the fortress through the more northerly breach in the west wall. This force would only have to cover a quarter of a mile to reach the Alcázar, though most of the distance was uphill.

The assault column under Major Torres would assemble in the Plazuela de San Lucas, half a mile directly south of the Alcázar. Since such streets as there were in this quarter were sinuous and narrow, the attackers would make their way to the Alcázar as best they could, to two rendezvous points. One group was then to converge upon the southwest corner and enter by the breach opened up by the mine. The other would make contact with two armored cars already parked near the Corralillo, and moving be-

hind them across the open common, overrun the defenders in the
Capuchinos and the dining hall.

The entire operation, Barceló told his commanders, was less an
attack than a mop-up. Doubtless there would be defensive pockets here and there, but no concerted resistance was anticipated.
Ten minutes after the explosion the first Republican wave ought
to be entering the fortress. If the "Flies" tried to surrender *en
masse*, the individual Republican commanders at hand could decide what to do. The Defense Committee had promised to turn
over all Falangist prisoners to the FAI, the militant wing of the
Anarchists.

Meanwhile in the superintendent's office, Moscardó sat at the
desk in the sputtering glow of a horse-grease lamp. In the log he
wrote, "All things possible having been done, we now commend
ourselves to God." Beneath this entry he drew a heavy black line,
as if he were marking the conclusion of his narrative.

On September 18 the newsmen at the Dehesa de Pinedo got up
early, wondering what sort of day it would be. What seemed at
first to be a fog proved to be a ground haze emanating from the
river valley. When the sun rose it burned the haze off the hillsides, so that the first visible object to the south was the squat
mass of the Alcázar, which looked as if it were floating on top of
a dense cloud. Behind the shapeless, ruinous north façade they
could see the erect southwest tower, the focus of their attention.
Even at this distance they heard the *paqueo* beneath the walls of
the Alcázar, and saw tracers from San Servando describing perfect arcs as they glided across the Tagus River.

At 6:00 A.M. this fusillade ceased abruptly, and the newsmen
were told that the militia who had occupied the barricades next
to the Alcázar were falling back to safer positions in the city.
The "Flies" were now up there all alone. At 6:05 the artillery at
Alijares, concealed from sight by scrubby ridges to the left,
opened fire on the Santiago Barracks and gradually extended their
barrage to the east wall, hoping to drive the garrison in the cellars
back to the west wall, where the mines were waiting for them.
At 6:18 the barrage ceased.

In the absolute silence that followed, the journalists grew

restive. They examined their watches, checked and rechecked the time, and muttered among themselves. Ten minutes passed, but nothing happened. Cranking the handles of their cameras, the newsreel photographers were cursing—they were wasting footage, but they dared not stop for fear of missing *the* moment. They fixed their eyes or their lens on the peak of the tower, but it told them nothing. Perhaps the trigger mechanism of the mines had failed to work. Perhaps the Alcazareños had surrendered— nobody could blame them if they had.

"*Qu'est-ce que c'est?*" asked a journalist.

"A five-and-ten-cent war," grumbled another.

"Thirty seconds late," fumed an English correspondent.

"Forty."

"I said it was a five-and-ten-cent war."

"Fifty."

At 6:31 the Alcázar exploded silently before their eyes. An immense black cloud erupted and immediately blew westward. Seconds later the newsmen felt the ground shake under their feet and heard the noise of the blast. Even two miles away, they obeyed their natural instinct to recoil or duck. In a field below, a flock of spectators sprinted to the rear; then, realizing how ridiculous they appeared, they wheeled around and ran back just as fast.

The southwest tower shot upward in a rocketlike surge, hovered briefly in the air, and fell apart as it plummeted down. Clearly visible from the Dehesa de Pinedo were sections of wall, steel girders, and smaller objects which some observers claimed were human beings. A segment of the tower landed on the slope of the crater, where it sat like a cottage—a nearly perfect cube, measuring fifteen feet on each side. A truck parked outside the carriage gate was hurled five hundred feet in the air; the engine block landed in the patio of a house half a mile away and was almost buried in the ground. A few seconds after the explosion Toledo disappeared from view under a wave of black smoke which rolled over it like molten lava. The noise of the explosion was heard in the suburbs of Madrid, forty miles away.

In the olive grove the journalists watched this awesome spectacle. They had expected the Alcázar to collapse like a dynamited building, not to erupt like a volcano. Soon their typewriters began to click. The first sentence of their stories was the easiest: "The Alcázar has fallen."

Even before the dust had settled completely, the Republican columns moved in for the kill—the Asalto shock force from the north walking up to the Zocodover as calmly as laborers going to work in the morning, while behind them came the militia, shouting, "We've killed the dogs! At them!" The Asaltos under Major Madronero waved their clenched fists at the Paramount cameraman before turning the corner beside the gutted Hotel Suizo and starting in single file up the Cuesta del Alcázar. After climbing over the rubble of the northwest tower, knocked down by artillery two weeks before, they encountered unfamiliar terrain, for the explosion had eradicated landmarks. Most of the houses next to the Alcázar, for example, had vanished, leveled by the blast. As they worked their way farther up the street, slowed down by loose rubble, they saw that a fifty-foot section of the wall beside the carriage gate had been sliced off as neatly as a wedge of bread cut from a loaf. Farther south the tower had been replaced by an even larger gap, leaving between the two spaces an upright section of wall that jutted upward like a gigantic incisor.

With Major Madronero leading them, the Asaltos pressed on toward the nearest gap, stumbling over the loose debris which had been spewed over the street. A mound of rubble led up into a shattered room on the courtyard level of the building; it had once been the chemical warfare laboratory of the Academy. When he reached the top of this steep slope, Major Madronero looked past the interior wall and saw the arcades in the courtyard, just a few yards away. To the south he could hear the cheers of the men under Major Torres, who were approaching the southwest gap. The time was 6:45. Fourteen minutes had passed since the explosion of the mines, yet not a shot had been fired at the attackers. They had only to hoist themselves a few feet and they would be able to walk into the deserted courtyard.

Within the Alcázar the explosion had been more felt than heard. The building shuddered as though the walls were breaking apart, the blast bowled people off their feet, and black smoke and dust swirled down the cellar corridors. It became so dark that many thought they had been buried alive, but the walls and ceilings held up on the north, east, and south, where nearly all the Alcazareños were sheltered. Paroxysms of half-strangled coughing were followed by the high-pitched screaming of women and children. Such sounds were reassuring—the dead do not call out.

Dr. Pelayo had a strange experience. At the moment of the blast he had been bending over a Civil Guard's wife who was in labor. The concussion knocked him down and extinguished the grease wick. The woman screamed and tried to raise herself off the workbench while her husband grappled with her and forced her down again. Regaining his feet, Dr. Pelayo groped for the women in the blackness and found a healthy baby girl, who had virtually been ejected from her mother's womb by the explosion.* Near by, another baby was aborted at the same time when something fell on the mother in the darkness.

Men moved around in the confusion, looking for signs of their families. As the smoke cleared from the passageways, shouts of panic gave way to intermittent cheers. The mines had gone off —but they were alive! A spasm of exhilaration surged through the cellars. They danced, they wept, they pounded or hugged one another. Cries of *"Viva Cristo Rey!"* echoed through the subterranean rooms. Some officers grabbed Lieutenant Barber, hoisted him on their shoulders, and paraded through the mob, shouting, "Long live our general of the Engineers!" The grimy, black-faced celebrants seemed oblivious to the Republican columns swarming up the rubble outside.

Several minutes passed before the officers came to their senses and began to shove through the mob. "All men upstairs! The Reds are coming! To your posts!" Soldiers clawed through the crowd toward the stairs as it dawned upon them that far from being over, the worst might only be beginning. Up in the courtyard, where a fifteen-year-old bugler blew "To Arms" with maniacal repetition, they saw through the gaping holes in the west wall the city of Toledo framed peacefully in the early-morning sunshine. Then a sound like the distant cheers of a bullfight reached them—the shouting of the advancing Republicans.

* This second child born in the Alcázar was named Josefa del Milagro ("Josefa of the Miracle"). She is today a schoolteacher in Spain.

The defenders stumbled through rubble to their rifle pits and parapets. But the men responsible for defending the west wall entered a baffling terrain, for this side of the Alcázar had been redesigned into bizarre shapes by the collapse of walls, the complete disappearance of whole rooms, and the tangled skeins of twisted girders. Those assigned to defend the second and third floors had no way of getting up into the rooms that remained, because the two towers which had supported the stairways were now gone. No fixed plan of defense was possible along the west, yet it was on this side that the Republican shouts were loudest.

A half-dozen Civil Guards reconnoitering in the Academy museum (the room next to the chemical warfare laboratory) were shocked to find that the blast had torn away the exterior wall at the southern extremity and that it was now possible to step out and slide down to the Cuesta del Alcázar. Across this gap lay the open space of what had formerly been the chemical warfare laboratory. Seeing that they alone were in a position to stop the attackers whom they could hear coming up from the Zocodover, they frantically began to build a brick-and-stone wall across the mouth of the hole; the situation was so critical that they did not have time to summon help.

Their barricade was only a few feet high when the first Asaltos, commanded by Major Madronero, began to climb the slope, and the Guards nervously withdrew into the deep shadows of the room. Unaware that it was occupied, the first Asaltos climbed past the barricade without noticing the Guards, their attention held by the open doorways leading into the courtyard. Noiselessly the Guards lifted their rifles and fired into the right flank of the Asaltos, only a few yards away. Three of the attackers jerked and fell backward down the incline, while the others, taken completely by surprise, scurried after them. Because the interior of the museum was dark and they were on a lower level, the attackers assumed that the room was heavily garrisoned, an assumption reinforced a few seconds later when grenades came tumbling out of the museum or were dropped into the Cuesta from the windows in the exterior wall. Therefore, instead of rushing in force, they fell back toward the Zocodover or began sniping at the museum from behind obstructions in the Cuesta.

The Asaltos appeared to be incapacitated by their discovery

that the enemy was alive and shooting. According to their briefing, the blast should have disposed of all Nationalists along the west side. This delay bottled up other Republicans coming along behind them, and they had to take cover in the doorways along the street. Small groups of Asaltos hurled themselves up the slope, but each time they were met by heavier rifle fire, for as each minute passed, more defenders found their way to the museum. The Civil Guards continued to pile bricks at the mouth of the opening until a frontal attack upon it would have been suicidal. Half a dozen men had momentarily fought off an assault column.

While Major Madronero was leading his men up toward the chemical warfare laboratory, Major Torres with half of his force had reached the southwest angle, which was expected to be the Achilles heel of the fortress. But he was dismayed by what he found. It was true that the tower had vanished, but in its place was a matted pile of twisted steel girders which blocked the entrance to the gap as effectively as a metal cheval-de-frise. Behind this lay a steep mound of rubble, and beyond that a twenty-foot-deep crater. Too late the major realized that he had neglected to bring scaling ladders. Although the route was accessible to lightly armed men moving forward individually, a frontal attack was out of the question. Determined *milicianos* twisted through the girders, climbed the mound, slid down into the crater, and then began climbing up the foundation wall of the Alcázar. But only a trickle of attackers was able to advance at once; the others piled up in the streets behind, waiting their turn. It was while they were packed together that the first Alcázar riflemen reached their posts in the southern windows.

The militia hurled grenades at the windows, but more often than not they bounced off the walls, back into their midst. The Alcazareños poured down a point-blank fire, driving the militia back behind the old barricades which they had occupied for the past two months. The men in the crater were cut off. Unable to move forward or backward, they burrowed in the debris, waiting for an opportunity to escape to their lines. Few of them made it. The Nationalists above dropped grenades into the crater, threw down stones on them, or picked them off with their rifles. It was as simple as spearing fish in a net.

Sniping continued all day at the southwest corner, but the issue was never in doubt. "Send us a tank," bellowed a *miliciano*. But Major Torres knew that a tank was useless here. If the Nationalists had constructed fortifications systematically, they could not have been more effective than those created, by chance, by the exploding mine.

Only on the Corralillo did the Republican columns have a clear field to maneuver and attack. Five hundred militia, led by two armored cars mounting machine guns, surged across this sun-baked pasture toward the dining hall, a hundred yards away. When the cars reached the wall of the building, they turned and moved back and forth, spraying the parapets with bullets. The men lying behind the parapets crouched low, unable to engage steel-plated vehicles.

Halfway across the Corralillo the triumphant militia broke formation and raced toward the dining hall. The isolated sniping which had greeted their appearance had almost entirely ceased because of the harassing fire power of the armored cars, which patrolled the width of the Corralillo while the other riflemen in shirt sleeves joined them by crawling out of windows and hoisting themselves over garden walls adjacent to the rocky common. Their objective was the south side of the dining hall, originally constructed almost entirely of glass, like a greenhouse. Since the panes had been knocked out weeks before, there was an immense area through which they could enter the gutted building, even though the window ledges were some eight or ten feet above ground level. Once they got inside, they would be in a perfect position to engage the Alcázar windows along the east. Moreover, it would be virtually impossible to dislodge them. Both the Santiago Barracks and the Gobierno would then be cut off from the Alcázar.

Just as the first *milicianos* were lifting themselves up to the window ledges of the dining hall, a machine gun spurted from a tiny, overlooked basement window of the Capuchinos. This window was in the laundry room of the Academy and had not been fortified previously because it faced the Santiago Barracks and the dining hall. But three Civil Guards had heard the militia coming across the Corralillo, had moved their gun into the window, and were waiting. It was an ideal position for an enfilading fire, because a single bullet might hit several *milicianos* as they gathered below the windows of the dining hall. The Guards dared not take on the armored cars, so they had held their fire and kept out of sight until the militia reached the windows. Then their machine gun opened up on the left flank of the attackers.

Asaltos might have been able to cope with an ambush, but the militia could not. Even before their leaders were able to pinpoint the gun, the men were in full retreat and did not pause to carry away their dead and wounded. Without infantry support the armored cars served no function whatever. Like scurrying beetles they jerked back and forth grotesquely because the drivers re-fused to approach too close to the Capuchinos for fear of a grenade attack. Finally, when it became clear that the undisci-plined troops would not return, the vehicles backed across the Corralillo. Fierce sniping continued for the remainder of the day, but the assault was not renewed.

Simultaneous with the attacks to the south, the southwest, and the west, the Republicans launched their men against the north-ern front. While machine gunners in the Santa Cruz peppered the windows of the Gobierno, and slingers on the rooftops threw dynamite petards across the Calle del Carmen, militia from the Zocodover pushed through the ruins of the houses at the foot of the north terrace and climbed up to the Zig Zag. Here they waited for the tank which was supposed to join them before they overran the northern breach and dropped down into the court-yard. Hidden by the embankment of the terrace, these clusters of militia were safe from snipers in the Alcázar, although they were exposed to riflemen in the Gobierno. Because of the vicious fire power mounted against the defenders from the Santa Cruz, how-ever, only eight of them could be spared to stop the militia from climbing the northern slope. Four of these, including Lieutenant José Espiga, were regarded as the best marksmen of the Gobierno garrison; the other four loaded rifles for them and cooled the barrels with dripping rags. On the whole, the militia ignored their harassing fire.

Meanwhile a tank nosed out of an alleyway beyond the Santa Cruz and rumbled awkwardly down the Calle del Carmen toward the iron gate. It was an immense, crudely made contraption that looked like a Diesel locomotive equipped with caterpillar treads. Constructed of thick steel plates fastened with hundreds of rivets, it mounted a light cannon under a cheesebox turret, in addition to machine guns in two steel bubbles along its sides. At any other time the sight of this fantastic machine, which at top speed moved no faster than a slow walk, might have excited mirth rather than fear, but Lieutenant Espiga and his sharpshooters quickly learned that it was impervious to bullets. The monster crawled inexorably toward them, undisturbed by the lead slugs that beat a tattoo against its thick hide.

Thrusting its muzzle into the stable approach, immediately below Espiga's window, the tank butted into the iron gate and chewed through the grating as easily as if it had been chicken wire. Beyond the gate was a truck weighted with stones, which it knocked over as if it were a toy. Grenades and bombs were in short supply, and the Alcázar officers had been ordered to save them for grave emergencies; now Espiga decided that this was one, since in a few seconds the tank would reach the entrance to the Zig Zag. He picked up a Lafitte bomb and slammed it down on the tank, leaning slightly out of the window to do so.* The bomb bounced off the tank and exploded in the air, filling the narrow roadway with jagged fragments. A Civil Guard at the next window was wounded in the shoulder, and Lieutenant Espiga, who had not ducked back inside fast enough, was hit in the arm.

In the tunnel-like roadway below, the tank stopped. The driver inside had almost no visibility. The machine was not damaged, but doubtless perceiving that if it were disabled it would be impossible for the crew to escape or to defend themselves, the driver backed out of the stable approach and drove to a place of safety. The Republican decision to by-pass the garrison at the Gobierno proved to be a costly mistake, for the militia clinging to the hillside below the north terrace now had to proceed unsupported. Gamely they hoisted themselves over the railing and

---

* The Lafitte bomb was so undependable that it is said to have required special instructions for its use: after triggering the bomb, one was supposed to throw it and at the same time run as rapidly as possible in the opposite direction.

streamed across the terrace from all directions. Dug in along the northern crest of the Alcázar were a few dozen Civil Guards backed up by scattered riflemen in the upper rooms on the east side. If these men failed to halt the attack, the Republicans would hold the mountain of rubble, which rose above the courtyard.

While the tank was forging its way through the stable approach, some of the Asaltos who had been forced back from the gap at the museum retreated to the north by hugging the west wall, but instead of returning to the Zocodover, they went up the path leading to the north terrace. Hiding behind the jutting foundation stones of the northwest tower, they found themselves in a corner untouched by the battle. Inadvertently they had discovered the blind spot of the Alcázar, a place not covered by any rifle. Piled against the outer wall, a loose stairway of broken stones leading upward into the west rooms tempted them. At first suspicious of an ambush from above, they crept up warily. The Asalto up ahead found a man-sized hole near the top, peeped through it cautiously, and saw only billiard tables, overstuffed armchairs, and ping-pong equipment. A few minutes later the others, accompanied by a female warrior nicknamed "Snub Nose," climbed through the opening and slipped into what had once been the cadets' recreation room, located on the second floor just above the museum. Immediately below them they heard shooting, and looking through holes in the floor, they saw the Nationalists whose rifles had driven them back from the west gap a short time before. Unnoticed by the Nationalists, a dozen Republicans had secured a foothold in the Alcázar.

Since the towers had contained the only stairways leading to the upper rooms along the west, the recreation room was inaccessible to the defenders, who had vacated this region before the explosion of the mines. Lieutenant Barber had been right: the rooms could be reached by attackers from the outside. The position of the infiltrators had but one drawback—their own men outside did not realize they were there.

While some of the Asaltos quietly constructed parapets from which they could open fire on the Nationalists in the courtyard below them, the others gathered grenades and crept to the holes in the floor. The museum was by this time filled with officers who, realizing that a disciplined force could enter through the blown-out wall, were throwing up a defense line within the room. Had anyone glanced up at the ceiling, he would have seen the faces of the Asaltos peering down at him. Suddenly grenades plummeted down. The museum erupted in a mass of flame, smoke, and shrapnel. Three officers were killed instantly and a half-dozen Civil Guards severely wounded. The attackers then opened fire on a reserve company of Civil Guards in the court-yard preparing to counterattack across the northern breach, should the militia gain the crest. The Asaltos were excellent marksmen. Their initial volley felled six or eight Nationalists.

Commanding in the courtyard was Major Méndez Parada, the artillerist, who had brought out one of the Academy howitzers to repel the tank which he had been told was pushing toward the north wall. Suddenly the reserve company standing near him was being fired upon, and men were falling like ninepins. Spurts of flames showed him that the enemy occupied the recreation room. He immediately sent his best riflemen aloft to the upper rooms on the east side of the courtyard, with orders to find out how the enemy had got up there and to wipe them out. In charge of them was a quiet, spectacled Infantry lieutenant, Benito Gómez Oliveres.

Lieutenant Gómez had no trouble discovering the leak in the defensive line and posted two soldiers where they could cover the blind spot, but to dislodge the Asaltos was not possible at the moment. No reinforcements would be able to climb up to the recreation room, but the enemy there had already cleared the courtyard of most resistance and were picking off the vital line of men who held the crest of the northern breach. When the militia attacked across the north terrace, they would be almost entirely unopposed.

While others cursed and fumed, Lieutenant Gómez took it upon himself to eject the Asaltos from the recreation room. While the bulk of his force maintained a harassing fire from the east rooms, Gómez collected a half-dozen Civil Guards and Falangists and slipped into the room beneath the Asaltos. He no-ticed the holes in the ceiling through which they had dropped grenades and realized that it might be possible to dislodge the enemy by climbing to the upper story through these holes. But how could they get a force up there? The distance from the floor to the ceiling of the museum was more than twenty-five feet. A quartermaster lieutenant, Enrique Castro, remembered that there were ladders in the cellars. Gómez had two of these brought up and lashed end to end with wire, but when they hoisted them up, they found that the ladders were still not long enough. Gómez was unperturbed. He had a display case dragged from the wall and placed directly under a hole. His men then shoved the top of the ladder through the hole and placed the other end on the case.

Lieutenant Gómez guessed rightly that the Asaltos would be too preoccupied with the Guards in the opposite rooms to suspect that anyone could or would climb up from below, so he cautiously began the ascent. The flimsy ladder was bending like a bow when Gómez reached the ceiling. He quickly stuck his head through the hole and withdrew it. Since no shot had been fired at him, he motioned his men to follow him, and slipped into the room. While others clutched the legs of the ladder and braced the chest with their bodies, Lieutenant Castro, more familiar with provisioning than fighting, climbed up gamely, followed by three Falangists.

Leading the way, Gómez burst upon the Asaltos from behind, his automatic pistol blazing. It was a total surprise. When Lieutenant Castro ran into the room, he nearly collided with an Asalto holding a rifle. Castro swung his pistol toward the man and pulled the trigger. It clicked. The Asalto and the lieutenant looked at each other in mutual surprise, then the man dropped his rifle and bolted toward the escape route, jumping feet first into the gap through which he had entered. "Snub Nose" also escaped. The others were shot down by Gómez and his raiders.* The Asaltos had tied a red banner to a girder protruding above the rubble at the northwest corner. Gómez climbed up through a hail of bullets and yanked it down.

The second floor along the west having been cleared of the

---

* Though Lieutenant Gómez was attached to an Oviedo regiment and had no association with the Toledo military establishments, Colonel Moscardó was so impressed by his bold attack that he arranged to have him made his special aide. Gómez served under Moscardó until the latter's death in 1956 and also wrote the official biography of his commander. In this book Gómez describes the counterattack on the recreation room in detail but without mentioning himself as one of the participants.

enemy, soldiers were sent up the ladder at once to establish a defensive line. It was none too soon, for the militia along the Zig Zag had already rushed across the north terrace and were climbing the rubble of the northern slope. As they advanced they threw grenades over the crest into the courtyard, but the defenders in the upper arcades were able to hold them back. The militia had not been told to expect stiff resistance, and having already witnessed the failure of their tank to forge past the Gobierno, they became demoralized. One by one they were hit, and slid down the slope. No reinforcements arrived. Men began to trickle toward the rear, until finally no militia remained on the terrace except the dead and the dying.

By ten-twenty both the Nationalists and the Republicans knew that the massive attack had failed. The Alcázar had not surrendered; its defensive perimeter remained unchanged.

As soon as the attacks had been repulsed, the batteries of 155's broke out again, battering the east walls. This was almost welcomed by the officers, for it indicated that the enemy acknowledged their failure. Each of the 272 shells which exploded against the Alcázar on September 18—the heaviest barrage to that date—testified to the impotent rage of the Republican command. Throughout the day the defenders remained at their posts in case the enemy should strike again.

Colonel Moscardó at once went with Lieutenant Barber to the cellars to examine the extent of the damage. Barber was worried about his assistant, Rodríguez Caridad, who had not been seen since early in the morning, when just before the explosion he had insisted on making a final check along the west to see that everyone had been cleared from the area. Surveying the damage below, Barber found that the main impact of the explosion had been vertical. With more patience, the miners might have dug secondary tunnels under the base of the west walls and brought down that whole side. As it was, the blast had been spectacular but very wasteful. Furthermore, the tons of stone had been ejected to the west, away from the interior.

The west cellars had been filled with heaps of rubble, but in the improvised chapel along the south Moscardó and Barber found the women praying in front of the image of the Virgin.

The statue had been knocked down, but it was only lightly chipped. Here was evidence, for those who sought it, that the power of God was stronger than the TNT of godless Asturians. While Moscardó dropped to his knees and prayed, Barber examined the wire barrier which he and Rodríguez had strung to mark what they believed would be the limit of the explosion. The wires were intact, but only a foot or so beyond them was a chaos of fallen rock and shattered masonry. The corporal could not be found. Evidently the mines had gone off while he was making his check. Entombed in the tons of debris with him were an officer and three Civil Guards who had been assigned to this sector to make certain that the Republicans would not sneak some militia in here, instead of detonating the mines.

Other than these men, no one was killed by the explosion itself, because almost everyone had obeyed strict orders not to move from the places assigned them in remote rooms. Teresa Gonzálcz, the meat dresser, had a narrow escape. In the quiet period just before the explosion, she and her husband had ignored the order and gone up into the courtyard, out of curiosity. When the mines erupted, they were thrown fifteen yards and were buried up to their necks in debris. Soldiers rushing past them to their firing posts a fcw minutes later were startled by what they at first thought were two heads without bodies lying on a mound of rubble. When they stopped to pull them out, Teresa said, "Don't bother with me. The Reds are attacking." They were extricated after the Republicans had been driven off, both of them having had a ringside seat at the battle for the recreation room. Except for bruises, neither was injured.

Most of the casualties had occurred when the Asaltos were in the recreation room dropping grenades or firing at the defenders below them. Antonio Rivera, "the Angel," had gone into action for the first time, as loader for a machine gun placed along the northern crest. Under a rain of grenades during the militia attack up the slope, the gun crew had run back to safety in a nearby room. Rivera decided to retrieve the gun. He reached the site and was dismantling the tripod when a grenade exploded only a few steps away, shattering his arm. While he clutched his rosary in the infirmary, this limb was amputated. The day's total amounted to thirteen dead and fifty-nine wounded in the Alcázar; Moscardó calculated that a hundred dead *milicianos* lay scattered about the precincts of the building, many of whom were dragged off by their comrades during the night. Some of the dead were women.

The Republican artillery pounded the Alcázar all day and all night. When darkness set in, the defenders built barricades, cleared passageways, and buried their dead under a few shovelfuls of earth in the Picadero. But this work proceeded slowly, for they were close to exhaustion. Because of the morning attacks there had been no time to butcher a horse; reluctantly Captain Cuartero had dipped into his emergency reserve in order to serve them a luxurious dinner of rice, beans, and sausage.

Having worked all night in relays, the soldiers resumed their posts before dawn. The night was uncommonly cold, a chilling wind sweeping down from the Guadarrama Mountains. Autumn had come to Castile, and it brought another physical torment to the men lying at exposed posts, waiting for the sun which would being them a little warmth and many militia.

10

ⅬⅬⅡⅬⅬⅡⅬⅬⅡⅬⅬⅡⅬⅬⅡⅬⅬⅡⅬⅬⅡⅬⅬⅠ

THE LAST ONSLAUGHT

BY THE EVENING of September 18, General José Asensio, the commander of government troops in central Spain, had acquired first-hand experience of what his superiors in Madrid were calling "the Toledan nightmare." All day he waited eagerly for news of the Alcázar's surrender. The red banner sighted in the morning should have been followed by a white one, but instead of advancing into the ruins of the fortress, his columns fell back. Even while Unión Radio was announcing that the Alcázar had fallen, the road leading to the railroad station was choked with ambulances trying to honk a path through the swarms of townspeople attempting to return to their homes, now that the terrible mines had been exploded. Not only had the Republicans been hurled back, but they had no clear indication of how much damage they had inflicted upon their adversary. Some officers estimated that there were less than fifty casualties in the Alcázar; others guessed that there were twelve hundred. Would a fresh assault meet little resistance, or would they fail a second time? Asensio could not know for sure, and he decided to take no chances. At a press conference he contented himself with saying that the defenders would be wiped out—and quickly.

First of all, the Gobierno's stubborn defense had to be crushed so that a tank could push up to the north terrace and the militia advancing up the Zig Zag would not be subjected to a fire from the flank. To accomplish this, Asensio requisitioned a gasoline truck from Madrid. His plan was to run a hose to the Gobierno, have gasoline pumped into the lower rooms, and then ignite it. After the fire had died down, *dinamiteros* would blow a hole in the wall to let attackers through from the Santa Cruz. At the same time a tank would force its way through the iron gate and ascend to the north terrace. The artillery at Alijares would continue to pound against the east wall of the Alcázar, concentrating on the door by the swimming pool in order to cut off possible reinforcements to the Gobierno. Rather than attempt to enter the fortress from four different directions, the Republicans would deliver a knock-out blow through the northern breach. Asensio set the attack for September 20.

The bitter night chill of the waning Castilian summer had lifted early in the morning of September 19, but the defenders lying exposed in the upper rooms were stiff from the cold. Moscardó had loads of horse blankets carried to the cellars so that the women could make overcoats out of them. No one down there needed blankets, for the fetid, steaming heat of hundreds of bodies piled almost on top of one another kept them warm, and except for the prized stallion Cajón and about a dozen mules, there were no animals left to worry about.

Having transferred most of their artillery from the Dehesa de Pinedo to Alijares, during the morning hours the Republicans furiously shelled the east wall nearest the last-remaining, south-east tower and the outlying buildings. The Academy was hence-forth entirely sealed off during the daytime from the garrisons at the Capuchinos, the Gobierno, and the Santiago. Since the curved passage had been buried under tons of fallen stone by previous barrages, the only available exit allowing for communication with the dependencies was the door on the east esplanade, leading down to the swimming pool. The militia artillerists knew this, and trained two 75's on the door and on the area just outside. Observers with telescopes mounted watch, and at the slightest sign of movement near the door they ordered a shelling so rapid that it became nearly impossible for any defender to venture outside.

In the afternoon the 155's pounded the washroom in the basement of the Capuchinos, where the Civil Guard machine gun had crippled their attack on the dining hall the day before. Their aim was nearly perfect. Shells whittled away the low window or slammed into the wall above, bringing down heaps of stone which buried the casement. The Guards pulled back into the room and waited for an attack, but none came.

Instead, militia crowded behind the gateposts outside the Santa Cruz, and then dodged across the street to the charred walls of the Gobierno in order to reconnoiter the building which they were going to attack the next day. After a half-hearted defense by the garrison inside, the attackers fell back to the Santa Cruz, convinced that a strong push would easily finish off the Gobierno. In the corridors and courtyards of the old convent, *milicianos* loaded steel-bullet clips and machine-gun belts. The outstretched arms of a terra-cotta apostle, whose eyes were imploringly fixed toward heaven, held a load of empty webbing belts. The militia were cheerfully expectant. They had heard about the gasoline truck, also that Prime Minister Largo Caballero was coming to Toledo to observe the attack on the morrow.

In the Alcázar, the junta debated among themselves whether to withdraw all units into the fortress proper, since the Gobierno and the Santiago could be cut off at any time, but they decided to wait a little longer. They did, however, map out a defensive plan in case the militia were to penetrate the Alcázar. Half the men would gather in the upper rooms and make a last stand, while the others would burrow into the cellars and defend the civilians to the end. Junior officers were impressed with one desperate fact: since those who surrendered would be shot by a firing squad, they might just as well die in the Alcázar with weapons in their hands.

The recreation room had been renamed "the Room of Death"; the rickety ladder constructed by Lieutenant Gómez was called "the stairway of Death." This was the most dangerous post in the Alcázar. If the Republicans seized this room again, it would be impossible for the defenders to escape. Moreover, the machine gun in the Magdalena Church raked the room regularly, and while it was usually possible to avoid being hit directly, the lead-nosed slugs ricocheted wildly. Sooner or later almost every man assigned to this post was hit, and the junta seemed to stick to a simple rule: once a man had mounted to the *"Sala de Muerte"* he was not permitted to descend again until he was a casualty, or a corpse. It took a strong stomach as well as a stout heart to climb the ladder covered with the slippery paint of blood that had dripped from the wounded or dead being lowered with the help of ropes.

The report for the day listed only eighty-eight heavy shells, four dead, and thirty-three wounded. At night a soft, steady rain began to fall over Toledo.

Half an hour after midnight on September 20 the enemy batteries opened fire upon the east façade of the Alcázar, concentrating on the southeast tower and swinging gradually over to the swimming pool door. The barrage lasted for five minutes and consisted of 150 shells of 155-mm. size—an average of one every thirty seconds. Sluggishly the men forced themselves awake, gripped their weapons, and waited. The bombardment, which was more intense than any other so far, must be the prelude to an attack. But at what point? Colonel Moscardó thought the Republicans intended to overrun the Capuchinos, where the men had not been relieved in over two days. He ordered the place reinforced at once, but his command could not be carried out— exploding shells filled the east esplanade with shrapnel, which clattered angrily against the walls. Wherever the attack struck, the men at that point would have to fight alone.

Hours before daylight the gasoline truck arrived in Toledo and was brought through back streets to a dark alleyway next to the Santa Cruz; throughout the sector, smoking was strictly forbidden. A pump was attached, and long segments of irrigation hose were fitted together; then the hose was run to an upper window facing the Gobierno. The nozzle was directed toward the wedge-shaped corner at the Calle del Carmen and the stable approach, and the stream of fluid turned on. The corner was soon flooded with gasoline, but when the militia tried to reach the middle section farther down the street, known as Stable No. 4, the pressure was inadequate. The floodlight in the Zocodover was cut off while *milicianos* carried the hose out the door and ran with it across the street to cram it through a window of the Gobierno. None of these men was armed, and in the darkness there was no covering fire from their comrades in the Santa Cruz. They stuck the hose through a window and turned it on. Nothing came out. Somewhere in the darkness behind them they heard a noise that sounded like water gushing from a broken pipe. While they had been positioning the hose at the window, someone had climbed out of a window in the Gobierno and slashed the hose in two with a machete. Now their precious gasoline was cascading harmlessly down the Calle del Carmen.

Someone threw a bomb. The whole area geysered into flames which instantaneously ignited the corner of the Gobierno and also ran along the hose back to the puddles spilled at the Santa Cruz. The militia worked frantically to put out the flames; somehow the pump was shut off and the gasoline truck, still half full, did not explode. The hose idea was dropped, but the militia collected wine bottles and buckets which they filled with gasoline; these would be thrown upon the Gobierno with their own hands when the attack was ordered.

The artillery barrage on the esplanade ceased at five-thirty, and the militia started to shower the Gobierno with petards hurled from slings, and with pieces of steel tubing packed with dynamite and lit by a cigarette. These forced the defenders back to the inner courtyards or into the basement of the building. The militia then attacked the corner in force. The Asturian miners crept along the wall until they reached that part of Stable No. 4 which had been partially opened up by the 75-mm. gun several weeks before. Here they laid a string of dynamite charges, lit the fuses, and bolted. At the explosion, one quarter of the wall crumbled down into the Calle del Carmen. Other *milicianos* then threw in buckets and bottles of gasoline and ignited the fluid with grenades. The men inside fell back along the corridor toward the east, and hastily built a crude barricade of rocks at the far end. With their backs to the wall, they waited for the enemy with the frantic rage of animals trapped in burrows.

The first militia to crowd through the breach found that they were brilliantly silhouetted targets for the desperate soldiers at the end of the passageway. They were cut down at once, several of them tumbling down inside. Those behind them tried to hurl grenades and gasoline bottles down the low-ceilinged passageway, but this was as difficult as to pitch a ball in a mine tunnel. They tried to bowl them, but the protruding horse stalls deflected the missiles. Throughout the day half a dozen young soldiers of the troop section would remain behind their precarious rock wall while *milicianos* potted at them, initially with straight fire but later by making the bullets ricochet off the walls like billiard shots, in order to reach their targets behind the barricade.

The Gobierno was now the scene of individual duels elsewhere in the building. In this room-to-room fighting the advantage lay with the Nationalists, who knew the building intimately. Furthermore, the militia had so often been tricked by their "play dead" tactics that they were wary and pressed forward slowly. The defenders had become more intent upon staying alive than protecting the Alcázar above.

At nine-thirty the Republicans launched their main attack on the fortress itself. Once again the tank pushed up the stable approach. This time there was nothing to impede its progress. Slowly it ground up the Zig Zag, its exhaust a cloud of thin blue smoke. Already several hundred militia lay waiting for it, crouched behind the embankment of the north terrace.

Lying along the crest in rifle pits scooped out of rubble or behind a head cover of metal ammunition cases filled with rocks, twenty to thirty Civil Guards braced themselves for the attack. Above them, in the ruined rooms and arcades, there were isolated riflemen, to give them some support, but most of these were dangerously exposed to the hail of bullets fired from rooftops near by. And at the south end of the courtyard a reserve company of Civil Guards waited with fixed bayonets to counterattack should the Republicans gain the crest. The snout of Major Méndez Parada's 75-mm. gun protruded over a mound of bricks, to engage the tank when it got to the northern breach. This gun had fired only blanks for twenty years, and no one knew for certain how it would behave when a live shell was used. Because the defenders were on a higher level, they could easily have driven off the enemy with grenades, but they only had a few dozen left.*

The tank announced its arrival on the terrace with hooting klaxon, the signal for attack. The militia surged forward over the

* At the beginning of the siege there were only 255 Lafitte bombs and about 60 incendiary grenades in the armory of the Alcázar. At the end of the siege there were 14 grenades left.

embankment and raced toward the slope while the light cannon of the tank blasted away the head cover of the Guards at the top. They took up positions behind the rubble at the base of the northern breach, and drove back the defenders from the upper rooms and arcades with grenades. The tank started up the slope.

The surface was very loose and the angle was almost forty-five degrees. In the first attempt the caterpillar treads did not get sufficient traction, so the cumbersome monster slipped back to the terrace. The driver backed off and tried again. Halfway up, the tank faltered a moment, then skidded back down. On the third attempt it almost reached the crest but butted into a length of steel girder which held it back like a metal prop. The treads spewed gravel down the hill behind, but the machine was unable to move forward. It sat there with its guns blazing and its klaxon screaming. The militia pressed upward.

Colonel Romero, who had taken charge of this weakening edge in the defensive line, realized that the tank squatting near the crest had to be driven off: its deafening cannon had already forced the Guards at the top to fall back into the courtyard and its klaxon seemed to be calling every unengaged *miliciano* in the city. He equipped his reserve company with bottles of gasoline and Lafitte bombs, and at his command, "Now!," the Guards tossed them over the crest. They exploded almost simultaneously, and the slope erupted in flames. The driver was forced to back down the mound; the tank paused at the bottom to fire a volley at the upper arcades, then pivoted and waddled slowly down the Zig Zag.

The reserve company of Civil Guards climbed up to the crest and bore down upon the militia with fixed bayonets. They did not fire a shot and did not have to. At the sight of cold steel, the militia at once lost their cohesiveness. They became a mob confronting avenging policemen. They bolted, vaulting the balustrade at the edge of the north terrace, and scrambled down the hillside toward the Zocodover. The Guards immediately returned to the courtyard, and the rifle pits along the crest were manned again. Colonel Romero was so enthusiastic that he sent the last five bottles of vermouth in the Academy commissary to the men posted in the arcades and along the crest. There was barely enough for a man to moisten his lips, but a ragged corporal shook his rifle and shouted, "Give us *coñac* instead of wine, and we'll grab the Zocodover for you!"

Isolated *milicianos* occupied the ruined houses between the Zig Zag and the Santa Cruz, from which they commanded the footbridge running over the stable approach—the most direct link between the Gobierno and the Alcázar. But the attack was over.

The Alcázar had lost contact with the Gobierno when the field-telephone lines were severed by a direct hit. In the early afternoon the guns at Alijares shelled the dependency heavily. Observers reported that an officer and four soldiers ran across the footbridge in what looked like an attempt to retreat to the Alcázar, but all of them were shot down. Scattered shots were heard coming from the Gobierno, but whether this indicated resistance or just mopping-up by the militia, no one could say. Had the garrison been wiped out? To find out, Moscardó requested volunteers.

The assignment was just what the Falange had been waiting for. Six of them volunteered, including their chief, Pedro Villaescusa, and while they were warned that it was tantamount to suicide to run through the barrage pounding the east esplanade, they insisted on trying. Huddling behind the swimming pool door, they waited for a lull in the bombardment. When the guns ceased for a moment, Villaescusa plunged out the door and dashed for the footbridge, closely followed by his men. The pitted ground slowed them down. They were about twenty yards from their starting point when a 155 shell exploded in their midst; red pulp plastered the east wall. Villaescusa and two others disappeared in a cloud of black dust; the others crawled back inside. Moscardó and Romero agreed that the Gobierno had to be abandoned after nightfall—provided there was anyone left alive in the place to return to the fortress. This meant that all the dependencies—the Santiago, the Capuchinos, and the dining hall—had to be vacated as well. The defensive line would henceforth be the Alcázar alone.

The Republican artillery fired the last of its 472 shells at six-thirty. As soon as it was dark, sixty Civil Guards crept out of the Alcázar toward the Gobierno in order to evacuate the building. Lieutenant Enrique del Pino warned his men not to enter the building through the windows, for if any soldiers were inside, they would doubtless be expecting raids by the militia. Noiselessly they slipped down into the stable approach and listened vainly for some telltale sound from the Gobierno. They heard nothing. Finally the lieutenant tapped lightly on the door under the footbridge. He heard a clatter inside, as if someone had knocked over a rifle, and was trying to decide whether or not to break down the door when he heard it being unbolted from within. It swung open and a private of the troop section peered out.

Lieutenant del Pino flew into a rage, "You stupid ass! We might have been Reds!"

"No," said the private wearily. "You knocked. The *'abisinios'* never do."

About forty or fifty half-starved, exhausted men were found in the Gobierno. Most of them were teen-agers of the troop section who had held this battered corner for two months. For the last time they assembled in the dungeonlike stables on the east side; they looked stooped and wizened, like old men. Shouldering their rifles, they filed into the stable approach and crawled up to the Alcázar, taking care not to be caught in the floodlights. Many of them brought back as souvenirs the name plates of horses which they had once groomed and later eaten. The relief party under Del Pino remained behind to round up the wheat stores and ammunition. Afraid that their glossy patent-leather hats might be spotted by the enemy across the river, the Civil Guards left them behind. The Gobierno was then set on fire, and at the windows of the Alcázar, doleful men gathered to watch the final agonies of the building which had formerly been the strongest link in the defensive chain around the Academy.

The evacuation of the dependencies had been carried out efficiently; nothing of importance was left behind. However, although no one was aware of it at the time, there had been a major blunder. Near the iron gate, in the stable approach, was the opening of a sewer which ran from the northeast corner of the Alcázar. It was a ready-made tunnel leading straight into the bowels of the fortress, and it was, moreover, wide enough for men to crawl through. It would be a simple matter for the Asturians to deposit TNT at the far end of this shaft and blow up the section which contained the greatest number of people. Everyone in the fortress had forgotten that this brick conduit existed.

The enemy barrage on September 21 was concentrated on the only remaining tower, on the southeast corner. The Cavalry library, next to the tower, was completely buried when the walls above crashed down on the esplanade, and books were scattered on the ground like seeds from a broken gourd. Atlases, bound volumes of the *Illustrated London News,* textbooks with titles such as *The Art of War*—all these littered the mound of rubble leading up to the space where the library had been. And just before sundown the great tower tilted outward and collapsed on the esplanade, burying the remnants of the old curved passage. After the day's bombardment of 238 heavy shells, nearly half of the east façade was stripped to the inner walls. There were few obstructions on this side. An attacking force would have little difficulty in climbing the gentle slope and entering the fortress through a dozen cluttered gaps on the levels of the courtyard or the first cellar immediately below.

During the bombardment Moscardó was holding a conference with his junta in the superintendent's office when a shell sliced into the room and exploded, scattering shrapnel among them. No one was killed, and only Major Méndez Parada was wounded seriously enough to be relieved from duty. The office was then transferred to a storeroom next to the south cellar. This completely dark cubicle, which was about the size of a small prison cell, became the last command post of the Alcázar.

At the end of the day there were five dead and twenty-five wounded, bringing the two-day total to twelve and eighty-three, respectively. Since the men were near complete physical collapse, the bodies of the dead were no longer carried to the Picadero for burial. Instead, they were dragged down to the swimming pool and braced upright in the locker-alcoves. Bricks and stones were piled loosely over them; here and there the bodies and the uniforms could be glimpsed through the uneven chinks of rock. Within twenty-four hours the odor became so nauseating that the civilians in the room had to change places with the horse and the mules stabled in the south cellar below. But the water in the pool was still used in cooking.

The Alcazareños did not know it, but the Army of Africa had that day broken the Republican lines at the village of Maqueda, twenty-four miles northwest, and this was the last important defensive position separating General Franco from his main objective, Madrid. Franco faced a crucial decision: should he attempt to relieve the Alcázar? Nationalist pilots reported that the Academy was almost unrecognizable and obviously of no further use; moreover, the garrison seemed ready to fall at any moment. Most of Franco's staff urged him to push on rapidly to Madrid and end the war with one blow, but Franco ordered General José Varela to push at once to Toledo with a column of the Spanish Foreign Legion and the Moorish Regulares. "Do you realize, General," asked Colonel Alfredo Kindelán, his Air Force chief, "that Toledo can cost you Madrid?"

"I know it. I have thought much about the consequences of my decision," replied Franco.

In the next two and a half years, the General would doubtless have many occasions to consider the consequences of his decision. He did not enter Madrid until 1939.

At dawn on September 22 the militia launched a heavy attack on the empty rooms in the Gobierno. Flame throwers licked the walls of this roofless ruin, which now looked like some archaeological remnant. Dynamite cartridges exploded in rooms suspected to hold pockets of Fascists, and it was not until afternoon that the militia rested, convinced that the place was vacated. Soon they began to occupy the other outbuildings, inspecting the cemetery in the Picadero with great care in order to record how many of the enemy had died and to estimate how many still lived in the fortress. They found sixty wooden crosses and promptly removed them. On the walls of the dining hall they wrote, in red letters: *"Viva Rusia!"* and *"Viva la República!"* They ate their rations off the heavy dinnerware, each piece embossed with the imperial seal of the Bourbons, and then broke the plates in contempt.

Journalists and cameramen followed the advance of the

milicianos, who crawled through the silent dependencies like wary cats, their backs hunched over and eyes alert. Two months as besiegers had taught these men that Fascist bullets were most dangerous after long periods of silence. An English correspondent was handed a mimeographed sheet of paper picked up in the Gobierno, and at first could not make out what it was. The heading at the top of the page read *"El Alcázar,"* and below it was the musical score for an anthem entitled "The Hymn of the Alcázar."

The artillery barrage was light, compared with others of the past. On this day only twenty-four heavy shells were fired; and observers reported that most of the guns had been dismantled and removed from their emplacements. They assumed that the pieces were being transferred toward the northwest in order to block the advance of the relief column; but in any event, since the Alcázar was already a shambles, artillery was no longer required.

The defenders knew that the militia were tightening the ring around the fortress, for the *paqueo* was swinging around to the east. This side of the Alcázar was especially vulnerable to attack because there was plenty of space on the esplanade to maneuver an assault column, and the burned-out trucks, shell craters, and mounds of rubble would provide adequate cover. The officers therefore posted their men in the windows and at loopholes overlooking the ravaged esplanade. Throughout the night they held their flare guns in readiness. But the sector was ominously quiet. Even though the enemy had not launched an attack, casualties for the day numbered two dead and twenty-seven wounded, most of them the victims of jagged-nosed ricochet bullets.

A fierce *paqueo* along the northern perimeter jarred everyone awake just before dawn on September 23, and at eight o'clock the tank mounted the Zig Zag, spearheading the militia against the breach once more. Out in front were the Asturians, some of them wearing alpaca jackets, and all of them fitted out with special bandoleers holding dynamite cartridges. Their ears were plugged with cotton, and their faces were etched with dust. Cigarettes dangled from their lips—they used them to light their explosives. At the bottom of the slope they hurled the dynamite sticks at the rifle pits on the crest, and covered by the fire power of the tank, began climbing upward. The noise was deafening—more terrifying than artillery shells—and the defenders fell back to the courtyard. The first wave of militia reached the summit and tried to rush down into the courtyard, but framed as they were against the skyline, they were instantly shot. However, the second wave dug in along the crest and used it as a parapet from which to exchange shots with the men below.

The tank plowed up the slope with its guns blazing. Once again it slipped backward to the terrace. The militia worked to clear a path through the rubble, and with the next effort the tank nearly reached the summit. The defenders drew reinforcements from the vulnerable east side and put these men in the arcades, from which they could fire down on the militia. Colonel Romero had bottles of gasoline sent up to the arcades, for the soldiers to throw at the tank. Both sides of the mound along the north exploded into flames and soon became a gigantic bonfire fueled by gasoline, dynamite, and Lafitte bombs. The heat drove the militia down to the terrace, and the tank followed. The klaxon screamed like a beast in pain. Soldiers in the arcades heaved down boulders and rocks on them. But for the tank, the spectacle lacked only a kettle of boiling oil to become a reasonably complete enactment of a battle in the Middle Ages.

When the fire died down, combatants on both sides of the mound rushed toward the summit. The Nationalists reached it first, and the tide of battle changed—the militia fell back to the embankment. The tank lumbered down the Zig Zag, leaving in its wake the putrescent remains of militiamen killed days before, which were squashed to jelly under the iron treads. By noon the attack had ceased.

In the afternoon the very last gun—a 155 planted in the Dehesa de Pinedo—battered the northern mound, doubtless to open a path for the tank. After twenty-nine shells had been thrown, the crest of rubble had been lowered by some five or ten feet, about the position reached by the tank in the morning attack.

At six o'clock the militia attacked again, but the tank did not advance beyond the Zig Zag. For an hour and a quarter they skirmished with the defenders on the crest, but they did not attempt to break through.

The worst blow came in the evening. Civilians in the cellar at the northeast corner reported that they had heard the sound of digging. With haggard, frightened faces they watched Lieutenant Barber probe the walls and floor with the borrowed stethoscope. "It is nothing. Nothing," he repeated, not wishing to upset them. But it was something indeed. Barber told the officers that the Republicans were placing another mine at the corner—it was then that they remembered the old conduit near the iron gate. Barber thought that the Asturians were digging by hand, probably enlarging the tunnel at the end in order to pack their explosives in it. Moscardó forbade the officers to speak of this matter to their men or to the civilians, for nothing could be done about it. As things now stood, they could not even transfer the people in the cellars to a safer position, because all habitable rooms were already crammed full.

News of the mine was particularly disheartening, for the same evening Radio Portugal announced that the Army of Africa was nearing the town of Torrijos—only eighteen miles from Toledo.

By midmorning the next day the single remaining 155 shelled the crest of the northern breach with a slow rhythm, demolishing the rifle pits which the soldiers had built following the attack the day before. All day long, observers watched buses, trucks, and automobiles arrive in Toledo. They were packed with militia, but their objective was not the Alcázar. Instead, they veered off at the Bisagra Gate and took the Ávila road toward Torrijos. The junta concluded that the Republicans were fortifying the eastern bluff of the Guadarrama River, an easily defended embankment commanding the level plain across which the Army of Africa would have to march. If this line held, the relief column might be delayed for several weeks. Yet, Moscardó bolstered spirits in *El Alcázar* by assuring the garrison that they would be saved within a few hours.

Even though the Republicans were making a major effort to block the Nationalist advance outside Toledo, none of the besieging troops had been withdrawn. As a matter of fact, during the night the militia dug trenches on the east esplanade only fifty yards from the walls of the fortress. Whenever they liked, they could mass undetected in the dining hall and rush the Cavalry library breach. But the enemy did not attack; they waited for the completion of the mine. Time was now running out for both besiegers and besieged.

At night a newscaster on Radio Portugal mentioned "Guadarrama River," but reception was so poor that the radiomen in the Alcázar cellars could not understand the context.

Dawn of September 25 was gloriously clear and sparkling, though very cold for the season. Expecting some sign or trace of the approaching relief column, most Alcazareños had been unable to fall asleep in their excitement. Even before the sun rose above the horizon, they were gathering silently in the courtyard, trembling from the cold. Observers in the upper rooms scoured the arid landscape to the west with their binoculars, looking for a trace of movement out there, while the crowd below stood quiet, straining to hear the sound of distant artillery.

Suddenly a fifteen-year-old bugler shouted from his post aloft, "I hear them! I hear them! Attention! Can't you hear them?" The people below stiffened; some of them cupped their hands over their ears. Then they heard something, too. It was the sound—a great distance away—of an artillery duel. From the galleries to the cellars the news was transmitted like an electric shock. Someone shouted, "The Alcázar for the Holy Virgin!" but few had the strength left to cheer. Most wept. Bearded soldiers slumped to their knees and sobbed like children. Then machine-gun fire from the enemy barricades drowned out the far-off artillery. The siege was by no means ended.

Later in the morning three Nationalist bombers hurtled over the city and bombed the Republican gun in the Dehesa de Pinedo, and minutes later Nationalist artillery opened up on the same target. After two months the enemy artillerists found out how it felt to be shelled. Then *milicianos*, on foot or in trucks, poured into the city from the west. At the Bisagra Gate they swung north along the Madrid road, but by midafternoon the same groups were seen returning to Toledo. Actually, they had been cut off by a Nationalist pincer movement toward the north. Soon the area around the *plaza de toros* and Tavera Hospital was cluttered with men, horses, trucks, and equipment. Confused, the soldiers raced back and forth, dimly perceiving that they were being deflected into a trap. The only escape route lay to the east, toward Aranjuez, but the militia chiefs refused to allow their men to take it. They must halt the Fascists at Toledo, no matter what the price in human lives. Among the militia the story circulated that the Army of Africa was rushing toward the Alcázar in order to seek refuge in the fortress.

The militia were crowding back to Toledo because their commanders had not tried to hold back the Army of Africa at the Guadarrama River bluffs near Torrijos. The Republicans had blown up the bridge, but the stream was narrow and fordable. The Nationalists crushed the militia with professional ease and drove them back from poorly prepared defensive lines. Turbaned dispatch riders on magnificent Arabian horses splashed across the river and galloped across the landscape. "A storybook war!" exclaimed H. R. Knickerbocker, an American correspondent with Varela's army. The road to Toledo lay open. The cobblestones were splashed with blood. Sometimes Knickerbocker was able to follow a specific red trail for miles—of a wounded man unable to stanch his bleeding. All the way from Maqueda the road was littered with Republican corpses. Torrijos was devastated—"not one house in the place unruined," wrote the American, while his Spanish driver muttered sadly and with disgust, "Spaniards! All are Spaniards!" Nationalist officers were carrying newspaper clippings showing pictures of executions in the Montaña Barracks; they took no prisoners.

In the Alcázar everything was quiet. Around two o'clock in the morning on September 26, the *paqueo* flared up but died out just as suddenly. The Republican gun engaged some invisible target far to the northwest of Toledo; from this the defenders conjectured that a portion of the relief columns was continuing to swing north to block the Republicans from retreating in that direction. Despite the diminution of enemy fire power directed against the fortress, Moscardó was more apprehensive than usual. He made a personal tour of all positions, convinced that the enemy was planning to spring a surprise attack. He warned the weary men not to become overconfident, and above everything else, not to let anyone come near the building without his specific permission. He was very much afraid that the militia might disguise themselves as Nationalists and capture the Alcázar by trickery.

The sky above the Alcázar was the setting for dogfights. In the afternoon three Republican fighters shot down a Nationalist trimotor. Three specks bailed out. One of the fighters machine-gunned the dangling figures, but those watching through binoculars could not tell whether the men were hit, since dead men hang in parachutes the same way as live ones. Observers in the Alcázar did not witness the aftermath. The plane crashed behind the Nationalist lines, and the three fliers landed close to the city. The pilot defended himself against a band of militia, shooting three of them with his pistol before being killed. The second flier was dead when he reached the ground, and the third was captured alive. The dead men were thrown on the rear luggage rack of a car and hauled to town, their hands dragging along the road. The live flier was bound and turned over to a group of women, who worked him over for seven hours. They slashed him with razors, trampled him, beat him until his body was converted to "a mass of bleeding pulp," according to one witness. The only words he uttered were "Oh! Mother!" Finally some Asaltos heard about this, broke up the entertainment, and brought the victim to Madrid because he was said to be the brother of a prominent Anarchist; this saved his life. But of greater importance, the officers of the Army of Africa learned the fate of the fliers and promised to pay the Republicans back in full—which was done, at a usurious rate of interest.

For all in the Alcázar this final period of waiting was unbearable, but for those who knew of the mine it was anguish. To be blown up or to be overpowered, with the relief column only a few miles away, after they had endured so much for so long, would make it all seem a cruel mockery by a malevolent deity. They refused to believe that such a thing could happen, but at the same time they knew it might. Some men were so weary, so emaciated that they did not seem to care. After the attack on September 23, discipline and self-control had snapped like a taut wire—ten weeks of siege had weakened their bodies and corroded their wills. Soldiers in the upper rooms refused to come down for their food rations. It was too difficult, even dangerous, to climb up again. At some of the higher parapets the stronger men used ropes to haul up those who were too weak to make it unassisted. The upper rooms were so chewed up by the bombardments that soldiers dared not move around at night; too many comrades had plummeted through a hole in the floor because they did not want to relieve themselves in the place where they fought.

Meanwhile the militia in Toledo passed the word to the townspeople that they should evacuate the city again. The mine was to be exploded the next morning. Few people obeyed the order. Throughout the night additional militia were brought up to the dining hall and other posts along the east esplanade. The mine, they were told, would tear out the northeast corner of the building, and they would attack through the space and occupy the cellars while others struck at the Cavalry library gap and the breach on the north. To save precious minutes, the militia would not be withdrawn to positions of safety prior to the explosion: they would have to expose themselves to the hazards of their own mine. All of them knew that this would be their last opportunity to humble the hated Alcázar. The mine contained one ton of TNT.

At five-thirty in the morning of September 27 the artillery piece in the Dehesa de Pinedo threw twenty-nine shells at the northeast corner. No sooner had this barrage ceased than the whole building shook at the impact of the mine explosion. On a hill four miles away, officers of Varela's army were training their field glasses on the military academy which most of them had attended. They were looking for a red-and-yellow flag to assure themselves that Moscardó's garrison was still holding out. With them was Harold Cardozo, the *Daily Mail* correspondent, who later described what they saw: "There rose an immense column of smoke and dust which went up like a huge plume for some hundreds of feet in the air and then slowly spread out so that it looked like a gigantic pyramid of fuliginous smoke. A great boom resounded, and we knew that yet another mine had been exploded. . . . Was it not, perhaps, the last blow?" It depressed them to think that they had fought halfway across Spain merely to occupy a ringside seat from which to watch the final agonies of the Alcázar. Had they arrived one day sooner, they would have prevented the disaster.

On the east esplanade militia leaders blew their whistles and urged the men toward the fortress hidden in the dense fog of black smoke and dust. From the dining hall the militia scrambled up the slope leading into the Cavalry library, and another wave surged toward the swimming pool door. Others swarmed up the Zig Zag to the mound of rubble at the northern breach. They were a mass of desperate, determined men; the weak-hearted had deserted many days before, when the Army of Africa neared the city.

In the Alcázar the sudden blinding explosion and stifling smoke had come as a total surprise to most of the garrison. It felt like an earthquake. The defenders clutched their rifles and peered outside, but there were no visible targets, only the yells of the militia in what seemed to be all directions. They were at a loss to know what had caused the explosion or to assess its damage. A black cloud covered the esplanade and shielded the attackers as effectively as a smoke screen. The men at the windows did not aim; they simply jammed cartridges home and fired into the dark, acrid cloud.

The first wave of militia clambered up the debris toward the Cavalry library breach. A Civil Guard standing behind an upright piece of wall at the top was peering into the gloom when a figure in blue overalls materialized in front of his eyes, not five feet away. Too startled to think of his rifle, the Guard lashed out with his foot and kicked the attacker back down the slope. Then he shouldered his rifle and pumped shots down the incline. When the smoke had cleared away, there were half a dozen militia grotesquely sprawled on the esplanade. The others had fallen back to the dining hall.

From the start, things went badly for the militia attacking the northwest corner. Seven yards from the walls they had tumbled into a deep hole, twenty feet deep and a hundred feet wide. This was the crater formed by the explosion of the mine; the building was entirely undamaged. But the militia scrambled out of the pit and rushed the swimming pool door. However, this had been partially blocked with a loose-rock barricade, behind which was a machine gun. Even in the smoke, the militia were silhouetted against the sun as they rushed the entrance; the machine gun cut them down. Half a dozen times other militia launched toward the door, but each time they were stopped. They used the edge of the crater as a trench from which to engage the defenders in a rifle battle at a distance of twenty feet, but as soon as the smoke dispersed, they came under the fire of other defenders in the windows above. Someone in the crater shouted, "Eagles of Liberty, attack!" but no one did. A few days later forty bodies were hauled from the crater.

The most serious attack came on the northern front, where the militia came up the Zig Zag dragging a hose with them. It was connected below to a tank of gasoline. They sprayed the breach with it and ignited it with grenades. A tall vertical cloud of smoke rose, and below in the cellars the women screamed as liquid fire dripped on them through the ventilation ducts. But stones will not burn and there was little else in the rubble of the northern slope. When the militia attacked, the defenders reached the crest first and drove them back. Two half-naked Anarchists boldly set up a heavy machine gun in the middle of the north terrace in order to clear out the posts in the upper arcades. They worked calmly and rapidly, ignoring the bullets spitting into the ground at their feet. But it was a doomed effort. Without any cover, they were able to fire only a short burst before being shot down. No other *milicianos* took their places. At one point in the fighting every defender along the north was *hors de combat*, but the militia did not know this and substitutes arrived in time. After less than two hours the enemy force melted away.

By midmorning the attackers began to fall back, leaving their dead comrades scattered along the slopes and beside the walls like harmless sea animals stranded by a falling tide. They had failed to subdue the Alcázar. And with the Legion and the Moors sweeping toward Toledo from the north and west, the time had come for them to flee toward the east.

After ten weeks of siege the hunters had become the hunted. The Alcázar had not surrendered.

11

▯▮▯▮▮▯▮▮▯▮▮▯▮▮▯▮▮▯▮▮▯▮▮▯

THE END AND AFTER

TOLEDO was a bedlam. Some units occupied defensive positions in town or near by, like the seminary or Tavera Hospital, preparing for a last-ditch resistance, while others pledged themselves to defend the city and then slipped away at the first opportunity. When the last attack was turned back at the Alcázar, many of the militia fled down side streets to the river bank, where they found a squad of Asaltos with a machine gun on the far side of the Alcántara Bridge. The corporal ordered the *milicianos* to go back, warning them that he had been instructed to fire on anyone trying to leave the city without a pass. "They won't shoot us! We are comrades!" cried an Anarchist, leading his fellows across the bridge. The machine gun sputtered and the leading militiamen toppled over. The others fell back. Without pausing to return the fire, they dropped their weapons and scrambled down to the edge of the water. They crossed the Tagus by boat, by crude rafts, by swimming. A few who did not know how to swim dived into the river, came up floundering, then sank out of sight. Along the shore the Tagus was tinted red by wounded Republicans. Disgusted with this senseless slaughter, the Asaltos took down the machine gun and abandoned their attempt to prevent the panic-stricken refugees from deserting Toledo. The way then lay open for a retreat toward Ocaña and Aranjuez.

Shells began to fall on the city from a battery three miles west. Governor Vega, who had been led to believe that ten thousand reinforcements were being rushed to Toledo from Madrid, went up to the roof of the Diputación to find out whose artillery was firing. No sooner had he picked out the white turbans of the Moors near the battery than a shell burst above the building. "Let's get out of here!" he yelled. Running downstairs with his entourage, he was stopped by an anxious militia captain who asked, "Governor, what should we do?" "Save yourself, if you can!" replied the governor, brushing him aside, and stepping into an automobile waiting in the street. Governor Vega and his official party rolled off to Ocaña.

Major Barceló, however, was not ready to give up so easily. He decided to defend Toledo with the same plan Moscardó had used ten weeks before: by fortifying the Cambrón and Bisagra gates, the Central School, and Tavera Hospital. Throughout the morning, as the militia were driven back by the Nationalist attacks from the west and north of the city, they were herded into these buildings and exhorted to fight to the death. Barceló himself wandered through the hilly section of town, trying to round up scattered bands of militia and send them to the new defensive positions.

The correspondent for *La Dépêche*, Clara Condiani, visited the Zocodover late in the morning. It was a confused, yet colorful scene out of Goya. The deterioration of the Republicans could be seen by their uniforms: blue capes of Loyalist officers, dark caps of Asaltos, red-and-black neckerchiefs of Anarchists, overalls of the militia. Men in business suits fired lazily at the Alcázar. Sitting on top of a barricade was a barefoot dwarf with a huge, deformed head. Major Barceló, wearing a brown leather jacket, argued with a truculent Anarchist leader.

"Ammunition! We need ammunition!" demanded the Anarchist.

"Ask the captain at the supply dump for them."

"I did. He wasn't there. Nobody was there. We're leaving. We're not going to be shot down by the Rebels like so many pigs!"

"No, man, don't go," begged Barceló. "You're wrong. Don't leave your post like this."

Another Anarchist pushed in between them and interrupted, "Let's go toward the Capuchinos. We can get up on a roof and see what's going on outside of town."

They left Major Barceló standing alone. A spectator, having overheard the conversation, walked over and offered his advice. "Major, you ought to impose your authority on these men." "Authority!" Barceló bellowed. "I can't impose it, because I don't have it! What can I do?"

Mlle. Condiani followed Major Barceló back to his office at the post office. For two hours she listened while the Defense Committee discussed their top-secret plans with the doors wide open. It came to nothing. And with each passing minute the Moors and the Legion closed in upon the doomed city.

When the battery was firing on the Diputación, the men of the Alcázar had their first tangible proof that the relief column was close at hand. The homemade Nationalist banner of red and yellow was brought out. Four Civil Guards were instructed to carry it up to the highest projection at the northwest corner, but since they lacked the strength to scale the wall, the banner had to be tied to a steel girder protruding from the rubble along the north. Almost at once they picked up a message flashed by heliograph: "*Venemos. Varela.*" General Varela was coming. At noon the defenders along the northern ramparts spotted men moving down the hill from the cemetery, headed toward the arms factory. These were skirmishers of the Spanish Legion, men whose private cheer was "Long live Death!" * With them were the Regulares, the Moors, who were about to enter the city for the first time since their ancestors were driven out of Toledo in the year 1085.

* The Legion was founded in the 1920's by General José Millán Astray and was similar to its French counterpart except for the peculiarly Spanish emphasis upon death which its founder implanted in his men. Arturo Barea has recorded a speech which he once heard Millán Astray deliver to recruits of the Legion: "You were finished, dead, when you arrived here. You have risen from the dead. You came here for a new life, for which you must pay with death. It is to die that one joins the Legion. You are 'the Betrothed of Death.' Long live Death! *Viva la Muerte!*" Gibberish perhaps, but also powerful medicine. Along with the Moors, the Legion were regarded by the Republicans as the most ferocious fighters they encountered in the course of the war.

The appearance of these troops set off a discussion among the officers in the Alcázar about what they could do to co-operate with them. Captain Vela requested permission to lead a counter-attacking force which would make contact with the Army of Africa and assist them in knocking out Republican pockets in the city. Moscardó absolutely refused. He could not spare a single man. He reasoned that the men they saw might be militia in disguise. But he did unbend enough to allow the artillerists to place the 75-mm. gun at the Cavalry library breach. Major Méndez Parada had been carried below a few hours earlier, after being wounded by a shrapnel during the morning attack. He was now carried up again, and supervised the firing of the gun, which shelled the Aranjuez road, packed with fleeing Republicans. For ten weeks the major had waited for this opportunity. He shelled the road beyond the river until the militia disappeared.

Along the northern breach, now strangely quiet, a group of Civil Guards squatting behind a parapet were discussing what they might do to aid the relief columns. One of them felt that since the Santa Cruz was one of the most famous buildings in Spain, they ought to be allowed to push down the hill and recapture it. "What do you think of the idea?" they asked a nervous youngster who had spent the past ten days in the defense of the northern slope. "If it's all the same to you," said the boy, "I'd just as soon let the Director of Tourism take it."

By the middle of the afternoon the Moors and the Legion had driven the militia back to the vicinity of the Bisagra Gate and had captured the arms factory (which, contrary to the vow of the responsable, was not blown up but surrendered without resistance). Three bombers, covered by five fighters, flew back and forth above the clusters of militia on the roads, bombing and strafing. General Varela halted the advance of his troops, for he preferred to give the Republicans an opportunity to evacuate Toledo during the night. In the open fields toward Aranjuez, a blighted plain without a shred of cover, they would be easy targets for his aircraft the following day, whereas if they holed up within the city it would be a serious nuisance to ferret them out.

The officers, however, had developed a strong urge to sleep in the Alcázar that night. Each one wanted to be the first to enter the fortress. Varela, a sportsman who went into battle wearing soft kid gloves and a chamois hunting jacket, decided to establish a contest between the Moors and the Legion to see who could reach the Alcázar first. Here was a rare opportunity to settle a familiar army argument as to which were the better soldiers. The Legionnaires were more competitive: one of their pastimes was to wager who could swallow the biggest piece of broken glass or who could urinate the farthest, or the highest. But in infiltrating an enemy position, the Moors were second to none. Lieutenant Luis Lahuerta with twenty Moors was chosen to compete against Captain Carlos Tiede with twenty Legionnaires.

Since the Bisagra Gate was still defended by a group of Republican machine gunners living their last evening on earth, the units swung to the east, through the Covachuelas quarters, and ducked through an obscure, undefended gate near the Tagus. Here they separated, the Moors climbing straight up to the Zocodover, and the Legion following the river downstream to scale the bluff near the Santiago Barracks. All were indifferent to warnings that the city was still swarming with *milicianos*.

Lieutenant Lahuerta reached the arcades of the Zocodover without encountering any sign of the enemy. He and his Moors stopped in the square filled with litter and debris, fascinated by the mysterious silence of the place. Suddenly a rifle crackled from a window overlooking the square. Two Moors, like highly trained animals, sprinted on bare feet toward the building, converging upon it from two sides. One Moor flattened himself against the wall and tossed a grenade through the window while the other sprang through the doorway. Minutes later the second man came out again, carefully wiping his knife blade with a rag.

At the sound of this firing, Isidoro Basarán, a defender in one of the west rooms of the Alcázar, was so startled that he spilled his plate of food. It was six-thirty, and he had just been served a heaping ration of rice and beans, a special treat offered by Captain Cuartero instead of the usual horse-meat stew. He cursed, and then stuck his periscope, a mirror on a stick, out of the window to see what was going on. There were men in the Zocodover! During the siege it would have meant certain death for a Republican to expose himself there. Basarán spread the news.

While Alcazareños crowded to the western windows to

watch, the outsiders climbed up to the north terrace. They were barking like terriers—the characteristic battle cry of the Moors. But the officers on the northern slope were not convinced; they ordered their men to shoot down the intruders if they tried to cross the terrace. Rifle bolts clicked, and the defenders peered into the fading light.

"Who goes there?" Captain Angel Frejo called out in Arabic. There was no reply. He repeated his question in Spanish.

"Spaniards," came the answer. "Don't fire. We are friends. Where do we enter?"

"Who are you?" demanded Captain Frejo.

"We are the Regulares of Tetuán."

The figures on the terrace could not be clearly seen, but this made no difference. A delirium swept over the defenders. Ignoring the officers' orders, soldiers struggled out of their rifle pits and stumbled down the slope toward the Moors while a Civil Guard on a parapet shouted hoarsely, "The Moors! They're on the terrace!" When the Moors saw the soldiers coming down toward them, they leaped up the slope like buck deer and embraced them; they lifted them up like sacks of straw and carried them up to the crest. Captain Frejo sagged and fell into the arms of Lieutenant Lahuerta. It was six-forty on September 27, a Sunday.

Choking with emotion, the men straggled out of the cellars to feast their eyes on the Moors. They wanted to hear them speak, and to squeeze them to prove to themselves that they were flesh and blood. These were the first friendly faces from the outside that they had seen in seventy days, the first human beings who did not want to kill them. The Moors were as gentle as children. They stripped off their packs and distributed tobacco and food. When a haggard Civil Guard with a fierce-looking black beard burst into tears, a Moor patted him on the back and said, "There, there. Be calm. Tonight you will eat well so that tomorrow we can go out together and kill all the Reds."

Five minutes later Captain Tiede and his Legionnaires filed into the Alcázar through the swimming pool door. Embroidered on their tunics was the emblem of the death's-head. Both Tiede and Lahuerta were nearly crushed by Alcazareños who would not let go of them. They were like revered gods who had descended from heaven. Captain Cuartero produced three bottles of domestic champagne which he had put aside for the first men to enter the Alcázar. No women joined the celebration. Ashamed to be seen in their condition, they remained in the dark cellars.

The men of the Alcázar begged for only one thing, cigarettes. One of them chain-smoked four in a row and keeled over in a trance. Not to be outdone by the generosity of their liberators, they prepared a banquet. Lieutenant Tomás Rabina brought in a tray piled high with "horse tarts." They smelled like rotten flesh, but the Moors and the Legionnaires bravely tried to eat them.

"Isn't this good?" asked Rabina. "Don't you like it?"

"But," stammered a liberator, "is this what you eat in the Alcázar?"

"Not always," replied Rabina, biting into a tart, "but today we are celebrating."

For most, the siege had ended, but not for Moscardó. While others slept or caroused like drugged men, he made the rounds to all the posts every hour to assure himself that Republicans had not crept into the fortress under cover of darkness. Even though the Moroccans assured him over and over that the enemy had been overcome, he nervously walked through the ruins, unconvinced that his responsibility was over. Not a sound was heard in the city below, yet Moscardó recalled this last night as "the longest and most painful of all." One of his deepest fears was that during these last hours the militia would commit reprisals on Nationalist prisoners in the city. To prevent this, he penned a short note promising that the Nationalist forces would be merciful when they entered the city, provided that the militia committed no crimes or atrocities. His side desired nothing more than "peace, work, justice, and a Spain completely Spanish," that was to say, non-Marxist. One of the hostages carried this note to the Republican lines.

Later in the evening Moscardó and Varela communicated by means of flashlights. Moscardó signaled that he had promised fair treatment to any militia who surrendered, but Varela showed little interest in the information. Instead, he wanted details of the siege to pass along to the journalists attached to the Army of

Africa. The foreign newsmen were pestering him for permission to enter the city, but Varela ignored their petitions. He was actuely aware of public relations. Although the epic of the Alcázar was first-rate publicity for the Nationalist cause, the mop-up of the militia by his Africans clearly would not be. Neither he nor his troops wished to be bothered with prisoners; therefore, with the exception of a small number of Nationalist journalists— whom he could trust not to print everything they saw—General Varela did not permit the newsmen to visit Toledo for two days.

It was now the turn of the Republicans bottled up in Toledo to fear the coming of dawn. Perhaps the waiting was easiest for those who believed what their leaders had told them—that ten thousand reinforcements were en route from Madrid. The truth was that these reinforcements existed only in someone's imagination and that their leaders, including Major Barceló, were already speeding along the highway to Aranjuez.

It had been a perfect night, with a beautiful moon and crystalline sky. At dawn those in the Alcázar heard cocks crowing in the city and not the crackling of rifles from a nearby barricade. At six o'clock the Moors and the Legionnaires who had stayed over-night forced open the door to the Plaza de Capuchinos, flooding the corridor with early-morning sunshine. After the Moors had checked their knives and the Legion their machine guns, they marched off briskly to begin their day's work—cleaning out pockets of militia in the city. Some of them smiled and waved cheerfully to bystanders in the Alcázar. Out of habit, Moscardó was disturbed by the sight of the open door, but he did not order it closed.

Little time was needed for the Army of Africa to push the militia, their ranks now depleted by desertions, away from the walls and back into the city. Varela's troops struck the Republicans in a three-pronged movement. In the center the Moors took Tavera Hospital at knife point and climbed over the city walls near the Bisagra Gate with scaling ladders. On the flanks the Legion advanced with fixed bayonets toward the Cambrón and Alcántara gates, on the extreme western and eastern edges of town. Out in front was a thin file of grenade experts. They pushed aside resistance as easily as if it did not exist, and forced the militia back toward the center of the city. Even the priests who accompanied them, and who usually minimized Nationalist atrocities, admitted that the slaughter was dreadful. A wide-eyed *miliciano* was pursued into a blind alley, sank to his knees, and surrendered to the Legionnaire who was chasing him. The soldier bayoneted his victim with such force that the rifle sank into his chest up to the bolt and could not be pulled out. Men of the rear guard had to spring across wide puddles of blood when they passed through the Bisagra Gate a few hours later.

Some of the militia scattered, taking refuge in garrets, gardens, church towers, and sewers. If they had a friend among the Nationalist sympathizers, they had a chance to escape, but such associations were rare. Others threw away their weapons and tried to pass themselves off as noncombatants, but Nationalist officers were accustomed to this deception. They examined the man's coat sleeve where it joined the shoulder, and if they found signs of unusual wear, they concluded that the captive had been firing a rifle at the Alcázar and shot him. The best-disciplined militia, however, fell back to their barracks in the city and prepared to sell their lives dearly.

The militia in the Colegio de las Hermanas Marianistas shot down the first Nationalists who incautiously approached the building, but soon they suffered a furious besieging fire. A Legionnare managed to crawl up to a window and hurl an incendiary grenade through it. The interior exploded in flames. One or two *milicianos* jumped out to the street and were shot instantly. The others were driven into the upper floors by the flames. Knowing that surrender was useless, they kept going up. Eventually they were driven to the roof, from which they threw themselves, one by one, to the street below. Most of them were ruptured by the fall, or by the hail of bullets which sliced them to pieces as they lay upon the pavement. Intestines and brains "sizzled like sausages" on the hot cobblestones.

Seventy militiamen barricaded themselves in the palace of the senior bishop, but after a platoon of Legionnaires under the command of a lieutenant in his late teens surrounded the place, the men came out with their hands over their heads. As soon as the building was cleared, the lieutenant lined them up against the wall and had them shot one by one. But another group of militia continued to hold out in the seminary.

The siege of the Alcázar ended officially at 10 A.M. on September 28 when General Varela climbed up to the fortress from the Zocodover. The morning was sunny and warm, and in the style of African campaigners the general was in shirt sleeves. He wore no hat. A pistol belt was strapped around his bulging midriff. His face was as round and smooth-featured as a young boy's. With him went his personal bodyguard and a priest, Padre Pujal of the Society of Jesus, who had been granted the honor of holding the first Mass. Moors fixed their sharp eyes on windows which might hide Republican snipers. Someone observed that on this day the Pope walked on the arm of Mohammed.

The official party climbed aimlessly around the rubble by the walls, unable for a time to find a way inside. Two soldiers trampled the debris ahead of Varela to make certain that the general did not accidentally step upon an unexploded shell or grenade. When they finally got into the courtyard, they found an apathetic crowd of defenders, too weary to produce much more than a perfunctory "viva." Moscardó, however, snapped a salute and announced, *"Mi general, sin novedad en el Alcázar."* The phrase "Nothing new in the Alcázar" did not impress those who heard it so much as the fact that it was followed by nothing else. What else could one say? The broken walls, which seemed to sway in the sky, the scarecrow men in ripped, baggy uniforms, and the skull faces with sunken eyes—all these told a story better than words.

The fanfare would be delayed until the next day, when General Franco and the gentlemen of the press were scheduled to make a tour of inspection. Until then, there was little to be done. Father Pujal went below to arrange a Mass for the survivors. At noon Moscardó left the Alcázar with members of his staff and walked down to Hotel Castilla, where he began his duties as the new military governor of the province. During the siege this hotel had been the headquarters of the Asaltos, and the floors were still littered with cartridge casings, scraps of papers, and empty food tins.

On the Cuesta del Alcázar, Moscardó was wondering about the fate of his family, when a man he did not know stepped up and congratulated him on his victorious defense. The colonel lightly tipped his hat and started to pass by, when the man added, "And I offer condolences for the death of your son Luis, which took place on August twenty-third."

Moscardó stood still, as though he had been struck a blow. "But why? Luis? No! What has he done?" he stammered.

The man ignored the questions and added immediately, "Also, they shot your son Pepe in Barcelona, you know."

Moscardó's knees gave way. He stifled a sob as two aides lifted him to his feet again. "Is this the price of glory?" he muttered, half to himself. The stranger had not mentioned his wife and Carmelo; he found them waiting for him at the hotel. They had both been liberated from the insane asylum earlier in the day; an attendant had hidden them under a pile of straw in the stable, so that militia bands were not able to find them.

Señora Moscardó was too weak to rise when the colonel came into the hotel. Husband and wife looked at each other strangely. They were both so changed that they did not recognize each other at first.

The last act of the Alcázar drama occurred on September 29 with the visit of General Franco. He walked up from the Zocodover amid cheers, applause, and popping flashbulbs. Two bombers buzzed so low over the fortress that the correspondents could see the pilots raising their arms in the Fascist salute. General Franco wore a simple khaki uniform and scarlet sash of the Infantry. Hovering around him were half a dozen Legionnaires with automatic rifles, all of them as alert as panthers. There was nothing to fear. Each window was draped with a white flag and was occupied only by silent women, young boys, and old men. One window near the Zocodover contained a red flag, but over the sill hung the motionless body of a man. A line of machine-gun holes traced a path along the wall bisecting the window.

The denouement had been carefully rehearsed. The demolition squad cleared a path through the rubble at the west wall, and the general and his entourage carefully picked their way through the loose stones, entering the Alcázar through the breach. In the courtyard Franco paused to salute the flag attached to the upper ruins. Moscardó was dressed in his powder-dusty uniform. He stepped forward and repeated the phrase *"Sin novedad en el Alcázar,"* this time adding, "You will find the Alcázar destroyed but its honor intact." Franco embraced him while the cameramen cranked their machines, the bombers thundered over the ruins, and spectators shouted *"Viva España!"*

After pinning the Cross of San Fernando, the highest military decoration in Spain, on Moscardó's tunic, General Franco delivered an appropriate speech: "Spain will not forget . . . among our ancient heroes . . . an example to the New Spain . . . rise from the ruins of the Alcázar." This ceremony was suddenly interrupted by the high-pitched voice of a little old man who screamed, "The dogs!" Everyone stared at him in surprise. "The dogs! The dogs! they thought they could whip us. Ha! Ha! Ha!" The spectators took up the blood-curdling laugh.

A tour of the Alcázar followed. It was a short one. After a few paces into the cellars, the odor of fetid humanity—a pestilential stench—nearly drove them back. In one room a delirious soldier cried out, "They attack! Don't let them in! The guns! To the cellars!" The swimming pool was the most ghastly place of all, for here they could see half-buried bodies sticking out of stones piled against the wall. A journalist asked an Alcázar officer, "For God's sake, why didn't you cremate them?" The officer was shocked at the idea. "Señor," he said, "we are *Catholics!*"

As a souvenir Franco was given one of the small black rolls which had been the daily bread ration. To the reporters he gave a statement: "The liberation of the Alcázar is the most important thing of my life. Now the war is won." The following day General Franco was named Head of State by the military junta and entrusted with conducting the war for the Nationalist cause. No other Spanish general was in a position to compete with "the Savior of the Alcázar."

The newsmen continued to explore the ruins. People trickled up from the cellars, and half-blinded by the light, hobbled down through the rubble to their homes in the city. But there were many others who refused to leave these catacombs. Living like shadows, they cowered piteously when flashbulbs exploded in the darkness. Most of the Civil Guards' families remained because they had no other home, and the five nuns stayed with them to cook and care for them. Outsiders entered the Alcázar with baskets of food. H. R. Knickerbocker, the American correspondent, saw ten survivors grabbing food from baskets and stuffing it down while a vast crowd around them cheered and wept in delight. Later, while he was poking around in the ruins, a woman shoved a piece of bread in his hand, the size of an egg and the consistency of brick. "Try eating that with mule fat!" she told him.

In describing the faces of the survivors, almost every journalist alluded to the faces found in El Greco paintings. "They had that ghastly pale-green colour, that gaunt expression and that faraway mysterious look in the eye," wrote Harold Cardozo, the English correspondent. "One hardly expected to hear them talk or see them move. Though they had been relieved for over twelve hours, not one of them laughed or smiled." But if El Greco had drawn these faces, Dante had designed the setting. The walls which remained were either blackened by fire or yellowed by sulphur vapors, and their weird shapes seemed sculptured by the hand of a demonic being. "A chapter torn out of a medieval book," reported the *New York Times*.

What the journalists found was ruin, desolation, stench, and hunger; yet there was a nobility here, too. The survivors formed a hierarchy of endurance. Sitting in the sunshine, the soldiers munched white bread without releasing the grips on their rifles. These men had become heroes, not because they wished to, but because they had to. Few of them would ever figure in the front pages of history again, but for the moment they had become part of a contemporary legend. And for a short time they would be pointed out as "men of the Alcázar."

In a cellar room Knickerbocker stumbled upon a rawboned mule on skinny legs eating the cardboard cover of an ammunition box. This was one of the four mules left at the end. The famous gelding, Cajón, had withered away to a Rosinante, but true to their promise, the officers had spared his life.

None of the women and children was killed in the course of

the siege. But many of them refused to show themselves until fresh clothes had been sent in to them. The lice-infested garments they had worn for the last ten weeks were thrown into a pile in the courtyard, where the last five gallons of gasoline left in the fortress were sprinkled over them; then they were burned. Outsiders helped the women, children, and old men down the slopes of rubble to the Cuesta del Alcázar. Ahead of them lay painful revelations—loss of home, of savings, of friends, and of relatives. The world which they crept into once again was drastically changed; history would pay them little heed.

In Hotel Castilla, Colonel Moscardó was now General Moscardó. But since his home had been looted during the siege and the only uniform he owned was the one he wore, he did not have time to have the insignia sewn on his sleeve, because of so many pressing duties. There was, for example, a large pocket of militia barricaded in the seminary; moreover, General Franco wanted a statistical report at the earliest possible moment. Because of his *"Sin novedad en el Alcázar,"* he had acquired a reputation for being a master of understatement. Journalists hounded him, more than willing to create an image of a latter-day El Cid. What they found, however, was a tired old man with a look of death about the eyes, who prefaced most of his observations with *"Todo fué un milagro en el Alcázar."* Since it was nearly impossible to build a hero out of a man who reiterated that "everthing was a miracle in the Alcázar," they stopped trying, and Moscardó completed his report. This is part of what it contained:

Days of siege: July 21–September 28	70
Shells fired at the Alcázar, 155 mm.	3300
" " " " " , 105 mm.	3000
" " " " " , 75 mm.	3500
Mortar shells fired at the Alcázar	2000
Hand grenades thrown " "	1500
Petards thrown at the Alcázar	2000
Air attacks	30
Bombs dropped on the Alcázar	500
Enemy assaults	8
Mines	3
Fires caused by shells and bombs	10

Total number of combatants	1100
Dead*	92
Wounded**	504
Deserters	35
Births	2

While Toledo was celebrating the relief of the Alcázar, the road to Madrid lay open, with *milicianos* jamming the roads toward the capital. The ditches were strewn with heaps of clothing, rifles, bandoleers, blankets, tin plates, mugs, bottles of wine, silverware. But there was confusion in Madrid as to whether the enemy had really taken Toledo. The Ministry of War continued to deny that the militia had withdrawn from the Tagus River until noon of September 28, when Largo Caballero broadcast that "for reasons purely strategic the high command has ordered a retreat." By dinnertime a rumor was circulating that the first ambulance train was arriving at the Atocha Station, full of wounded Republicans. The station was mobbed by people who learned the truth about Toledo a second time.

The following morning André Viollis, a French newspaperwoman, pushed down the Toledo highway to ascertain whether the rumor was true. Scrawled on buildings beside the road were the words "*No pasarán!*" in red paint. Seven miles from Toledo her automobile was flagged off the highway. Mlle. Viollis could go no farther. She found a hundred militia lying in a ditch, badly demoralized by enemy aircraft.

"What about Toledo?" she asked.

"It is ours!" came a chorus of voices.

"You may be right," said an officer, "but I'm not sure. The road is cut a hundred yards from here."

At that moment a reporter of the Madrid *Heraldo*, a Leftist newspaper, walked over to Mlle. Viollis and said, "This morning

* This figure does not include five others who died of natural causes during the siege and ten more who died afterward as a result of wounds. There were also three suicides.

** Many of these, of course, were wounded more than once. (Major Méndez Parada holds the record; he was wounded four different times.) This figure also includes four civilians—two women and two small boys—three of whom were wounded when the first mine was exploded.

at eleven o'clock I was in Toledo myself. I swear to you that it was completely quiet."

But when Mlle. Viollis asked him some questions, the reporter fumed, "Are you doubting my word? Do you call me a liar. Toledo is in our hands, I tell you!"

At that moment Franco and the newsmen were exploring the Alcázar. The only corner still in Republican hands in Toledo was the seminary, the former barracks of the Anarchists. Thirty militia were still trapped there.

In the afternoon of September 30, the Legion received orders to drive them out. They rushed the building, set fire to it, and began battering the front door with a beam. The Anarchists inside shot through the wooden panels of the door and wounded two Legionnaires. Howling like infuriated animals, the Legionnaires smashed the door off its hinges and sprang into the seminary. Inside, there were only seven Anarchists still alive. One of them leaned against a wall, put his pistol barrel in his mouth, and pulled the trigger. Three others bolted out of a rear door and were shot down instantly. The remaining three won the admiration of the Legion by their desperate fight through the echoing corridors of the building, but finally they were trapped in a room at the end of the second floor. While the Legion crept near, the leader wrote a message on the wall with a piece of charcoal:

> Manuel Gómez Cota, *miliciano* of the Republican Left of Madrid, on the 27th took charge of this seminary. After making a strong fight against the enemy and putting the women, old people, and children at liberty, we set the place on fire. It is five in the afternoon. The place is burning; the only ones left are ourselves.
> Manuel Gómez (chief of the Red Lions)
> Tomas Parques (sergeant)
> Eduardo Ruíz (Socialist)
> *Viva Azaña! Viva la República!*

Then they shut themselves in a narrow closet and exploded a Lafitte bomb. "Those men knew how to die!" said the Legionnaires, specialists on the subject. Thus ended the last episode of the Toledo siege.

EPILOGUE

IT WAS OCTOBER 6 before the Nationalist offensive toward Madrid was resumed. General Emilio Mola facetiously remarked that he would be drinking coffee in the Puerto del Sol by October 12, and General Francisco Franco promised a speedy capitulation of the city and an end to the war. But by swinging southeast at Maqueda to relieve the Alcázar, the advance of the Army of Africa had been delayed for three weeks, and once lost, the momentum of attack was not easily resumed. The Republicans had sufficient time to regroup and to hold a defensive line at the outskirts of Madrid. The loosely composed militia groups were placed under a unified command and stiffened by the arrival of the international brigades, comprising anti-Fascist volunteers from nearly every country in Europe. These men dug in and blocked the advance of the enemy at Carabanchel, at Casa de Campo, at University City. What began as a rising of the Army became a full-scale civil war. Even though Madrid went under siege and the government fled to Valencia, the People's Army stood fast and blocked the passage of the Nationalist war machine. When Madrid ultimately fell, the Second Spanish Republic was already dead, despite the scattered Republican resistance in the field. Even then, Franco did not capture the city by force. The surrender was negotiated, and many of the victors rode into the center of Madrid on subway trains like commuters.

Without the Alcázar, José Moscardó would have had no biography. But there *was* the Alcázar, and Moscardó was the hero of the drama. He went into the Academy as Colonel What'shisname and came out ten weeks later as the biggest celebrity in Nationalist Spain. The elite circle surrounding General Franco were surprised to find that Don Quixote was really El Cid, at least so far as public opinion was concerned. They had to find employment for him commensurate with his reputation as worker of military miracles, but at the same time they had to be sure that he was not placed in a position which would expose his limitations. And this was done.

Early in October, Brigadier General José Moscardó was transferred to the militarily stagnant front in the province of Soria, a bleak region principally known for the worst winter weather in Iberia. Ironically, his first assignment was to capture the thousand Republicans besieged in the cathedral at Sigüenza. What might have become an Alcázar in reverse did not turn out that way. The militia surrendered in just three days.

In a grandfatherly kind of way, Moscardó was popular among his men. He retained his fondness for football players and found young women irresistible. His men regarded him as an "easy disciplinarian." When a young lieutenant was threatened with court-martial for bringing his mistress to the front, Moscardó intervened and got him off. His phrase *"Sin novedad en el Alcázar"* became the most famous *bon mot* of the war. It was soon followed by *"Sin novedad en el frente"* ("Nothing new at the front"), literally true in the Soria sector, although the phrase also implied something else ("Nothing new in the forehead"), as sarcastic junior officers were quick to point out.

When the Italians moved upon Madrid from the northeast in the spring of 1937, General Moscardó anchored their right flank with the 72nd Division. The Italians were cut to pieces at Brihuega, and Moscardó, like many other Spanish officers, was secretly pleased that the conquerors of Ethiopia had failed to take Madrid.

In the fall Moscardó was transferred to the Aragon front. Before he left Soria, a delegation of townspeople, wishing to honor him, asked what they might give him as a memento. Without hesitation Moscardó asked for an altar. Hence the little Romanesque church of Santo Domingo in the town of Soria contains an altar dedicated to the Virgin of the Alcázar. During the remainder of the war Moscardó commanded an Army corps, but for the most part in the quiet sector between Zaragoza and the Pyrenees. By the end of the war he was a major general.

In his letters Moscardó began to allude to "my Alcázar."

Moscardó made a trip to Germany, after all. In the winter of 1941 he visited the "volunteers" of the Spanish Blue Division, a unit fighting with the Germans on the Russian front. He was widely feted, and held "secret" conversations with Hitler. He was immensely pleased to find a frozen outpost of the Blue Division called "El Alcázar de Toledo."

At the London and Helsinki Olympics, in 1948 and 1952, Lieutenant General Moscardó represented Spain. He was now Count of the Alcázar of Toledo, a nonhereditary title. After his retirement from the Army, Moscardó liked to spend his free time in Toledo, where he conducted visitors of state through his ruins and told them how it all happened. At the Venta de Aires restaurant, waiters would point out Moscardó and explain in whispers who he was. Under the sporty greatcoat he always wore a black necktie in mourning for his two dead sons.

After his death at eighty in 1956, Moscardó was posthumously promoted to the rank of captain general. Many a back alley and narrow street in Spain bears his name, but invariably the avenues are named for others.

What of the other "Knights of the Alcázar," as the newsmen called them? No other survivors attained great prominence in the military hierarchies of Spain. Colonel Pedro Romero, Colonel Manuel Tuero, and Major Méndez Parada dropped out of sight. Captain Emilio Alamán, the officer who brought Major Rojo into the Alcázar, rose to the rank of general. Captain José Carvajal, the aide who handed the telephone to Moscardó on the day Candido Cabello called the Alcázar, also became a general; he now occupies Moscardó's old post as director of the Central School. Lieutenant Benito Gómez, who led the counterattack on the recreation room, eventually reached the rank of major and became Moscardó's biographer. Captain Julián Cuartero, the conscientious commissary officer of the Alcázar, remained at the

Academy where he had once taught history, and enjoyed escorting parties through the ruins. Every shot fired at the Alcázar had been a personal affront to him, or so he told his guests. Time has swallowed up Lieutenant Luis Barber, the Engineers officer, and Lieutenant José Espiga, the bold junior officer of the Gobierno defense.

Many of the defenders came to rest in anonymous graves during the two and a half years of war that followed the siege. Captain Emilio Vela, one of the bravest of them all, recruited a company from among the survivors, which called itself the *"Bandera del Alcázar,"* and was killed in the terrible fighting which occurred in December, 1936, in the outskirts of Madrid, in the Casa de Campo. Vela did not live long enough to achieve his ambition of commanding a tank company, and his *bandera* was badly decimated in the Madrid fighting.

Of the deserters from the Alcázar, two were picked up after the war and jailed. Today they may be seen among the crowds in the Zocodover. The others were killed by the Republicans, by the Nationalists, or simply vanished.

Other than Moscardó, perhaps the most celebrated figure in the Alcázar drama is Antonio Rivera, "the Angel of the Alcázar." As soon as the siege had ended, he was carried to his father's home in Toledo, but his amputated arm failed to heal. Large crowds came to see the young man who had been converted from pacifist to soldier, and they carried away the memory of his "perennial smile." He died in mid-November. Joaquín Arrarás, the Nationalist historian, visited him just before his death and told him, "You remind me of an ascetic in a Zurburán painting, with the aspect of a saint." The label "saint" has not been forgotten. From time to time there is public agitation to have Rivera canonized, but this has not yet come about.

The epic of the Alcázar has figured many times in contemporary Spanish arts and letters. Countless poems have been written about it, but the history of the siege has been more meaningful than the poetry it has inspired. Some critics have attempted to exalt Moscardó's pedestrian "Diary of Operations" to the level of the classic Spanish epics, but no one else takes this very seriously. Ignacio Zuloaga's painting "The Alcázar in Flames" depicts

the city of El Greco ablaze while donkeys graze in the fore-
ground. Patriots have argued the superiority of this painting over
the "decadence" of Picasso's "Guernica," without great success
in converting world opinion.

El Alcázar, the mimeographed newssheet, is still being published, but it is now one of the great newspapers of Spain.

Almost three decades have passed since the siege. The awesome
heap of ruins on the highest hill of Toledo has been carted away
and in its place an exact reconstruction of the original Alcázar is
being completed. Men in blue *monos* swarm over the building,
but they carry not rifles and grenades but hammers and chisels,
with which they peck at the massive walls. These men are the
heirs of the same *milicianos* who razed the detested fortress in
1936; now they rebuild it. One wonders whether they would destroy the building like their fathers, if given an opportunity.

Spain is a poor country, and the reconstruction of the Alcázar
costs millions of pesetas. The fortress will have no practical function, because a new military academy has already been erected on
the bluffs across the river. The new Alcázar is a cold, stiff building with the marks of newness on every stone. It is a Disneyland-
Gothic castle, a grotesque monument to Spanish pride, a mauso-
leum which hints that the Republic is buried therein. The rubble
spoke of pride, courage, and nobility far more eloquently.

Present tours of the Alcázar concentrate on the lugubrious
cellars, which have remained almost as they were thirty years
ago. Plaques on the corridor walls record the telephone conversation between Moscardó and his son, in French, English, Italian,
Japanese, Arabic, Greek, and nearly every other widespread
language—except Russian. The guides are all survivors of the
siege. There is a small museum, which contains the motorcycle
used for grinding the wheat, the smashed metal container
dropped from Franco's airplane, the swab used for wiping the
blood off the operating table after amputations, a bottle of horse
fat, a tiny blackened wheat roll, and other mementos of the siege.
At one end of the museum the wall is covered by mildewed photographs of men—some bareheaded, others in tricorn hats—who
were killed in the siege, but the guides no longer remember their

names. Many of the spaces are empty, indicating that no photograph of the dead soldier was ever taken or else one could not be found.

The tour of the Alcázar is climaxed by a visit to Moscardó's office, which looks as it did when he walked out of it the last time, except that Azaña's photograph has been replaced by an oil portrait of Moscardó in thick, dark-lensed glasses, flanked by another oil, of Luis in shirt sleeves. The wooden floor and the plaster walls are gashed by bullets; the ceiling is ripped and hangs in long thin strips like tattered banners. Out in the middle of the courtyard the statue of Charles V stands on a new pedestal. One place absolutely off limits for visitors is the swimming pool, which is still cluttered with debris from the bombardments of September, 1936.

The Republican artillerists built an ammunition road leading up to their gun emplacements in the Dehesa de Pinedo. Though this road is marked on maps of Civil War vintage, it is washed out, forgotten, impassable. One has to walk up to the olive grove. But for rabbits bolting from clumps of thistle, the hillside is deserted. As at Verdun or Petersburg, the gun emplacements are still visible, mound-shaped like huge graves. The immediate area has been tamped flat and the soil poisoned by picric, so that nothing grows here. The blade of a shovel brings up the corroded husk of a sardine tin. The Republican soldier who dropped it there three decades ago doubtless believed that Spain belonged to the future and that contemporary history was stronger than medieval tradition. He was wrong. The Alcázar rises from its ruins, and the chief exports of Toledo are still soldiers and priests.

READING NOTES

1 THE RISING

Moscardó's trip to Madrid is most fully treated in Alberto Risco's *La Epopeya del Alcázar de Toledo*, a manuscript read and approved by Moscardó himself prior to its publication. The present discussion of Moscardó's life before and after the siege is based upon Benito Gómez Oliveres' biography, *General Moscardó*, written after twenty years of close association with his subject. Moscardó's vociferous anti-Republicanism is sketched by Claude G. Bowers in *My Mission to Spain* (1954). The premature plot of the Falange to march on Madrid is explained in Stanley Payne's *The Falange;* Gómez discusses Moscardó's reaction to it.

All important accounts of the siege testify to Captain Emilio Vela's outstanding role. His assembling the cadets and bringing them to Toledo is recounted by Risco; in *Heroes of the Alcázar*, by Rudolphe Timmermans, the account is supported. Vela's part in the earlier "revolt" of the cadets of the Toledo Academy and their "exile" to Alijares is discussed in detail by Gómez. Biographical information about Lieutenant Luis Barber is found in Risco. In *The Spanish Civil War*, Hugh Thomas describes the funeral of Barber's uncle, Colonel Calvo Sotelo.

Moscardó's return to the city and his activization of the Alcázar defense is derived from both Risco and Gómez. Details pertaining to Colonel Romero's mobilization of the provincial Civil Guards come from *La Epopeya del Alcázar* by D. Muro Zegri, who also outlines the original plans for the defense of the city. The results of the outburst in the Zocodover on the evening of July 18 are discussed in Risco. Vela's part in assembling the Toledo Falangists is recounted by Muro, although Stanley Payne gives the best account of the objectives of this organization.

2   THE BLUFF

Beginning with July 19 the official log of the Alcázar, "El Diario de Operaciones" (reprinted in both *El Asedio del Alcázar de Toledo* by Alfredo Martínez Leal and *El Sitio del Alcázar de Toledo* by Joaquín Arrarás and L. Jordana de Pozas), contains a sketchy but accurate record of each day's events. Whenever details in other sources conflict with those in the "Diario," I have relied on the "Diario," which chronicled only those things seen and known.

Moscardó's telephone conversations with General Cruz, Colonel Hernández Sarabia, General Pozas, and General Riquelme are recorded line for line in *Historia de la Guerra de España* by Manuel Aznar. They are also summarized by Risco and Muro. That Moscardó was pleased with the success of his deception is shown by his statement to Gómez: "I answered personally all the orders with the most absurd pretexts I could think of: that I needed a written order, that said munitions would not go to insurrectionists, that a telegram was not sufficient since I could not consider it a written order, and so on."

The withdrawal of the munitions from the arms factory to the Alcázar is described in Muro and Risco. The same authors also discuss the fight at Tavera Hospital, as does Geoffrey McNeill-Moss in *The Epic of the Alcázar*. The photographs taken by Rodríguez are reproduced in Arrarás and in McNeill-Moss; the subsequent role of Rodríguez is based upon private interviews.

There were hostages in the Alcázar, and Nationalist authorities have never tried to deny it, although the assertion of the leftwing press that all the women and children in the Alcázar were hostages is mere folklore. In his *Memoirs: 1921–1941*, Ilya Ehrenburg claims that he saw thirty-eight photographs posted at the militia barracks, all of them hostages said to be held in the Alcázar; the militia were encouraged to remember the faces lest these people be killed when the fortress was overrun. The display of a photograph does not, however, prove the existence of a hostage. Arthur Koestler, whose information about the Alcázar in *Spanish Testament* (1937) is based upon second-hand material, speaks of a fourteen-year-old kitchen maid who escaped to the town through a sewer and who swore that she had been violated by eight or nine officers of the Alcázar. No other pro-Republican writers on the siege have credited this story. In *Man's Hope*, André Malraux admits that the legend of the hostages was greater than their real number, and I have no doubt that he is right. My opinion, based on conversations with survivors, is that there were between ten and twenty hostages in the Alcázar.

3 "THE ALCÁZAR WILL NEVER SURRENDER!"

The fullest account of the withdrawal from Tavera and from points within Toledo to the Alcázar is given in Muro; McNeill-Moss adds little to the summary of events found in the "Diario." The Moscardó-Barnés conversation is recorded by Aznar; Gómez relates Moscardó's disappointment at finding some officers willing to surrender.

El Alcázar mentions that a census of the defenders was taken on August 25; the name and status of every person in the Alcázar are listed by Martínez and by Arrarás. Food and armament inventories are found in Muro.

The most detailed discussion of the "Red Terror" in the city of Toledo is found in Risco's book, particularly Chapter Eight, devoted entirely to militia atrocities. Risco was more inclined to search out such details (and, perhaps, to believe them all) than were other investigators, such as Muro and McNeill-Moss, who were far less emotional about them. For a general evaluation of the murders, Red and White, during the war, the reader is referred to Hugh Thomas, *The Spanish Civil War*, Appendix II. The El Cristo de la Vega incident is taken from Arrarás.

The definitive account of the Moscardó family's movements about Toledo, the capture of Luis, and the telephone conversation between the colonel and his son, is found in Manuel Aznar's "The Alcázar Will Not Surrender," a monograph written expressly to demonstrate the authenticity of the last episode, which had been viewed skeptically by Herbert L. Matthews in his book *The Yoke and the Arrows* (1957). Gómez, however, says that Moscardó did not really believe the Republicans would carry out their threat to kill his son.

4 WAITING FOR MOLA

No accurate statistics exist concerning the number of armed militia surrounding the Alcázar, and it is doubtful that even the Republican commanders knew exactly how many men they had. Aznar estimates seven thousand, Muro ten thousand. That the Republicans continually feared a counterattack by the Alcázar is shown by accounts of neutral observers such as John Langdon-Davies in *Behind the Spanish Barricades* and Henry W. Buckley in *Life and Death of the Spanish Republic* (1940). Buckley and others believed that the Nationalists should have been able to break out of the Alcázar. This might have been possible, but they could not have seized the town, and if they had fought their way out of the town, they would have found no place of refuge more secure than the Academy.

The mission and fate of Captain Alba is discussed in nearly every piece of literature pertaining to the siege, although specific details vary. Risco, for example, claims that twenty drunken *milicianos* burst out of the Venta de Hoyo tavern when the automobile was wrecked, and shot Alba fatally. Muro took more pains in checking the details of the episode, and my account is based upon his. The open garbage truck hauling bodies of dead Fascists through Madrid streets was a familiar sight during the summer of 1936 (described in *The Forging of a Rebel* by pro-Republican Arturo Barea).

In *The General Cause*, Moscardó states that Unión Radio announced the surrender of the Alcázar as early as July 23 and 24, but the "Diario de Operaciones" does not allude to this until July 25, the day when Alba departed on his mission to Mola. The earliest newspaper headline of the alleged surrender which I have seen is that of the *Ahora* (Madrid), dated July 28. However, the Alcázar "surrender" was reported many times during the siege, and there is little reason to doubt the entry found in the "Diario."

Activities of belligerent and nonbelligerent tourists in Toledo are discussed by Barea and Malraux, and in H. Edward Knoblaugh's *Correspondent in Spain* (1939).

The short-lived social events in the Alcázar during the lull in the bombardment in late July are described by Risco, Arrarás, and Martínez.

5   BOMBARDMENT

The "Diario" claims that the contents of the granary belonged to the Bank of Toledo, not the Bank of Bilbao, and that knowledge of its presence was "through a confidence." Although Gómez reports that the Frenchman's name was Ratier, Muro gives Clamagiraud, which is more likely, since a baker by that name was indeed in the Alcázar during the first weeks of the siege. In any case, Moscardó told Gómez that the unexpected presence of the wheat store was proof to him that God had intervened in the siege; further, Moscardó said of the Frenchman: "I am sure that the gentleman had no other purpose in the siege than to provide us with the knowledge of the wheat." Much more astonishing, however, is the reaction of the Republicans. Deserters must have revealed the existence of the granary, but inexplicably they made no effort to shell it or block raids, either of which they could readily have done.

The Mercedes Durán incident is summarized by Arrarás; Martínez lists him among those killed during the siege, but in a separate category headed: "Assassinated for Having Refused to Fire Upon the Alcázar."

Al Uhl's account of the unnamed artillery officer killed by the Republicans is found in Knoblaugh.

Muro and McNeill-Moss describe the gasoline attacks on the Gobierno. The aperture in the upper wall of the Santa Cruz from which the hose protruded can still be seen. Risco summarizes the contents of the radio broadcast from Radio Lisbon on August 17.

6 DISCOVERY

It was Muro who charged that Margarita Nelken was responsible for bringing the Asturian *dinamiteros* to Toledo. In *The General Cause*, Moscardó writes that the Republicans dug three mine tunnels toward the west wall, but this is not true. During the last days of the siege the Asturians set off an explosion in the vicinity of the carriage gate, but this was not a subterranean affair.

Beginning on August 1, the "Diario" listed the number and the caliber of each shell fired at the Alcázar; prior to that time only the hours of the barrages are noted. Martínez records the anecdote about Privates Carrión and Garrido.

The fullest account of the first airdrop is found in Muro. In his book, Martínez reproduces a photocopy of Franco's letter. All writers on the siege agree that the first Nationalist plane brought the strongest encouragement they knew during the siege. Moscardó told Risco that he was overpowered by the thought, "We are saved!" A few days later some of the defenders organized a Brotherhood of the Alcázar: their emblem would consist of four dates: day of the rebellion, day of Franco's airdrop, day ending the siege, and day of final victory.

As a reward for silencing the gun, Palomares received a battlefield promotion to the rank of corporal on September 4. Muro's book contains the incidents regarding Lieutenant Espiga and Colonel Tuero at the Gobierno.

Delaprée's visit to Toledo is described in his *Mort en Espagne*.

7 "FLIES" AND "ABYSSINIANS"

Muro quotes sample broadcasts from "Radio Cigarral." Both Risco and Martínez tell of the pet dog and cat of the Alcázar. The fullest treatment of the women of the Alcázar is found in Risco, whereas it is Arrarás who quotes the page from a child's diary. The story of the defenders in masquerade costumes is repeated in most sources. The words and score of the Alcázar anthem are included in Martínez's book, which is to be expected, since he wrote the words. Arrarás mentions an interview with the surgeon and prints a picture of the operating room. Koestler and other pro-Republican writers allude to three women who committed suicide; however, the official records list only two women who died in the course of the siege, "of natural causes."

The executions at the Matadero and at the Paseo del Tránsito are discussed, at length, by Risco and Muro; the latter estimates that eight hundred people were killed during the period when the Republicans occupied the city, a figure that seems too high, although impossible to disprove. The murder of the proprietor of Venta de Aires is recounted by McNeill-Moss and has been confirmed by his daughter, the present owner of the restaurant.

The fullest account of the reprisal executions on August 23 is found in Aznar's "The Alcázar Will Not Surrender," which is also the source for the subsequent moves of Carmelo Moscardó and his mother. For Aznar, the principal villain is Candido Cabello, but Muro felt that he was responsible for preventing much aimless slaughter. The dramatic escape of Clamagiraud is taken from Arrarás.

The description of Toledo during the siege is based upon the following eyewitness accounts: John Langdon-Davies, *Behind the Spanish Barricades;* Arturo Barea, *The Forging of a Rebel;* Louis Delaprée, *Mort en Espagne;* Ilya Ehrenburg, *Memoirs: 1921–1941;* Franz Borkenau, *The Spanish Cockpit;* André Malraux, *Man's Hope;* and Henry W. Buckley, *Life and Death of the Spanish Republic.*

Muro refers to the Peugeot being driven up the Corralillo road, but a fuller account of the incident (and a picture of the burned-out vehicle) is found in McNeill-Moss.

8 THE THREE EMISSARIES

Muro, Risco, and Martínez are in agreement concerning the details of this chapter except for small discrepancies in time, which are established by referring to the "Diario" and *El Alcázar.* The anecdotes about Moscardó and his reactions to the visits by Rojo and Camarasa are found in Gómez. Muro has the most complete account of the Fink sortie.

Rojo's mission to the Alcázar was covered, on the Republican side of the lines, by Delaprée, whose story was, in turn, used by Koestler. For Camarasa's visit, including the exchange of razor blades, tobacco, and taunts, I have used Ehrenburg, Malraux, and Delaprée. The mention of Camarasa's departure from Spain and exile in France is taken from Arrarás, who quotes French newspapers. The fullest account of Núñez Morgado's abortive visit is found in Arrarás.

The escape of Corporal Gutíerrez is described by Muro. Martínez, who was inside the Alcázar at the time, tells of the wretched creatures who haunted the fortress. The fullest account of Rivera "the Angel" is found in Gómez.

9 EXPLOSION

The chant of the militia is recorded by Muro, who also presents the most complete information about the deserting officer, Barrientos. Further, his account of the evacuation of the city is the most complete. The two mine mouths were located at No. 20 and at No. 6 in the Calle de Juan Labrador, two blocks west of the Alcázar. Most accounts say that the exploding device was located at the town hall, although Martínez claims it was at the seminary—very unlikely, when we consider that this was the Anarchist headquarters. Barceló's plan of attack is one of the few Republican documents of the siege which is extant; it was found in the Colegio de las Hermanas Marianistas and is printed in full by both Aznar and Arrarás.

McNeill-Moss is the best authority for the reaction of the journalists in the Dehesa de Pinedo. The explosion itself has been recorded on motion picture film. The specific time of the explosion is variously given: the "Diario" and McNeill-Moss say 6:31, while Muro and Moscardó (in *The General Cause*) say 6:21.

Details concerning the birth of Josefa de Milagro are taken from Risco. Although McNeill-Moss reports that the tank reached the north terrace on September 18 and describes its efforts to break into the courtyard, both the "Diario" and Muro report explicitly that it was turned back before it reached the Zig Zag. Either McNeill-Moss was fictionalizing his narrative or else he was confusing the events of this day with those of a day or so later.

All sources speak of Gómez's exploit in the recreation room—which quickly became one of the favorite stories of the siege; in his own book the modest lieutenant recounts the episode, though referring to his own role in third person. Gómez is the authority for the description of the mine damage in the cellars of the Alcázar.

10 THE LAST ONSLAUGHT

Scenes describing the militia in the Santa Cruz are taken from Delaprée and Malraux. The latter, however, must be used cautiously as a source; he describes, for example, fighting in underground passages connecting the Gobierno and the Santa Cruz. At one time these buildings were connected by a covered bridge over the Calle del Carmen, but I can find no evidence that there was a subterranean corridor. Knoblaugh confirms the gasoline attacks. The fullest account of the defense of Stable No. 4 is in McNeill-Moss.

Muro and McNeill-Moss contain the most information about the attacks against the northern front. No source other than McNeill-Moss mentions the Civil Guard counterattack over the crest with fixed bayonets.

The Franco-Kindelán dialogue is taken from the latter's book, *Mis Cuadernos de Guerra* (n.d.). Martínez specifically states that noises were heard under the northeast angle of the Alcázar prior to the explosion of the third mine there; but the "Diario" and most other sources contend that the explosion came as a complete surprise.

The breakthrough at the Guadarrama bridge is described in *The Siege of the Alcázar* by H. R. Knickerbocker. Risco records the reaction in the Alcázar to the first sounds of the relief column. In *The March of a Nation*, Harold G. Cardozo, a correspondent with Varela's forces, writes of the last mine explosion and its effect upon the officers of the relief columns. Knickerbocker saw the Nationalist airplane shot down and the men bail out; Risco describes the aftermath.

11 THE END AND AFTER

The attempt of the Asaltos to stop the flight of the militia and the account of Governor Vega's escape are taken from Muro. The Clara Condiani dispatch is quoted in Arrarás. The anecdote of the young Guard who preferred to leave the Santa Cruz to the Director of Tourism is from Risco.

The slaughter in Toledo after the arrival of the relief columns is based upon accounts by Knickerbocker, Cardozo, Malraux, and Mc-Neill-Moss; even Nationalist writers such as Risco and Muro make no attempt to conceal it. Koestler estimates that two thousand militiamen were killed by the Nationalists in three days, but this figure seems exaggerated. According to Langdon-Davies one hundred Anarchists were killed after the Nationalists surrounded San Juan Hospital. But neither of these reporters was in Toledo at the time, and estimates of dead and wounded during the Spanish Civil War tend to be grossly exaggerated by both sides. The vagaries of reporting are seen when we compare Langdon-Davies' story with that of Geoffrey Cox in *The Defence of Madrid* (1937), who writes that the Moors shot down the doctor at San Juan Hospital and proceeded to kill *four hundred* of the wounded by throwing hand grenades into the ward.

The fullest accounts of Franco's visit to the Alcázar are those of Knickerbocker and Arrarás, both of whom were present. There is, furthermore, no dearth of film recording this final act of the drama. Gómez describes Moscardó's departure from the Alcázar and is the best source for his later career.

For the confused Republican retreat toward Madrid, see Barea and Cox. The Viollis dispatch is quoted in Arrarás. The story of the final mop-up at the seminary is found in Muro and Risco.

SOURCES

For a comprehensive view of its subject, *The Spanish Civil War* (1961) by Hugh Thomas is unsurpassed and undoubtedly will remain so for some time. In *The Spanish Labyrinth* (1943), Gerald Brenan has examined the hopelessly tangled social, economic, and religious problems of twentieth-century Spain which led inevitably to the Spanish Civil War. *The Spanish Cockpit* (1937) by Franz Borkenau is another work which illuminates the background and early stages of the war with unusually keen analysis. Each of these is a classic in its own special way; each has been helpful in providing a foundation for my own narrative.

Many other general works were employed peripherally in this study, and deserve mention. *Reform and Reaction* (1964) by José M. Sánchez traces the interaction between Church and State; *The Falange* (1961) by Stanley Payne is a detailed study of Spanish Fascism; and *The Civil War in Spain* (1962) by Robert Payne is a useful collection of contemporary accounts of the war.

The siege of the Alcázar has been the subject of countless books, monographs, essays, and tracts. For the most part, these can be summarily dismissed as valueless repetition of a few important works listed below.

By far the most valuable study of the siege, despite its haphazard structure, is *La Epopeya del Alcázar* (1937) by D. Muro Zegri. When one considers that the author, a Nationalist sympathizer, was researching and writing his book at a time when the outcome of the war was not yet clear, the objective manner and the careful attention to detail of this author are all the more remarkable. One of the most useful works is *El Asedio del Alcázar de Toledo* (1937) by Major Alfredo Martínez Leal, one of the survivors of the siege. Later editions are more valuable. The fourth edition, for example, contains the journal kept by the author; complete lists of casualties and personnel who endured the siege; a printing of Moscardó's logbook, "El Diario de Operaciones," unquestionably the most important single primary document pertaining to the siege; and an appendix filled with maps and floor plans of the Alcázar.

Much more partisan is *La Epopeya del Alcázar de Toledo* (3rd ed., 1941) by Alberto Risco, a priest who arrived in Toledo shortly after the relief of the Alcázar. Risco was especially interested in interviewing survivors, a technique which occasionally yielded information of great value overlooked by other writers on the siege, but often he is gullible and polemical. Risco was also very interested in tracking down evidence of Republican "atrocities"—which, admittedly, were extensive. As one might expect, his book is the most popular Spanish account of the siege, while Muro Zegri's is almost impossible to find. Quite different from all these is *El Sitio del Alcázar de Toledo* (1937) by Joaquín Arrarás and L. Jordana de Pozas, an anthology rather than a study of the siege. It contains a reprint of Moscardó's "Diario de Operaciones"; important excerpts clipped from *El Alcázar*, the newspaper published by the defenders; a valuable collection of data pertaining to the siege printed in Nationalist, Republican, and European newspapers; and fragments taken from diaries and letters not found elsewhere. Another valuable source is *General Moscardó* (1956) by Benito Gómez Oliveres, who figured importantly in the "recreation room" episode. Although the emphasis of this book is, of course, on Moscardó, Gómez also writes of many events not mentioned in other books.

The General Cause (English translation, 1953), a Nationalist collection of documents prepared to indict the Republican government, contains a fragmentary account of the siege by Moscardó. Although he sometimes contradicts his own log, failing memory is undoubtedly the cause.

Summaries of the siege containing smatterings of information which do not turn up elsewhere are found in *Historia de la Guerra de España* (1940) by Manuel Aznar and the official *Historia de la Cruzada Española*, Vol. XXIX (1939–1943). *Resumen Histórico de la Academia de Infantería* (1925) by Hilario González contains a historical account of the Toledo Academy and valuable diagrams of the layout in the Gobierno. Files of *El Alcázar* proved to be more curious than valuable, since the daily newspaper was more concerned with lifting morale than dispensing news.

By far the most notable account of the siege in English is *The Epic of the Alcázar* (1937) by Geoffrey McNeill-Moss, who arrived in

Toledo just after the siege had been lifted, and remained for three months. He interviewed townspeople as well as defenders and was deeply moved by the history of the siege. In constructing his narrative, McNeill-Moss followed the outlines of Moscardó's log, expanding this by his own research. The strictly chronological arrangement is sometimes monotonous and flat, although he writes the battle scenes with unusual vigor. Less informed than Muro Zegri, McNeill-Moss nevertheless writes better.

The Siege of the Alcázar: A Warlog of the Spanish Revolution (1936) by H. R. Knickerbocker, an American correspondent, was the first book on this subject, although the title is deceptive. The author accompanied the Army of Africa northward from Andalucia, and most of his book deals with his observations en route rather than with the siege as such. Most of his information was picked up at second hand when he arrived in Toledo, but his account of the final days of the siege is of major importance. Another book in English, *Heroes of the Alcázar* (1937) by Rudolphe Timmermans, is the least dependable of all. The author arrived in Toledo after the relief, acquired some first-hand stories of the siege, and wrote his book too hastily.

No one has written a comprehensive account of the siege from the Republican perspective and it is unlikely that anyone will. There are, however, many fine fragments recounting days which the writers spent in Toledo during the fighting. Louis Delaprée visited Toledo many times; his *Mort en Espagne* (1937) is a book in which journalism is transmuted into literature. Ilya Ehrenburg's *Memoirs: 1921–1941* (1964) describes the city at the time of Camarasa's visit to the Alcázar. *Behind the Spanish Barricades* (1936) by John Langdon-Davies contains a chapter dealing with a day at the Republican firing lines. Arturo Barea's *The Forging of a Rebel* (1946) contains valuable commentary on the siege and an account of the fighting at Toledo. *The Patrol Is Ended* (1938) by Olaff de Wet, a flier with the Republican Air Force, describes air strikes.

In "The Alcázar Will Not Surrender" (1957), Manuel Aznar collected and published documents, letters, and testimonials pertaining to the telephone call between Moscardó and his son, which ought to silence permanently those who have attempted to deny this story. Moreover, the pamphlet traces the movements of the Moscardó family in Toledo during the weeks of siege.

Other journalists and observers have recorded their impressions of Toledo and the ruins of the Alcázar immediately after the siege was lifted. The most useful of these books have been *The March of a Nation* (1937) by Harold G. Cardozo, *The Road to Madrid* (1937) by Cecil Gerahty, and *Mine Were of Trouble* (1957) by Peter Kemp.

The most thorough study of the sequel to the Alcázar, the drive of the Nationalists toward Madrid, is *The Struggle for Madrid* (1958) by Robert G. Colodny.

Several novels have been written about the Alcázar. Michael Blankfort's *The Brave and the Blind* (1940) is exaggerated, but André Malraux's *Man's Hope* (1938) is less easily dismissed. The factual details of this novel are often inaccurate, but Malraux successfully captures the essential spirit of the *milicianos* besieging the Alcázar. Though it deals with the war in Spain as a whole, José María Gironella's *One Million Dead* (1963) throws light on the public reaction to the Alcázar victory.

Through the courtesy of the Sherman-Grinberg Film Libraries, of New York, I have been able to view the Paramount newsreels of the siege. Included among them were the explosion of the mines and the subsequent attacks, the artillery barrages on the Alcázar, and the relief of the fortress. Newspaper reports of the siege have not been a fruitful source of information, since too often they reported rumors or governmental communiques as fact. During the course of the siege the Nationalist press did not have any idea what was going on in the Alcázar, and the Republican press consistently distorted the truth for purposes of propaganda.

It should be borne in mind that in Spain "the War of Liberation," as the present government calls it, is a subject not yet viewed with objectivity and detachment. The issues of that war still simmer below the surface, and the outsider who rummages in the immediate past must feel, at times, as little welcome as a Lutheran minister in the Papal archives. The Spaniard is highly pleased that the *extranjero* displays interest in his history, but at the same time he is suspicious that one might uncover something—he is not sure what. The Nationalists won the war, but their cause has generally been cut to ribbons by self-styled "neutral" historians and observers. Therefore the appearance of a foreigner with a notebook and a habit of asking questions spells trouble: nothing good can come of this, or so the Spaniard says to himself. For this reason, if the foreigner wants to examine a copy of the 1936 register of cadets at the Toledo Academy, he can be involved in a series of introductions to personages ranging from the corporal of the guard to the military governor of the province. The experience is memorable: everyone is charming, but the register does not appear.

In the course of my field work I went over every foot of ground in and around Toledo. During the day I paid the regular five-peseta fee and prowled the Alcázar from top to bottom; cigarettes for the watchman were my pass at night. I talked with dozens of people who had been in the city or in the Academy during the siege. Spaniards are naturally helpful and garrulous, but few of them told me anything I did not already know. A major recoiled in horror when asked whether it would be all right to use his name in my list of acknowledgments. It would not be wise, he said. Would it damage his career? He thought not, but at the same time it would do it no particular good. So his name has not been mentioned, nor the names of the others who gave me specific information about the siege.

One other experience might be recalled here. The most important living eyewitness to the Republican side of the siege has now returned to Spain, after many years of exile. He alone could clarify the many details of the Alcázar saga, yet he cannot. Part of his promise to the present rulers of Spain is that he will not discuss the war without the proper authorization. Eventually he will have his say, but for the present he is silent. Spain is not yet ready to assume her obligation to the impartial judgments of history.

Perhaps the real difficulty is that history has never been impartial and just to Spain, and Spaniards know it. We remember the *Maine*, the Armada, the Inquisition, and we ignore Las Navas de Tolosa and Lepanto. Before we become too condescending about the Spaniard's defensiveness about his country's history, it is wise to remember our own locked chapters. History is a record not of what happened but of what somebody says happened. It is never impartial, but at the same time, not necessarily partisan. The wounds of the Spanish Civil War will be healed when the Alcázar is at last remembered not as a Nationalist victory or a Republican defeat but as a monument to man's determination to survive.

ACKNOWLEDGMENTS

My major debts are to the Conference Board of Associated Research Councils for appointing me lecturer at the University of Salamanca in 1962–63, thereby providing me with the opportunity to research this book, and to the administrative officials and trustees of Washington and Lee University for authorizing my leave of absence and for giving me financial assistance to write it. Further, I wish to thank the staffs of the following libraries—in the United States: Harvard University, the Library of Congress, Washington and Lee University, the University of Virginia, the Virginia Military Institute, and Duke University; and in Spain: the Biblioteca Nacional and the University of Salamanca.

Ramon Bela and Miss Matilde Medina of the Commission for Cultural Exchange between Spain and the United States, in Madrid, generously provided suggestions, introductions, and information. To them I owe fond recollections as well as thanks. I am grateful to Antonio Tovar and to Francisco Alonso for their information, of a general nature, about the whole epoch of the Spanish Civil War. For reasons given elsewhere, I do not publicly acknowledge specific informants in Spain; however, I have thanked them privately.

All books have godfathers—individuals who have contributed directly as well as indirectly through encouragement and sympathy. Mine are Frank Nulf and Paxton Davis. My thanks also go to Perry Knowlton of Curtis Brown, Ltd., who supported the book at each stage in its preparation; to Robert D. Loomis of Random

House, Inc., whose editorial assistance always went beyond the obligations of duty; to Barbara Willson, also of Random House; and to Patricia McGuire Eby, who helped in countless ways. Clare Eby supplied the last necessary ingredient—comic relief.

CECIL EBY first visited the ruins of the Alcázar in 1950. In 1962 he spent a year in Spain doing research while serving as a Fulbright lecturer (in American literature) at the University of Salamanca. He traveled 20,000 miles in Spain, collecting films, books, and pamphlets dealing with the siege, and interviewing survivors and spectators of the battle.

He is the author of *Porte Crayon: The Life of David H. Strother* (University of North Carolina Press) and the editor of Strother's Civil War journals. He has had numerous articles published dealing with American history and literature. He is now Associate Professor of English at the University of Michigan.

W

S

N

E

Capuchinos

CORRALILLO

Comedor
or Dining Hall

Curved Passage

Swimming
Pool Exit

ESPLANADE

Picadero
or Riding School

The Ramp

SANTIAGO
BARRACKS

Riding School Terrace

TAGUS
RIVER